Historical controversies and historians

Also by William Lamont and published by UCL Press

Puritanism and historical controversy

Historical controversies and historians

Edited by

William Lamont
University of Sussex

First published in 1998 by UCL Press

UCL Press Limited
1 Gunpowder Square
London EC4A 3DE
UK

and

1900 Frost Road, Suite 101
Bristol
Pennsylvania 19007-1598
USA

The name of University College London (UCL) is a registered trade mark used by
UCL Press with the consent of the owner.

British Library Cataloguing in Publication Data
A catalogue record for this book is a available from the British Library.

ISBNs
1-85728-739-8 HB
1-85728-740-1 PB

Typeset in Garamond by Graphicraft Typesetters Ltd., Hong Kong
Printed and bound by T.J. International, Padstow, UK

Contents

Notes on contributors

Colin Brooks: his admiration for the historian, Bernard Bailyn, stems from an interest held in common in the interaction between English and American studies in the eighteenth century. That interest led to the creation of an interdisciplinary course by Brooks with a fellow English colleague, Professor Angus Ross, *A city on the hill*, which is still running strongly in the School of English and American Studies at Sussex.

Peter R. Campbell: his *Power and politics in Old Regime France 1720–45* (London: Routledge, 1997), has been compared favourably by a recent reviewer with Le Roy Ladurie (one of the great *Annales* School of historians discussed in Campbell's own essay in this volume).

Saul Dubow has followed up an earlier full-length study of the origins of apartheid with his more recent *Scientific racism in modern South Africa* (Cambridge: Cambridge University Press, 1995): some of the findings in that study are incorporated in the essay which he wrote for this volume.

Michael Hawkins was a research pupil of Lawrence Stone (whose contribution to interdisciplinary history is measured by him in his essay in this volume), and he contributed an essay to the Stone *festschrift*: A. L. Beier, D. Cannadine and J. M. Rosenheim (eds), *The first modern society: essays in English history in honour of Lawrence Stone* (Cambridge: Cambridge University Press, 1989).

Gerry Holloway writes from an informed base on women's history, as the Membership Secretary of the National Women's History Network and as a committee member of the Southern Women's History Network; she has also recently published an essay in a collection edited by Eileen Janes Yeo, *Mary Wollstonecraft and two hundred years of Feminism* (London: Rivers Oram, 1997).

Alun Howkins: his essay in this book, and his earlier classic study, *Reshaping rural England, 1850–1925* (London: Routledge, 1992), both draw upon his own experiences as an agricultural labourer, before he came into higher education as a mature student.

Roderick Kedward for his essay in this volume on the French Resistance drew upon research material from his recent book, *In search of the Maquis: rural resistance in Southern France 1940–1942* (Oxford: Clarendon Press, 1993), which won the *Prix Philippe Viannay – Défense de la France* in 1995.

Malcolm Kitch: in the early days of Sussex University all Arts undergraduates (not just historians) did the preliminary "Historical controversy" course. All students had to choose between just three historians to study for a term: Burckhardt, Tawney and Turner. Kitch taught tutorials on Burckhardt, lectured on him, and now writes about him in this volume: paradoxically, he has published one of the best dissections of *Tawney*! *Capitalism and the Reformation* (Harlow, England: Longman, 1967).

William Lamont has edited this collection of essays by historians at Sussex University on the writing of history. They have all taught "Historical controversy" as a first-term introduction course to new undergraduates, and this experience inspired this book. It also triggered off Lamont's earlier work, *Puritanism and historical controversy* (London: UCL Press, 1996). His essay on R. H. Tawney in this volume had its roots in his editing of Richard Baxter's *A holy commonwealth* (Cambridge: Cambridge University Press, 1994).

John Lowerson: his *Sport and the English middle classes 1870–1914* (Manchester: Manchester University Press, 1993) has been in its own right a significant contributor to the shift in historical studies, from periphery to centre, of sports history, which he discusses in his essay in this collection.

John C. G. Röhl has spent a lifetime of research on the Kaiser Wilhelm II. A recent by-product of it, *The Kaiser and his court: Wilhelm II and the government of Germany* (Cambridge: Cambridge University Press, 1994), was joint winner of the *Wolfson History Prize* 1994. His documentation of the Kaiser's anti-Semitism makes more compelling his views on the controversy discussed here, about ordinary Germans' responsibility for the Holocaust.

Pat Thane has made the welfare state the focus of a number of essays and articles: particularly relevant to this collection are the essays which she co-edited with Gisela Bock, *Maternity and gender policies: women and the rise of the European welfare states* (London: Routledge, 1991).

Alistair Thomson is a specialist in oral history and his *Anzac memories: living with the legend* (Melbourne: Oxford University Press 1994) was shortlisted for the *Douglas Stuart Prize for Non-Fiction* 1994.

Richard Whatmore has written about theories of "modern citizenship" with particular reference to France at the end of the eighteenth century, and applies some of these insights to a re-reading of Max Weber.

Beryl Williams has written recent essays on Lenin and the problem of nationalities (*History of European Ideas* 15(4-6), pp. 611-17 1992) on ethnic conflict in the Soviet Union (with Kenneth Minogue) in A. Motyl (ed.), *Thinking theoretically about Soviet nationalities* (New York: Columbia University Press, 1992) and on national identity in late Tsarist and early Revolutionary Russia: L. Löb *et al.* (eds), *Forms of identity, definitions and changes*, (Szeged: Attila Jozses University Press, 1994), whose findings are incorporated in this essay she wrote on Soviet historians for this volume.

Blair Worden, who was elected a Fellow of the British Academy in 1997, has written some of the most definitive essays published on Oliver Cromwell. His most recent work was *The sound of virtue: Philip Sidney's Arcadia and Elizabethan politics* (New Haven, Conneticut: Yale University Press, 1996).

Eileen Janes Yeo co-edited as a young researcher with E. P. Thompson (the subject of her essay) *The unknown Mayhew: selections from the Morning Chronicle 1849-50* (London: Merlin, 1971), and has recently published a major study, *The context for social science in Britain: relations and representations of gender and class in Britain, 19th and 20th centuries* (London: Rivers Oram, 1996).

Brian Young is equally at home writing about the seventeenth and twentieth centuries (as he is here) as he is on his more familiar terrain, the eighteenth century (where Pope and Gibbon have been recent fields of inquiry).

Introduction

William Lamont

At school, history is often perceived as the most authoritarian of subjects ("learn the three causes of the repeal of the Corn Laws"); paradoxically, at university, history emerges as the most unauthoritarian of disciplines. How can that gap be bridged? Certainly not by a crash course on the philosophy of history. The sixth former, flushed with success in advanced level history, often only discovers at university a mind-blowing truth: historians disagree with one another. One is reminded of the Thurber cartoon, which shows a disconsolate figure at a party, ignored by all the other guests. The hostess explains devastatingly to a fellow guest: "he doesn't know anything except facts."

There is not much in the way of guidance for the history student in what we might call the age of transition from school to university (except that, as historians, we know that *all* ages are ages of transition). The group of historians at the University of Sussex who have contributed to this book hope that it will indeed fill this gap. The book derives from the course that they teach to all students in their first term called "Historical controversy". Its function is to communicate to students the exciting open-endedness of historical debate, where all opinions are challengeable and all conclusions provisional.

What could be less controversial, therefore, than a book about controversies? This is to reckon without a powerful contradictory school of thought, which would consign all controversies to the wings of history, and place facts firmly at the centre. That Thurber cartoon would need to be redrawn, on this view, to show the-man-who-doesn't-know-anything-except-facts as actually belonging at the centre of the stage – the very life and soul of the party. This school of thought recently commended itself to the government of the day, and it very nearly prevailed. It is a story which deserves retelling, because a book like this one, about historians and historical controversies, needs to be put in a political context.

That story now *has* been retold, by Duncan Graham, handpicked by the then Education Secretary, Kenneth Baker, to introduce the new National Curriculum for schools. *A lesson for us all* is a memoir of failure. He knew where to locate the blame for that failure. Other school subjects would make difficulties for the devisers of the National Curriculum, notably mathematics, science and English. But none would prove as prickly to handle as history. Graham called history "the Calais engraved on his heart" (even at its most cussed, history could thus still at least come up with the serviceable metaphor). Why should that have been so?

Graham knew why. History, he said, "was already riven by the argument over empathy, a concept which required children to imagine what it would have been like to live through a particular event or be alive at a particular time". Graham was fair-minded about the educational uses of "empathy", which he recognised as having both strengths and weaknesses. But his conclusions were unequivocal: "when the national curriculum was proposed in 1988 history syllabuses consisted largely of local history, where the evidence was more readily available, the study of documents, dramatisation, and relied heavily on empathy". "Empathy" did seem to annoy people. One can even see why. When a person imagines that he is Napoleon our instinct is to lock him up. This seems a natural and sensible reflex. "Empathy" was, however, lumped in the minds of critics with the Schools History Project. This had been set up in 1977 by the Schools Council (now itself killed off) to establish a base for understanding key historical concepts (of which empathy, in fact, was but one in a cluster). The State provided money on an experimental basis for a number of schools to pursue a syllabus which would test pupils' abilities to master such historical skills as reading documents, selecting evidence and writing personal dissertations. The content was, provocatively-almost, random. There was a short study of the American West, a thematic inquiry into medicine. No "British social and economic history 1750 to the present day". Those who pioneered this approach were, even if they didn't know it, following in the tradition of Mae West (the greatest of all educationists?), who sang the virtues of "A guy what takes his time". Now schoolteachers, like their university colleagues, freed at last from the burden of the-facts-that-must-be-told, were given the inestimable gift of time. But the idea that this constituted a revolution, which had then swept all before it, is pure myth. For example, between 1980 and 1984, in two of the major national examination boards, only 8–13 per cent and 6–10 per cent of pupils respectively were taking up this option. One is reminded of the contemporary comment on one of those occasional Tsarist reformist spasms: "There is much talk of revolution, and much chance of despotism". Perhaps the most telling insight into the real condition of history teaching was the survey of 9,000 early school leavers in 1968 which showed history as their "least interesting" subject and second-from-top of their "least useful" (edged out only by Classics).

Myths are as important as realities in history. There is no reason to question Graham's sincerity, when he made his despairing assessment of history before the reforms were mooted. But it was a hopelessly partial and misinformed analysis. Convictions like his, however, informed the selectors of the members of the History Working Party. Kenneth Baker picked, as its chairman, a retired naval commander, whose hobby was history, and who had his own castle in Kent. On the face of it, not a likely Trotskyite subversive. Nor indeed was he, although "objectively" (as Trotsky himself would have said) that would indeed be his role – at least in the eyes of his masters. In their view he perpetrated the worst of all crimes: he "went native". He and his fellow members (all vetted after personal interviews with the Minister) actually *listened* to what teachers had to tell them. And they came to the conclusion that attainment targets for history pupils could not be based on possession of facts. Their interim report to the Secretary in June 1989 recommended that programmes of study should embrace the body of historical knowledge, but the quite separate attainment targets should specify only understanding and skills. Baker was unhappy with the report, and was succeeded by MacGregor, who asked the group to look again at ways of including essential knowledge in the attainment targets. (When asked on Channel Four *what* constituted essential knowledge, MacGregor offered as an example "The Battle of Trafalgar in 1815".) There were other cavils: not enough chronology, British history, or the twentieth century. The group would give way on these points (thus, ironically, overloading the syllabus to the point where it would almost become unmanageable). But they would still not define attainment by knowledge of content. MacGregor sat on the report for two months before publishing it in April 1990. He did not make a formal response, however, because he said that he wanted there to be a period of consultation in which there could be a thorough public debate on all the issues raised. Mrs Thatcher's displeasure with the report was well known.

The Historical Association – the professional body of history teachers – had already produced their contribution to the debate. They had prepared for Baker a list of 60 topics for children, between the ages of 7 and 14, to study. There would be a balance in their syllabus between political history, "which might perhaps encourage pupils towards the political Right", and social and economic history, "which might encourage them to the Left", and cultural history and scientific and technological history, which presumably didn't encourage them to anything. They offered suggestions of five headings for British history: early invasions of the British Isles; on the edge of Christian Europe; powerful monarchs, religious conflict and a corrupt parliament; Britain becomes a strong commercial nation; Victorian Britain. This was the Prig Interpretation of History with a vengeance: a pusillanimous recrudescence of Little Arthur's History of England.

It was the Working Party who, in the end, saved the soul of history teaching. In their final report they warned of the very real danger of history in schools being hijacked for propaganda: "there will always be those who seek to impose a particular view of history through an interpretation of history" (in other words, what was sauce for the Thatcherite goose could be sauce for the Marxist gander). They rejected Mrs Thatcher's request that there should be a greater emphasis on the learning and testing of historical facts: "Names, dates and places provide only the starting point for under-standing. Without understanding, history is reduced to parrot learning and assessment to a parlour memory game". They reaffirmed to MacGregor their resolve to put "specific historical information in the programmes of study, which have statutory weight, and assessing pupils' acquisition and under-standing of that information through attainment targets which also have statutory weight".

Fortunately, university teachers now gave the group the backing which the Historical Association had signally failed to do earlier. *The Times Edu-cational Supplement* of 1 June 1990 carried this dramatic headline: "His-tory dons answer call to arms" (the nearest any of them would ever come to a battlefield). Twenty historians from the Council of the Royal Historical Society identified themselves with the aims of the Working Party's final report; forty more historians (half of them professors) were signatories to a supportive letter inside.

The report (amended by MacGregor) went to his successor, Kenneth Clarke, in December 1990. Three attainment targets now made up one profile component: "knowledge and understanding", "interpretation of his-tory" and "the use of historical sources". So knowledge had made it into attainment targets after all! But this was mere face-saving: knowledge of what? and, even when yoked with "understanding", only, anyway, one third of a skills-based whole. The group's insistence that knowledge of prescribed content was not the aim of history teaching had won the day. Were that point to be conceded, "rigidity" – always the danger in any prescription from the centre – would, they said, be made infinitely more likely.

This was not how Duncan Graham had seen it. He was no lackey to the Government: his book is intelligent and indeed idealistic. Here we had a social engineer *manqué*, who saw himself as a reformer of education like Forster and Butler before him. He advocated a National Curriculum not out of tidy-mindedness – though there clearly were gains from history pupils not having to endure "a double-dose of the Vikings" (maybe a triple even?) – but in pursuit of his vision. A National Curriculum was, in his words, "the gateway to a life of opportunity". And all that stood in its way was a crankish claque of historians, blethering on about the perils of historical content. It was not surprising that he called his book *A lesson for us all*. Should we however sub-title our book, *A lesson for Duncan Graham*?

Let us be a little more precise. We are offering two lessons, one for each Part of this book. Part I focuses on some famous historical controversies; the lesson it hopes to enforce is that history as a discipline gains immeasurably when it moves beyond the confines of political history. Part II reminds us that history is made by historians, and that we should look to it for contribution to debate rather than for the transmission of certainties. The essays that follow are not arranged chronologically: they do not, therefore, need to be read in sequence. But there is a logic in the order in which they are placed, and this is what I want now to bring out.

The role of the Resistance in the Second World War is still a touchy subject for French susceptibilities. This is brilliantly conveyed in Jacques Audiard's recent film, *A self-made hero*. It is a tale of twentieth-century self-fashioning: how a passive Second World War survivor turns himself into a post-war hero of the Resistance. Roderick Kedward would take his tape-recorder with him on many such explorations of memory in the course of his researches on the French Resistance, and would encounter many self-made heroes. But his essay, which opens Part I, is concerned with something totally different. In his own striking phrase, what interests him is "the women in the doorway" who observe his encounters with the head of the household. Their silences dominate his essay. Carolyn Steedman pursued a similar line of investigation when she reassessed E. P. Thompson's *The making of the English working class* ("A weekend with Elektra"). Her point is not the trite one, that Thompson's book has too few women in it. Rather, her concern is that "what women and the feminine *meant* is missing", and that these were actually "the feelings, beliefs and understandings which brought about the making of a class". Steedman turns to the world of Greek myth for an insight into the enigma which is Elektra: "at the heart of collective action that ushers in a new political order, Elektra is nowhere". And then she corrects herself, and in so doing links hands with Kedward: "Elektra is indoors perhaps, a woman in the house." And so the "home truths" of Kedward's title do turn out to be in fact truths about home. When (in Part II) Gerry Holloway discusses women historians, *her* title proclaims their aim as being to write women back into the story. Or, in Kedward's image, to take them out of the doorway.

The Holocaust is for German sensitivities what Vichy is for the French. The controversy which has divided Germans was sparked by Daniel Goldhagen's recent bestseller. His title says it all: *Hitler's willing executioners: ordinary Germans and the Holocaust*. Bernard Rieger's article on the controversy it inspired was entitled "A Daniel in the lion's den". There was irony intended, and John Röhl's essay makes clear why this should be so. There may be something Daniel-like about a young historian taking on a fairly complacent historical Establishment, but some balance is lacking in the outcome. Röhl has shown more clearly than any previous historian the extent of Kaiser Wilhelm II's anti-Semitism, but it was not deep enough to forgive his fellow-countrymen for what they did to the Jews in 1938. This is the balance missing in Goldhagen: his instrument is too crude to pick up such refinements. Like father, like son? Goldhagen's father, Erich, blows the most damaging holes in Albert Speer's plea that *he* was not Hitler's "willing executioner" (Gitta Sereny, *Albert Speer: his battle with truth*). A pity then that he should buttress an already strong case with a fabricated quotation. When challenged on this by Gitta Sereny over the telephone, he brushed it aside as unimportant. "I didn't agree" was her comment. She was content to call herself a journalist; Goldhagen was the historian. And who would have known?

Gallipoli is for Australians what these other historical shames have been for French and Germans. Percy Bird and Fred Farrall are not names to conjure with; they were ordinary survivors of Gallipoli. Alistair Thomson uses his attempts to draw out from them the truth of what happened to make the case for oral history (and also to highlight its dangers). These are not "self-made heroes" in the obvious sense, but theirs are tales that have been, perhaps, too often told. Thomson is the kindliest of interrogators, but interrogation is the right word for his testing of evidence. "Sympathy" is too collusive a term; that much-maligned word "empathy" seems better to describe his approach.

Who better than our leading historian of Oliver Cromwell to take us through the vicissitudes of his historical reputation? Blair Worden does not take us into the twentieth century, although he rightly refers in passing to the use made of him in the Second World War to topple the Chamberlain Government. The late Raphael Samuel noted how the Army Officers' Manual of 1941 stressed the importance of having men under them who "know what they fight for and love what they know": a direct quote from Oliver, but unattributed – itself a remarkable tribute to the way in which he has become part of our shared cultural assumptions. Worden leaves Cromwell's Irish reputation out of his fascinating account. Just as well, would be the obvious retort. But historical research continues to excite us by coming up with the unexpected. Toby Barnard has recently written a ground-breaking essay on "Irish Images of Cromwell". He shows how the Irish lost interest in Cromwell after the Restoration, how King Billy would prove a much better hate-figure for Irish Catholics after 1690, and how it was effectively not until 1865 that the Irish Cromwellian silence was broken. In that year an Irish barrister, J. C. Prendergast, produced his *Cromwellian Settlement of Ireland*, which was his effort to set the record straight about Cromwell and Ireland, in the teeth of Thomas Carlyle's heroworship. The missing years were soon caught up, and Cromwell-the-demon-of-Irish-history is with us to this day. But who of us, before Barnard, would have thought that it all began again as late as 1865 with an obscure Irish barrister? The coming of the Welfare State would seem the least problematic of the historical controversies so far discussed. But Pat Thane persuades us otherwise. Hers is no triumphalist "Whig" mini-history of how the State came to extend its provisions for the old and the poor. She raises awkward questions. From a feminist perspective, can the Welfare State be seen as "the triumph of paternalism"? How much does it owe (for better or worse) to its Poor Law antecedents? Was Correlli Barnett right to think that the Labour Government pursued the shadow of a New Jerusalem and in the process sacrificed the substance of post-war economic investment? These are the questions that she addresses, and her answers – written just in time to accommodate into her argument Labour's landslide electoral victory in 1997 – may have fresh light to throw upon The Strange Death of Tory England.

That may, or may not, have been predictable. What we can say with certainty is that nobody could have forecast, even a few years ago, that a future Communist Party would be outlawed in Russia and be a partner in government in South Africa. Saul Dubow, in his essay, relates theories of race in South African historiography to these and other shifts in politics. Racism was, for 1930s liberals, an irrational ideology; for their successors of the 1950s and 1960s, it was an over-reaction to imperial wrongs; for Marxists of the 1970s, it was one stage in the development of capitalism. Now, what these reactions have in common – despite their internal disagreements – is an indifference to the *contents* of racial ideas, as opposed to what they represent. Dubow shows how this is changing: to historians' taking an interest in how stereotypes are formed, to their re-evaluating Victorian experiences, and finally to their recognising how physical anthropology, from the mid-1920s debates onwards, has shaped the historical agenda on race.

Alun Howkins shows how treacherously beguiling are images of the countryside. He begins – where better? – with Thomas Hardy, but does not end there. His interest indeed is not with Hardyesque permanence, but with change. He explores what it means to talk about an "agricultural revolution". He shows how historians disagree about the period in which it should be located, and over the very meaning of the word "enclosure", and then warns of the perils of imposing "models" based upon pastoral readings of history. His essay ends, not with Hardy, but with a vision of the future as cheerless as anything Hardy ever wrote.

We turn in Part II from the controversies to the historians who inspired them. *The English Historical Review* is the voice of the History Establishment. Two of the most influential books in the last fifty years have been Sir Keith Thomas's *Religion and the decline of magic* and E. P. Thompson's *The making of the English working class*. What else do they have in common? Thomas once wryly pointed this out to me: they were never reviewed in *The English Historical Review*. That is not quite true: the recent (Penguin) edition of Thompson's work in 1968 was reviewed by Brian Harrison in the journal for July 1971. However, I know of no single more compelling instance of the timidity of the old, when confronted with the shock of the new. It makes the case for the History Working Group's assertion, against

xvii

its political masters, that agreement on a core curriculum was a path on the road to inertia.

To give an instance. Who would have included witchcraft among the topics to study in an undergraduate curriculum of 1948? The date chosen is deliberate. In that year, Lucien Febvre wrote an essay entitled "Witchcraft: nonsense or a mental revolution?" And in that year the expected answer would have been: "nonsense". And it continued to be when I had finished my undergraduate studies seven years later; when I knew everything about the Petition of Right, and nothing about witchcraft. And I don't believe that my experience was uncommon. In England the landscape would be transformed with Thomas's masterpiece of 1971, which truly seemed to relate witchcraft to Febvre's "mental revolution" (the theme of Peter Campbell's essay later in this section). In his earlier essay, "The origins of the French Reformation: a badly-put question", Febvre had set out the *Annales* programme for the future. It was not enough, he argued, to demonstrate that ancient institutions had lost their vitality, as if that in itself *explained* the Reformation. The more ambitious task was to re-create the thought processes of the reformers themselves and, in particular, in Febvre's case, of one of them, Martin Luther. Wasn't this precisely what Thomas gives us in his work? *Up to a point* he does. The village outcast, refused charity, gets her (nearly always it is "her") revenge by casting spells on her neighbour. That is a familar enough picture to us now. But to understand why agent and victim could have a common belief in the efficacy of the curse, it was necessary to re-create the mental world of those who lived in the early modern period; in a word, to be made aware of what it meant to inhabit a universe governed by providence. This was what Thomas memorably achieved. But it still wasn't quite what Febvre had asked for, and the title of Thomas's book gives us the clue as to what got in the way.

Religion and the decline of magic is a deliberate echo of R. H. Tawney's *Religion and the rise of capitalism*. Both Thomas and Tawney believed that the Reformation in England marked a decisive break: that a world of community reciprocity gave way to a harsher one of competitive individualism. The Protestant Ethic transformed the world of business and economics on the larger stage, and at the smaller level, of village relationships, it set individual against individual, especially the prosperous against the deprived. From Aquinas to Norman Tebbit, as Tawney didn't say (although it is the sort of thing he might have said, and in the way he might have said it). That wasn't necessarily the wrong tack for embarking on a study of what caused witch hunts. And what was understandably crude in the early formulations could be refined, and was, in later researches (many of them immensely valuable). There would be an emphasis in the newer works on the importance of gender which was lacking (although not to the extent some have claimed) in the works of Thomas and of his then research student, Alan Macfarlane; there would be evidence from other counties which would modify Macfarlane's findings based on Assizes records in Essex alone; there would be an effort to relate the psychology of child accusers to repressions within the family, and so on. These would all be chalked up as substantial gains for our under-standing of the *mentalité* of the earlier period, but something was still lacking.

That gap has now been filled by Stuart Clark's magisterial *Thinking with demons: the idea of witchcraft in early modern Europe* (Clarendon Press, Oxford, 1997). His is not an investigation into witchcraft prosecutions (as, in their very different way, all the other preceding studies were). Rather, his aim is to try to do for the "demonologist" of the sixteenth and seventeenth centuries what Febvre tried to do for Luther: to re-create the mental map of those who argued for witchcraft beliefs. We are nervously tiptoeing our way to the concept again of "empathy". Clark presents the "demonologist" to us, wrapped in these inverted commas, because he insists (correctly) that the people who wrote about witchcraft were neither obsessionals nor aberrants, nor (more neutrally) even specialists in the subject. Rather, they were men who turned to the subject to make sense of *their other concerns* as "theologians, priests, philosophers". If one feels that Clark has now written the book which Thomas almost wrote, this in no way diminishes the original, although of course it underlines the achievement of its successor. What it does do is to place Thomas's work itself in the context of when it was produced, and then help us to see in 1971 why he would feel the need to fit his answers to questions that were first set by Max Weber and R. H. Tawney. With hindsight even, we can see that it diverted Thomas down a *cul de sac*, but *Religion and the decline of magic* is no mean diversion, no mean *cul de sac*.

We start Part II appropriately enough, therefore, with the historians who were still helping to set that agenda in 1971. What Weber, Tawney and Lawrence Stone have in common is a belief that, in England, the Reforma-tion is a watershed, and its consequences spill out into the worlds of capit-alism, politics, science and family life. Weber made the famous link between capitalism and the Protestant Ethic; Tawney developed and qualified his thesis and, in turn, saw the rise of the gentry class as the key factor in the origins of the Civil War; Stone supported the latter claim by demonstrating to his own (but not to Hugh Trevor-Roper's) satisfaction that the decline of the aristocracy matched the rise of the gentry. In his essay Richard Whatmore is less concerned with tracing these later controversies set off by Weber, than by rooting Weber himself in the intellectual milieu which shaped his work. My essay on Tawney is similarly restricted. It confines itself to a con-sideration of what Geoffrey Elton meant when he said that "there is not a single work which Tawney wrote which can be trusted". It is difficult to imagine a more damning verdict. Patrick Collinson reaches back for a parallel to the sixteenth century, and to Peter Ramus's verdict on his predecessor: "whatever Aristotle said is false." Elton doesn't say that Tawney was a bad man (not anyway an easy case to make), but that he was a good man who was a bad historian. He even seems to imply that Tawney's goodness as a man (humanity, compassion, a feeling for the underdog) was actually what got in the way of his being a good historian. That is the proposition I address in my essay. But, suppose he were right at least in this, that a good man *could* be a bad historian. What of the opposite proposition: could a bad man be a good historian? It is the question that Brian Young addresses when he ponders the implications of Anthony Blunt's treachery. Can we compartmentalize him, as to some extent he did himself: perfidious Soviet spy and consummate art historian? The Fellows of the British Academy thought not, when they took away his Fellowship. A. J. P. Taylor thought the opposite, and resigned his own Fellowship of the British Academy in protest. One is reminded of Lynn Thorndike's judgement on Francis Bacon: "a crooked Chancellor in a moral sense and a crooked naturalist in an intellectual and scientific sense. He did not think straight." Brian Young considers whether Blunt's crookedness (now explored in fictional form in John Banville's magnificent *The Untouchable* (London: Picador, 1997)), disqualified him from understanding Poussin any more than Goldmann's idiosyncratic Marxism made him the wrong man to interpret Blaise Pascal. We can read Blunt sideways by juxtaposing him with Philby, Burgess and Maclean, or we can read him backwards (as we have done here) by placing him after Jacob Burckhardt. How that great Romantic historian blazed a trail for future historians of culture, almost made Blunt-on-Poussin possible, is the subject of Malcolm Kitch's essay.

"Study the historian before you begin to study the facts": this is the commonsensical recommendation in E. H. Carr's enormously influential *What is History?* (London: Random, 1967) That influence has been, on the whole, beneficial; that injunction is, after all, what we seem to be following in our various essays in Part II. But a cautionary note needs to be struck (actually, two cautionary notes need to be struck). Not all of Carr's common sense makes sense; sometimes his advice is downright perverse. When he tells the student, before reading that work by Jones of St Jude's, to ask a friend at St Jude's what bee he has in his bonnet, this seems incontrovertibly sane. He speaks indeed of facts in history as being "like fish swimming about in a vast and sometimes inaccessible ocean". That may be true, but what the historian/fisherman often catches is, dare we say it, cod psychology. Weber's Bismarckian father and evangelical mother *explain* the Weber thesis on this line of reasoning (and Weber's breakdowns in health). In similar vein, A. J. P. Taylor's Bismarck is *explained* by having a Junker father whom he reveres, and a neurotic mother whom he resembles (and it is a Taylor bonus that we learn from him that "blood and iron", if pronounced at all, would be in a high-pitched voice, and that Bismarck would invariably weep in a crisis). However entertaining, these exercises can take us only so far, and taken further can become crudely reductionist. This is Michael Hawkins's plea for Lawrence Stone: a mind on the move, ever ready to explore new fields, but whose interests are not determined by his genes. Bernard Bailyn, the American historian, resembles Stone in the range and evolution of his writings, but Colin Brooks, in writing about him, also has a bone to pick with Carr. It is another proposition in *What is History?* which angers him: that history is only interested in the cricket century-makers, not in those who make ducks. Brooks argues for Bailyn's greatness precisely because of his interest in the losers of history, of whom there can be no finer example than Governor Thomas Hutchinson. The losers in history remind us of contingency: the best antidote to hindsight cocksureness.

Both Stone and Bailyn are receptive to new currents of thinking about what is the proper content of historical study. In the next three essays, Gerry Holloway, Peter Campbell and John Lowerson show respectively how feminist historians, historians of *mentalité* and historians of sport have transformed the discipline. To my own surprise I find myself in the third of these chapters. Lowerson starts his essay with myself and my old Professor of History, S. T. Bindoff, at a Wembley Cup Final. What he doesn't say is how we got there, but that too reinforces the serious point he wants to make. We were the guests of Charles Korr, who followed up a first book on Cromwell's foreign policy with a second on the history of West Ham Football Club. One perk for the "born-again" historian was complimentary tickets for his friends. Lowerson shows how sport has moved in very rapid time from diversion to scholarship. Korr on soccer indeed received an accolade denied to Thomas on magic and Thompson on culture: a sympathetic review in *The English Historical Review*.

E. P. Thompson inevitably is most revered for that stunning early book, *The making of the English working class*. But Eileen Janes Yeo shows there was much more to him than that: her title reminds us of the importance of his last book. *Witness against the beast* is his posthumous study of William Blake. It was inspired by his life-long obsession with the artist. He believed that Blake had been a Muggletonian. In pursuit of this belief, he tracked down the existence of the last twentieth-century survivor of that seventeenth-century sect, Philip Noakes, and the archive of which he was custodian. Although Noakes (whom perhaps brashly we have called "The last Muggletonian") died in 1979, the 88 volumes of his archive are now housed in the British Library. Ironically they now prove beyond doubt that Blake *never had been* a Muggletonian. Thompson clutched at one straw. Catherine Hermitage, Blake's mother, *might* have been a Muggletonian. If so, would she have been crooning a Muggletonian hymn to baby William on her lap? Thompson allows himself this brief fantasy, and then discipline asserts itself. Thompson the historian checks Thompson the romantic: he pulls himself together with the recognition that this is nothing more than "a pleasant fiction". And so his destination ultimately is a *cul de sac*? Only in the same sense that Thomas may have strayed too close to Tawney in his discussion of the Protestant Ethic. If *cul de sacs* are roads that the historians should not travel, we would all be the poorer for it. Lawrence Stone's *The crisis of the aristocracy*, as Hawkins reminds us, is another brilliant book which does not sustain the thesis that inspires it; in many ways it can be described as a proof of a non-crisis. Thompson called himself a "Muggletonian Marxist", a friendlier animal altogether than the Soviet custodians of ortho-doxy in the past 70 years. Their dismal hegemony is the theme of Beryl Williams's gripping final chapter of this volume. Her last sentence in it, the final sentence in the book in fact, is this telling quote from Khruschev in the 1960s: "historians are dangerous, they need to be controlled". To which Thatcherites would add a fervent "Amen". But not all Prime Ministers, not even all Conservative Prime Ministers, would have reacted in a similar way. Here is an illuminating exchange between Winston Churchill and R. A. Butler in 1941. The new Education Minister was told by his Prime Minister to introduce a note of patriotism into the schools. "Tell the children that Wolfe won Quebec" was his injunction. Butler replied that he would like to *influence* the education content, but this was always difficult (different times, different customs). But Butler remembered Churchill's immediate reaction: "Here he looked very earnest and said: 'Of course, not by instruc-tion or order, but by suggestion'" (quoted in: Neal Ascherson, *Games with shadows*). I want to conclude this Introduction with two personal anecdotes. The first relates to the theme of Part I: historical controversies cannot stay with the political. The second relates to the theme of Part II: history cannot, in Carr's phrase, be "a corpus of ascertained fact", separated from those who produced it and to be placed at the service of a political master (be that master English Thatcherite, Russian Leninist – or, in this case, Chinese Maoist). When I began teaching history in school, it was to 11-year-olds. My subject in one lesson was the Anglo-Saxon Witan. The lesson was not going well, but I was reassured by the consensus in the staffroom that this lot were "dim". In the middle of my exposition of constitutional niceties, a hand was raised. Now I had learned some educational theory, or at least enough to know that this could not be construed as insolence. "Well?" I said. "Please, sir, did the Anglo-Saxons wear gloves?" I was disorientated by the question: Bishop Stubbs's *Select charters* had not prepared me for this. I blustered: "Well — yes — er — no. Let's get back to the Witan." At the end of the class I set a homework on the topic. Dim they certainly were. No knowledge revealed about the Witan, but every sentence beginning: "The Anglo-Saxons were a group of people who did not wear gloves". I made a personal resolve then that, whatever else I did as a history teacher, it would be history-with-the-gloves-on.

Move on to more recent times, and I would face an audience of three hundred Chinese history teachers in Tianjin, a few years after the Cultural Revolution had ended. The impending debate in England on the National Curriculum already cast its shadow, but I tried to explain how the degree of personal autonomy which, up to then at least, historians at university and school had enjoyed, made it possible for history to be an educationally enriching pursuit. Controversies in history, I argued, were its glory, not its weakness: conversely, there was no body of information which historians *had* to communicate. All this was not going down too well, I suspected (any more than myself on the Witan had entranced my 11-year-olds many moons ago). That the State should keep out of the business of prescribing content must have seemed to them absurd. This was pluralism gone mad: the world turned upside down. And that students should learn about controversies, not about conclusions – what an abdication of responsibility! I knew that my forebodings were justified when I heard the uncomprehending first question from my audience: "Please, how big is the school textbook in England?" I should have replied, but didn't: "Historians of the world unite! You have nothing to lose but your gloves."

Suggestions for further reading

The references in the Introduction are to the following works:

Duncan Graham, *A lesson for us all* (London: Routledge, 1993).

Carolyn Steedman, A weekend with Elektra, *Literature and History*, 3rd series **vi**(1), pp. 17–42, Spring 1997.

Bernard Rieger, A Daniel in the lion's den, *History Workshop*, 43, pp. 226–33, Spring 1997.

Gitta Sereny, *Albert Speer: his battle with truth* (London: Picador, 1995).

Toby Barnard, "Irish images of Cromwell", *Images of Cromwell*, R. C. Richardson (ed.) (Manchester University Press), 180–206, 1993.

Stuart Clark, *Thinking with demons: the idea of witchcraft in early modern England* (Oxford: Clarendon Press, 1997).

E. H. Carr, *What is history?* (London: Penguin, 1961).

Neal Ascherson, *Games with shadows* (London: Radius), 11, 1988.

Part One
Historical Controversies

Chapter One

**French Resistance:
a few home truths**

H. R. Kedward

One of the most powerful and emotional visual images of the 1930s was the newsreel footage of Spanish refugees crossing the Pyrenees on foot, in a desperate attempt to escape from the ravages of the Civil War. They were Spanish republicans who had hoped for military aid from republican France, but now, defeated by General Franco's rebel forces, straggled across the mountains, the men often on crutches, the women in shawls clutching bundles of belongings, and small children in clogs, slipping on the steep paths which were covered in ice and snow. Over the border in France there had been widespread collections of money and clothes, organized by humanitarian groups and the political parties of the Left, and volunteers had been recruited by the Communist Party to fight in the International Brigades, defying the non-interventionist policy of France and Britain. By 1939 it was clear that the Spanish republic had lost, and the distress of the refugees symbolized the collapse of a cause which had fired the political commitment and the poetic imagination of a generation. A year later in France itself, in May 1940, as the tanks of General Guderian broke through the French defences on the Meuse, the French poured on to the roads in a gigantic flood of refugees, fleeing from the advancing German armies of Hitler's Reich. An estimated six to ten million people took to roads and rail, with horse-drawn carts, bicycles, cars with mattresses on the roof, farm trucks and wheelbarrows, in a flight which mirrored and compounded the military catastrophe. The desperation of the refugees in the Pyrenees was terrifyingly echoed in the plight of those on the roads of northern and central France, from Picardy to the Limousin, from Brittany to the Auvergne.

With younger men mostly mobilized, this civilian exodus during the battle of France was a story of initiative, suffering and despair by women of all ages, older men, and children. The terror of the refugees, attacked by German fighter planes as they tried to get as far into central France as possible, was dramatically re-created after the war in the opening shots of René Clément's film, *Les Jeux Interdits* (Forbidden Games, 1952), but, at the time, the mass movement of people in the path of the invading Germans was interpreted by certain British and American journalists as cowardice and blind panic. In Britain, Harold Nicolson, Parliamentary Secretary to the Ministry of Information, prefaced an account of the events in France with the words: "In the event of invasion of this island it is the duty of ordinary men and women to stay put and not to block the roads. These extracts from *The Road to Bordeaux* will give a vivid picture of what happens to a population which disregards these instructions." The booklet, taken from the eyewitness narrative of the fall of France by Denis Freeman and Douglas Cooper, was called simply *Panic.*

This was not the way the French experienced it. They saw it not as a "disregard of instructions" but rather as the failure of the government, who left Paris for Bordeaux, and of local authorities who failed to provide a lead in civilian defiance. In Versailles, for example, on 13 June 1940, the town hall was said to have been abandoned, leaving behind a typed notice headed "Evacuation Orders" followed by a single sentence: "La mairie invite tout le monde à fuir" (The municipal authorities call on everyone to take flight). Information was either non-existent or contradictory. For several weeks it was a civilian nightmare. Most remember with relief the broadcast on 17 June by Marshal Pétain, announcing that he had taken over the reins of government and was seeking an end to the conflict. His heart, he said, went out to the refugees on the roads, and he offered himself as a "gift to France" to alleviate the country's suffering. It was the beginning of a Pétainist cult, which took on religious proportions. In simple words he called on the French to "Go home". He would look after the affairs of state: the people had only to follow and obey. It was a paternal relationship he offered to France, with himself as wise and benevolent father and the population as his children. His leadership was constituted in a new regime, the Vichy State, and from the start traditional principles of home, family and patriarchal values were pivotal to the politics of Vichy's "National Revolution", a programme to settle people back on the land, to introduce a corporatist industrial structure outlawing trade unions, and to mobilize male youths into disciplined work in labour camps. In a climate of scapegoating, uncontested by public opinion, a series of racial decrees and laws dating from as early as July 1940 excluded all Jews, whether foreigners or French, from full citizenship. By 1942 the Vichy police were assisting the German occupiers in the deportation of over 75,000 Jews. Pétain and Laval did nothing to forbid the use of goods trains which transported people like animals, nor did they investigate the increasingly insistent information which came through the Red Cross and other reliable sources that the destination was not "resettlement in the East" but extermination camps.

The racial acts of Vichy are now well known and documented, and any summary of its politics will include that dimension. Its other policies of collaboration with the Germans were either ideologically motivated or acts of expediency, depending on what aspect is under scrutiny, and there is a current tendency among historians to talk of Vichy in the plural, *les Vichy*, in order to highlight its internal inconsistencies. In the controversy over whether or not Vichy should be called "fascist", there seems no doubt about the fascism of its Milice, founded in early 1943 as a French version of the Gestapo, while in 1944 three of its ministers, Darnand, Henriot and Déat were squarely in the collaborationist, pro-German camp. Much of Vichy's ideology, it is often argued, was of a traditional, right-wing, nationalist nature, harking back to a pre-Revolutionary, rural age, with the accent on hierarchy and provincial values, and this competed with the technocratic modernism of some of its ministries. And yet it is this very synthesis of opposites, a familiar characteristic of fascist regimes, which suggests that Vichy, at least in its last two repressive years, was indeed a variant of fascism.

At the Liberation in 1944 Vichy in all its manifestations was swept away and declared illegal and treasonous. There seemed to be no historical or moral doubt that the Resistance, whether symbolized by General de Gaulle, or by the bands of *maquis* fighters in the woods, had rescued France from the ignominy of collaboration with Nazism into which Pétain, Laval and the Vichy regime had descended.

This bald statement of Vichy failure and resistance success does, however, mask fifty years of contested memory and history which have made the French Resistance into one of the most legendary, disputed and controversial elements in twentieth-century history. Two assertive narratives of resistance dominated in the post-war years, but both saw their hold on history weaken by the mid-1970s. There was a growing disquiet at the national status of the Gaullist version of Resistance, which featured de Gaulle's BBC "*Appel*" of 18 June 1940 and his leadership from London and Algiers as the mainspring for resistance within France. De Gaulle's frequent reference to "La France résistante" as if the whole nation had been involved in resistance activity, could not long survive his own death in 1970, and the powerful documentary film by Marcel Ophuls, *Le Chagrin et la pitié* (The Sorrow and the Pity, 1971) did much to refocus attention on Vichy and collaboration to the point that it was accepted as self-evident that resistance had never been more than the activity of a small minority. At the same time the Communist Party version, which portrayed the party as the only constant fulcrum of popular resistance, had to face mounting accusations of party inactivity, and even collaboration, before the invasion of Russia in June 1941, and there were escalating doubts about the actual number of party members whom it claimed had been shot in the German repression.

5

Revision is at the centre of the historical process. The more established the certainties of history, the greater the challenge to find ways of revising and reformulating the questions, approaches and conclusions. The prevalent mode of revisionism is to replace the term "history" with the term "myth", so that the Gaullist and Communist versions of resistance history become the Gaullist myth and the Communist myth respectively. It is a short distance from here to talking about the whole of French Resistance as a myth, a way of speaking which has carried many historians, journalists and film-makers along with it since the ideological watershed marked by the collapse of the Communist world in 1989. The power and indeed excitement of "myth" lies in its close relationship to opinion, representation and identity. The "myths we live by" denote an accepted form of consciousness about the past and its importance for present identity, but the very label of myth also creates an aura of interrogation and doubt and a hint of deliberate mystification. A myth, however functional to society, is never far removed from the notion of fantasy. For this reason historians need to use the term with care, particularly at a time when a new level of scepticism, with the philosophical status of post-modernism, is calling all meaning and values in history into question. This can be seen as a positive move providing that it opens up debate rather than closing it, but there has been a strong tendency in the 1990s to believe that revisionism in resistance history can only be in one direction: towards more and more doubt about its effectiveness, its size and even its very existence. Resistance as myth shades into resistance as merely image, representation or even fiction.

A review on 14 January 1996 in *The Washington Times* of a new book by Douglas Porch on *The French Secret Services* (1995) contained the words: "The section of the book that should excite hot fury in France is Mr Porch's contention that the fabled French Resistance played only a marginal role in chasing the Germans back to their own borders . . . Mr Porch does not denigrate the bravery of Resistance fighters, but he establishes a vast gap between legend and reality. He documents . . . the inability of the Resistance to engender broad popular support". Other reviews, matched by television debates, were even more triumphant in their confidence that the "myth" or "fable" of the Resistance had finally been exposed, and with it the comfortable view of the past which had buttressed French identity in the post-war world. But, meanwhile, in French, Italian, Greek, Belgian and certain British and American historical circles there has been a palpable rediscovery of resistance to Nazi-occupied Europe. From the late 1980s the previously dominant ways of monopolizing resistance history have been put into a much more pluralist perspective which highlights the range of different resistance groups and individuals and has launched a massive academic analysis of local detail to arrive at a new understanding of the motivations, sociology and culture of resistance.

Not least there has been a return to the dynamics of 1940, and Pétain's instruction to the people and refugees of France to "Go home". Metaphorically and literally this created a closed world. Vichy, with its doctrine of family and home, represented a turning inwards, leaving the big issues and decisions to Pétain. By contrast resistance can be seen as a breaking free of domesticity, a bursting out of the closed world, rebelling against the inward-looking, home-based, defensive philosophy of Vichy and the Armistice. If Vichy equalled the home, then resistance equalled the world outside. This formula is compelling, until the equation of Vichy and the home is pushed aside and the historian looks more closely at the connections between home and resistance. A whole dimension of resistance is there to discover, which has been missed because it is so basic and because the original metaphor is heavily gendered. After fifty years the history of resistance within, around, from, and to the home has still to be explored. Hence the title of this chapter: "French Resistance: a few home truths".

In the twentieth century the most potent symbol of unacceptable authority has been the invasion of the home, the violation of the family, and the brutal crossing of public force into the private sphere. There are the all-seeing television screens in Orwell's *1984*, and the arrest of Joseph K. in his bedroom at the start of Kafka's *The Trial*. There is the terrifying painting at the end of the First World War by Max Beckmann, called "The Night" in which a family in their own home are savagely tortured by intruders. The invasion of the home is the modern equivalent of violating the sanctity of the church in the Middle Ages. It is a sign of unlicensed power. Is that what is meant by the connection of the resistance and the home: the arrests and searches to which resisters were constantly exposed, often in the middle of the night? Yes, of course, but it is the most obvious aspect and the one which few people do ignore. Accounts of such incursions by the Gestapo or by the Vichy police are legion. It is important to start at the other end, from the home, from home life and the exigencies of everyday existence under the Occupation.

First of all the curfew, *couvre-feu* (literally, covering lights). It was imposed in most towns by German ordinance from 10pm or midnight until 6am, but often lengthened for various reasons in specific places to a full ten hours or even twelve. Confined for longer periods in the home, people read more, wrote more letters, and made love more often (the birthrate finally begins to go upwards). People were more conscious of neighbours, of other houses in the neighbourhood or flats on the same staircase, and more reliant on the concierge. Visitors were noticed, and unexpected happenings observed more sharply. This was not, on the face of it, ideal for clandestine purposes, and yet there was also far more noise of home activity, of repairs, hobbies, music-making, family quarrels, and listening to the wireless. Typing and duplicating tracts, together with tuning into the BBC or Radio Suisse were covered by the ambient noise, and much preparation of resistance material, including explosives, was done in the home. For example, France Bloch-Sérazin, who was eventually executed for resistance, set up a small laboratory in her two-room flat in Paris where she made explosives and detonators. Breaking the curfew was not just leaving the house but returning undetected. People discovered, often for the first time, the geography and topography of their home and their neighbourhood, the roofs, the fire-escapes, the back entrances to blocks of flats and the interconnections of ancient town centres. The Croix Rousse in Lyon was a paradigm in its lay-out of houses which connected on different levels through covered passages known as *traboules*. Many resisters in their oral or written memoirs will point to windows through which they leapt to safety or to passages which swallowed them into the darkness. And the discovery was prolonged into daytime activity, in the endless comings and goings for food and fuel, and the ingenuity of returning home and beating the police controls. It is often said that the only authority that French people resisted was the *Ministère de Ravitaillement* (Ministry of Provisions), and among some resisters there is a real contempt for the popular obsession with food. But once resisters start talking about the day-to-day mechanisms of revolt, one finds the same dynamic: the ingenuity used in cramming a flat with rabbits in the sideboard, and goats on the balcony, and of working out substitute recipes by using long-neglected ingredients, also went into the production, hiding and disposing of documents, false identity cards, arms and ammunition. Beating the system for food was most people's first, and often only, brush with illegality. But for many by 1944 it had gone much further.

Petty collisions with authority were frequently a breeding ground for more committed opposition, and there is now a renewed academic interest in forms of food demonstrations and protests, often spontaneous in 1942 and 1943, which took the anger of the home out into the streets. Although the experience of hunger and cold in the towns cannot be seen as an automatic prelude to resistance, it nevertheless played a role in leading many people to challenge the collaboration of Vichy which was seen as providing the German occupiers and French collaborators with the very goods which were denied to the French. Peasant producers in the countryside undoubtedly kept produce away from the public markets in order to sell it at higher prices to individuals and this is normally interpreted as stark self-interest, or, as the urban Vichy prefects called it, "the atavistic egoism of the peasantry". But for the same reasons as protesters in the towns, peasant villagers and farmers in some specific areas saw their actions as ways of undermining the German occupation and destabilizing Vichy, and in 1943–4 the passive or active support of the peasantry was a vital factor in the history of the *maquis* units who could not have survived in a hostile environment. It has also to be remembered that many of the *maquis* bands were themselves composed of young agricultural workers and villagers as well as workers from the towns, and that in many areas of the countryside the local people referred to the *maquis* as *nos gars* (our boys). Obsession with food, therefore, was not always a diversion from resistance, but was, in a substantial minority of cases, related to resistance on a sliding scale of illegality and protest.

The experiences of scarcity, crisis and disaster are held to bring people together and to obliterate social divisions, but that is rarely more than a half-truth. Social divisions can also be intensified by the same factors. Increasingly in occupied France those who had enjoyed good food and heating, clothes and comfort were seen not just in class terms, but as friends of the German authorities and as Vichy supporters. What makes people angry is a necessary question when looking at the origins of resistance, and for many families the anger started in the home, particularly among working people for whom Vichy's idealized family was nothing more than a sick joke. Some of the most violent newspaper articles produced in the resistance underground press were aimed at exposing the fraudulence of Vichy's incantation of family virtues, and *la fête des mères* (mothers' day) was increasingly ridiculed, particularly in the communist press aimed at women in both the home and the factory.

These initial ways of putting the home back into the history of resistance are not easy: most histories choose to ignore them. In the past ten years certain revisionists have insisted that only organized military actions can be called resistance, so that civil resistance, still less resistance in the home, is not even credited. The ones to suffer most from this military definition are predictably women. Putting their resistance actions into social and historical perspective involves an evaluation of their role in the home, which can easily be interpreted as a regressive form of analysis. But the light that this sheds on the realities of the time is crucial. In my own case it was the process of interviewing ex-*maquisards* in rural France during the 1970s which underlined the gender conventions and finally disclosed new research possibilities. I would arrive in the resister's home for the interview and a table would have been prepared with chairs, one clearly intended for the *maquisard* and another for myself, with the tape-recorder on the table. During the interview, the wife or sister, who had frequently been fully committed to resistance, would stay at the doorway, nudging the man's version of events along with corrections of detail or forgotten names and dates, but only rarely agreeing to sit at the table. The "woman in the doorway", I realised, was clearly a fixed social and cultural role, as indeed it appears in *Le Chagrin et la pitié* in the filmed interviews with the peasant brothers, Alexis and Louis Grave, when the wife of Alexis Grave made all her contributions from her vantage point at the door. If the doorway was a site of women's action and possibly power which people took for granted, it would certainly have been significant under the Occupation, and I began, therefore, to look for "the woman at the doorway" and the exercise of that power in the police reports of the time, which had only recently been made available in the archives. The abundance of cases that I found was overwhelming, from well-known resistance names to anonymous villagers. Two examples can stand for them all:

> In November 1941 the French police and Gestapo knocked at the door of a flat in Paris in which arms, documents and plans were hidden. De Gaulle's niece, Geneviève de Gaulle, was living there with another of her uncles Pierre de Gaulle. Geneviève went to the door and held up the police for several minutes by what she called social chatter, the sort of talk expected by men from a woman at the door. Meanwhile one relative inside hid or destroyed material and another escaped from a back window to alert Geneviève's mother who was due home with a bag of documents. The search revealed nothing.

> Madame le Bars in Ussel in the Corrèze successfully prolonged a police interrogation at the door in November 1943, while the cleaning woman stowed resistance documents in a shopping bag, filled it with potatoes and sent it out with nine-year-old Nicole, who hid it in a meadow.

Reports from local gendarmes, investigating young men who had refused compulsory labour service in Germany and had gone into hiding, are full of references to women at doorways who used a network of addresses in the country to misdirect the police search. Part of growing gendarme co-operation with the resistance in certain areas was to accept these directions, investigate them at excessive length and enter scrupulously detailed accounts concluding with the words, "The search led nowhere".

It is widely observed by oral historians that women resisters often refer to actions of aid, cover and refuge as "natural", whereas men, in giving their own histories, emphasise their "choice" and "commitment". Can the actions of women at the doorway, which they themselves represent as natural, be considered acts of resistance? The same question can be asked of a myriad of small but significant actions within civil resistance whether by women or by men. The work of the historian at this juncture relates closely to that of anthropologists who have charted the numerous cultural practices, seen as "normal", which have been put to resistance use – for example, actions by peasants of Malaysian villages in the Kedah against the excessive demands of landlords, as studied in 1978–80 by James C. Scott. In his book called *Weapons of the weak. Everyday forms of peasant resistance* (1985) Scott examined forms of resistance which mark everyday behaviour and by which the peasants defend their interests as best they can. These forms comprise such actions as "foot-dragging, dissimulation, false-compliance, pilfering, feigned ignorance, slander, arson and sabotage". Such resistance, he says, should not be romanticized, but it is not trivial and it is certainly effective: it amounts over time to "a social avalanche of petty acts of insubordination".

The historian of resistance in the Second World War can borrow much from Scott's insights, not least the very discovery of resistance within cultural practices, which did not have to be learnt, except in the ways that all cultural roles and behaviour are transmitted from one generation to the next. This is largely what is meant by "natural", just as Protestants in the village of le Chambon-sur-Lignon and in the Cévennes, who sheltered Jewish children and families in their homes and saved them from deportation, claimed that they "naturally" handed down the memory of Protestant martyrdom in France which made them responsive to those seeking refuge from persecution.

The use by women of culturally accepted roles and behaviour to cover and extend their resistance activities outside the home is now increasingly analyzed and documented. From house to house, for example, the safest means of transporting documents, light arms and ammunition was to use shopping bags, children's satchels and prams. A woman's behaviour was less likely to be questioned if she were pregnant or carrying a child, and the story of Lucie Aubrac's rescue of her husband from a death sentence at the hands of the Germans in Lyon has become a classic story of combining ruse and invention with pregnancy to outwit the Gestapo. And yet the history of the woman at home still needs far more research: it is either relegated to the history of Vichy and its ideology of hearth and family, or to what historians, but not anthropologists, often tend to dismiss as the unexceptional history of daily life. It should not need stressing that the use of culturally "normative" behaviour for resistance purposes still involved choice and commitment. It was only a minority of "women at the doorway" who responded in this way, however "natural" their actions seemed to be. To this extent the historian, who has to explain the specificity of action, and the anthropologist who charts general cultural practices, have different but complementary aims.

Whichever approach is used, the "natural" action needs to be historicized and given its full context and meaning. We can take one further instance, the study of wives and mothers of the *maquisards*, the women who stayed at home when their menfolk took to the woods. It is acknowledged that their support was vital to the successes of the *maquis*, but we have few first-hand insights into the choices and commitment of these women who bore the brunt of raids by the Vichy Milice, by the German army and the Gestapo in the hunt for the *maquisards*. The local archives contain frequent police reports which state, "The men had all left the village: order was given to set fire to *x* number of houses as a reprisal." In the history of the *maquis* it is the men in the woods who are normally at the centre of the action and those who supported and fed them occupy the periphery. But it was the "periphery" that was caught up in these raids and the women left in the village had to resist the threats and inducements of the invading forces. If the fighting front is where the enemy is, then at those precise moments the front was in the home. This inversion of traditional wartime distinctions, common to all occupied countries involved in resistance, must involve a shift of discourse from the gendered metaphor with which we began. The home cannot simply be equated with passivity, nor did all breaking out lead directly to confrontation with the enemy.

To some extent the importance of the home was recognized in the subtle resistance novel by Vercors, *Le Silence de la mer* (The Silence of the Sea, 1942), with its story of a billeted German officer and the daily reaction of an uncle and niece to his presence. The total collapse of the cultured officer's belief in the cause of Germany is the sting in the tail of the novel, but the silent protest of the niece is the constant throughout. A later resistance novel, by Elsa Triolet, *Les Amants d'Avignon* (The Lovers of Avignon, 1944), has a young woman resister, Juliette, journeying from farm to farm in the hills as a liaison agent between town and country. It is this latter type of resistance figure, rather than the niece in her home, which the histories of resistance have preferred to explore. Triolet's heroine was no fantasy: there were hundreds of resistance women on whom she was realistically based, carrying information, guns and ammunition, and their histories are finally being written and analyzed, after years of neglect. By contrast, historians still turn their back on the essential home-based infrastructure of resistance, because it seems so ordinary. But it was the use of the ordinary, the continued exploration of the possibilities of everyday life and behaviour, which enabled a growing minority of French men and women to create resistance openings and defy both Nazism and Vichy. "In fact", said resister Odette Sabaté, "my resistance was the logical consequence of a whole series of happenings, the sense of action which gripped our home . . . the support given to the victims of repression and the daily struggle of life itself."

In the urge to dispel myths and revise all apparent historical certainties it is often forgotten that the certainties themselves may have been inadequately researched and presented. For some the French Resistance is simply ripe for deconstruction and demythification, but for others the real challenge is the realization that huge areas of resistance, both in France and elsewhere, still need primary research and more accurate and imaginative concepts. In all controversies it is important to find new ground.

Suggestions for further reading

A wide-ranging study of women in the French Resistance, based on extensive interviews, and aimed at both the general and the specialist reader is: Margaret Collins Weitz, *Sisters in the Resistance. How women fought to free France 1940-1945* (New York: John Wiley, 1995). An important pioneering article on the subject, which is essential reading, is: Paula Schwartz, "*Partisanes* and gender politics in Vichy France", *French Historical Studies*

16(1), Spring 1989. Excellent comparative material is to be found in Margaret Higonnet, Jane Jenson, Sonya Michel and Margaret Weitz (eds), *Behind the lines: gender and the two world wars* (New Haven: Yale University Press, 1987). Lucie Aubrac's own account of the planned escape of her husband, and much good detail on everyday resistance, is available in translation as *Outwitting the Gestapo* (Lincoln: University of Nebraska Press, 1993). The central role of women in the rural history of the *maquis* is one of the themes in H. R. Kedward, *In Search of the Maquis* (Oxford: Clarendon Press, 1993), and the same author's *Occupied France* (Oxford: Blackwell, 1985) forms an introduction to both Vichy and the Resistance. A two-volume history of the period which is full of different aspects and approaches, and which awaits translation, is: Jean-Pierre Azéma and François Bédarida, *La France des années noires* (Paris: Seuil, 1993). Meanwhile there is Jean-Pierre Azéma's earlier treatment, *From Munich to the Liberation* (Cambridge: Cambridge University Press, 1984). The classic study of Vichy is still by Robert Paxton, *Vichy France: old guard and new order* (New York: Knopf, 1972), to which must be added the translation of the equally classic history of the memory of Vichy which continues to stir controversies and confrontations: Henry Rousso, *The Vichy syndrome: history and memory in France since 1944* (Harvard University Press, 1991). Also translated is the important new approach not so much to collaboration but to accommodation with the German occupiers: Philippe Burrin, *Living with defeat. France under the German occupation 1940–1944* (London: Arnold, 1996). Collaborators, and many of those studied by Burrin, were purged at the Liberation, with punishments which featured the shaving of women's heads, probably the most criticized act carried out in the name of resistance: see the section on gender in H. R. Kedward and Nancy Wood (eds), *The liberation of France: image and event* (Oxford: Berg, 1995). Finally, for an original and perceptive book on the inter-war years which is at the frontier of gender history see Siân Reynolds, *France between the wars. gender and politics* (London: Routledge, 1996).

᳁

Chapter Two

Ordinary Germans as Hitler's willing executioners? The Goldhagen controversy

John Röhl

When the Allies landed in Normandy in 1944, the fiercest resistance they encountered was from the 12th SS Panzerdivision "Hitler Jugend", whose members, when wounded, preferred to "die for the Führer" rather than accept medical help from the enemy – until they were threatened by a fate worse than death, transfusion with Jewish blood.

In his highly controversial book *Hitler's willing executioners: ordinary Germans and the Holocaust*, the Harvard political scientist Daniel Goldhagen does not go quite so far as to ascribe such fanatical attitudes to the German people as a whole, but he comes close. Well over 100,000 "ordinary Germans", perhaps as many as half a million, were directly involved in the slaughter of European Jewry in those terrible years 1938–45; they acted – so Goldhagen argues – on the basis of two centuries and more of "eliminationist anti-Semitism" with "joyful" enthusiasm (his words) and gratuitous cruelty, and refused to stop even when Himmler, for egoistical reasons, ordered them to do so at the very end of the war. What is more, because the killers were "ordinary Germans", it follows (so he claims) that any number of other Germans – "*the* Germans" – would have behaved in the same way had they been called upon to do so. Many millions knew and approved of what was being done to the Jews.

Success . . .

Whatever else we may think of this thesis, there is no doubt that the book which advances it has been an astonishing success. Even before its American publication, the Harvard dissertation from which it sprang was awarded the prestigious Gabriel Almond Prize of the American Political Science Asociation. A revised version of the thesis was published in the US by the very reputable Alfred Knopf company and has sold 150,000 in its first year. Published in German translation by the Siedler Verlag in August 1996 – just five months ago – it has already passed the 160,000 mark. At the tender age of 36, Daniel Goldhagen has made well over a million dollars from his dissertation, and the French, Italian and Japanese editions are not even out yet.[1] The Nobel prize winner Elie Wiesel has praised the work as something every German schoolchild should read. Gordon Craig, the doyen of German historians in America, has extolled it as breaking important new ground in an area of the deepest significance in human history – laying bare the behaviour and motivation of many thousands of common killers operating not in the notorious death camps, but in the villages and towns of German-occupied Poland and Russia. Throughout Europe and America, hundreds of thousands of people are reading about the Holocaust as seen through the eyes of Daniel Jonah Goldhagen. Seldom can a doctoral dissertation have made such an impact, for better or for worse.

... and savage criticism

But bright light casts dark shadows. Criticism of Goldhagen's work, by Jews and Gentiles, Americans, Britons and Germans, has been severe. The grand master of Holocaust studies in Israel, Yehuda L. Bauer, has publicly asked what on earth went wrong at Harvard, that such a work should have slipped through the filter of critical scholarly assessment and been awarded a doctorate. Another Israeli writer, Moshe Zimmermann, has commented that the Goldhagen book has caused barely a ripple in Israel itself simply because its thesis never rises above the level of the prejudices and oversimplifications current in the Israeli population as a whole, which are far removed from the highest standard of international scholarship. Gulie Arad, a third Israeli voice, explains the commercial success of the book in America in terms of (a) massive media hype and (b) the psychological and socio-political attractions for American Jews of the "culture of victimization". The leading Israeli historian of the Wehrmacht, Omer Bartov, who teaches at Rutgers University in the United States, has accused Goldhagen of oversimplification and arrogance, of intolerable contempt for his fellow-scholars, and of ignoring most recent research on the Holocaust in order to lay a false claim to originality. These are devastating criticisms.

The reception in Germany

For obvious reasons, the reception of Goldhagen's book in Germany was observed with intense interest by many, not least because of two important

[1] This text was written in January 1997. Both the French and Italian editions have since appeared.

and related literary–historical events which preceded it. 1995 saw the publication of Victor Klemperer's wonderful diaries chronicling in the most painful detail his life as a Jew married to a German in the Third Reich; though they cost nearly 100 marks, the two volumes sold some 100,000 copies in a short space of time. The same year, 1995, saw the huge success of the travelling exhibition *Vernichtungskrieg* which demonstrated, again in graphic detail, the mass participation of "ordinary Germans" – in this instance the soldiers and officers of the Wehrmacht – in the massacre of over four million Soviet prisoners of war, some three million Jews and perhaps five million so-called "partisans" and their families on the eastern and south-eastern front in the Second World War.

Inevitably, the German edition, too, was launched with much media hype. Goldhagen skilfully heightened the sense of expectation by refusing to answer any questions put to him by German journalists until the German translation was on the market. The translation – even the title – was subtly modified to suit German sensibilities. When he toured Germany in August 1996, the Bonn government gave him a level of armed protection normally accorded only to visiting statesmen. In three lengthy television debates he succeeded, by means of charm, youthful good looks and innocent protestations that he had been misunderstood, in winning the studio audiences and much of the general public over to his side against his elderly professorial inquisitors, who were widely perceived as having failed in their duty to provide truthful, meaningful and readily understandable explanations of the Holocaust. In March 1997 he was awarded the Democracy Prize by the editors of a leading journal of international politics, the laudation being spoken by the eminent philosopher, Jürgen Habermas.

Goldhagen's German critics

Goldhagen's German critics were on balance more negative than the early American commentators had been, although the range of arguments used was much the same and there was much praise there too. But even those Germans who admired the book – Volker Berghahn, Julius Schoeps, Volker Ullrich, Joseph Joffe and Ignaz Bubis, for example – criticized its one-dimensional, oversimpified message and its zealous, pamphleteering tone. Other highly-regarded experts like Eberhard Jäckel and Hans-Ulrich Wehler condemned him for causing "immense harm" to Holocaust studies and accused him of seeking to make a name for himself by shrilly refuting theses which no-one had advanced for decades: who on earth now claimed, they asked, that the killing of millions in the Second World War was the work of a small band of fanatical Nazis lording it over a terrorized German population? Some went so far as to describe the work as an act of revenge for the sufferings of Goldhagen's father, who had only just escaped

17

near-certain death in the Holocaust in Rumania. Many complained that Goldhagen's book was a throwback to the days of "Re-education" in the late 1940s and 1950s, when young American GIs saw it as their mission to civilize the "barbaric" Germans. The general view was that it failed badly to take into account much of the careful research that had been undertaken in the last 15 to 20 years.

German praise

At the same time there was widespread praise in German academic and literary circles for three sections of the book which together make up almost half of its 620-page volume – those sections on the deadly activities of the Police battalions, the so-called labour camps, and the death marches in the final stages of the War.

Police battalions

The harrowing Chapters 6–9, on the activity and mentality of Police Battalions in Poland, are by common consent the most successful in the whole book. There were 38 such Battalions at work, comprising some 19,000 men in all – "ordinary men", family men in early middle age from middle-class or lower middle-class backgrounds, from good homes with good jobs, only a third of them members of the Nazi Party, only one in thirty of them in the SS, yet they were responsible for the brutal slaying of between one and three million Jews, young and old, men and women. They were all given the chance by their commanders to opt out of their deadly work, but only 10 or perhaps 20 per cent seized it, even though there is not one case on record of anyone being penalized for refusing to kill. More shocking still than these statistics are the eyewitness accounts Goldhagen provides of the "joyful" blood lust of these "ordinary" killers – of the policeman who, in full view of his smiling commanding officer, urinated on his elderly victim before firing his rifle into the old man's skull, of the 900 Jews forced into the synagogue in Bialistok where they were incinerated, of the wives who were invited to come and watch the policemen at work, of the snapshots proudly sent home.

Some critics have pointed out that another American scholar, Christopher Browning, had already published much of the information on the activity of one of these Battalions, the Reserve Battalion 101 from Hamburg, and have complained of the hectoring manner in which Goldhagen ceaselessly attacks his distinguished rival, but others have been quick to defend him, pointing out that vigorous scholarly debate, and coming to different conclusions on the basis of the same evidence, is a legitimate and necessary process in the search for truth.

The labour camps

The next three chapters of the book, on the 10,000 "labour" camps set up by the Nazi regime, have provoked less comment, but they are also extremely moving accounts of a bestial system deliberately designed to kill Jews through overwork and starvation; no fewer than 940 such camps were set up in occupied Poland specifically to torment and kill Jews at a time when millions of slave labourers were being forcibly transported into the Reich to work. There is widespread agreement that these camps, in contra-distinction to the Auschwitzes and Treblinkas, Dachaus and Buchenwalds, have been largely neglected by researchers, and that Goldhagen has per-formed a useful service in drawing our attention to them.

The death marches

Finally, the deadly marches from the extermination camps and concentration camps on the occupied periphery to the German heartland in the last months of the war are described by Goldhagen in vivid and almost unbearable detail and have received much praise for their originality and scholarship. He estimates that of the 750,000 people who were forced to participate in these marches through German villages, towns and cities in 1945, between one third and one half – in other words between 250,000 and 375,000 men, women and children – died or were killed on the way. The marches con-tinued even after Himmler, who was insanely hoping to negotiate with the Allies, gave the orders for them to be disbanded, and even though naked self-interest should have told the perpetrators that they should throw away their weapons and drift away homewards. Once again, Goldhagen is able to argue that such behaviour can only be explained in terms of voluntarism.

The problem

The central problem of Goldhagen's book concerns not so much these nine empirical chapters, but the overall interpretative framework into which he places them. His accusation that "the Germans" were so imbued with "eliminationist anti-Semitism", as he calls it, to the point where, by 1933, they became, actually or potentially, Hitler's willing executioners has under-standably provoked outrage and anguish in Germany. Hans-Ulrich Wehler and Eberhard Jäckel – both distinguished historians of the Left – have called Goldhagen's thesis "biological collectivism" and accuse him of "a regression to the most primitive of all stereotypes". Numerous critics point out that the German henchmen were willingly assisted by countless Poles, Lithua-nians, Latvians, Ukrainians in the East and by Dutch and French militiamen – though not by Danes or Italians – in the West. Others have questioned the monocausal explanation provided by Goldhagen – anti-Semitism – in view of the many millions of non-Jews – Soviet prisoners of war, Russian and Serb "partisans", Poles, gypsies, the mentally and physically handicapped, homosexual men – who were killed in that same unbelievable orgy of death which was compressed into the seven brief years between 1938 and 1945. Many complain of the complete lack of any attempt on the author's part to compare anti-Semitism in Germany with other versions of anti-Semitism working their poison elsewhere in Christian Europe. They ask how, if "eliminationist anti-Semitism" – in which category he includes assimilationism – had been so all-pervasive in German culture, the German Jews could have contributed so miraculously to its flowering in the nineteenth and early twentieth centuries; indeed why the Jews stayed in Germany at all. There is also disbelief that Goldhagen, in a throwaway remark tucked away in a footnote on page 582 of his long book, should aver that the German national character was not "timeless", and that in 1945 the Germans had in fact become "just like us"!

But at least one highly-respected German historian, Ulrich Herbert of the University of Freiburg, has pointed out that, however overstated and one-dimensional it might be, Daniel Goldhagen's thesis *has* raised an important question not previously or adequately addressed by historians: how extensive *was* anti-Semitism in Germany before Hitler? He rightly criticizes his German colleagues for becoming so obsessed with their impenetrable and arcane structuralist explanatory models that the intentions of the executioners has slipped entirely from view. Herbert estimates that at the time of Hitler's rise to power perhaps half of the German population was moderately anti-Semitic, but that this was more than enough to provide Hitler with his executioners once the regime had legitimized mass murder.

Whatever else it has achieved, then, this deeply flawed book has provoked much impassioned public debate on an issue of immense concern to the whole of humankind – an issue, it might be said, that is too important to be left to structuralist historians.

Suggestions for further reading

Hitler's willing executioners: ordinary Germans and the Holocaust, by Daniel Jonah Goldhagen, was published in March 1996 by Alfred Knopf in New York, USA and by Little, Brown & Company in London. It is now available in paperback. The German translation is entitled *Hitlers Willige Vollstrecker* (literally: Hitler's willing *executors*, rather than executioners) and was published in Berlin by the Siedler Verlag August, 1996. Aggressively marketed on both sides of the Atlantic, the book provoked mixed but increasingly critical reactions. The early reviews in America and Britain were generally favourable, but they were not written by professional historians.

See Robert Harris's review "The Awful Truth" in *The Sunday Times*, 24 March 1996 and Richard Bernstein's comments "Was Slaughter of Jews embraced by Germans?" in *The New York Times*, 27 March 1996. The Nobel prize winner Elie Wiesel added his influential endorsement in a brief article entitled "Little Hitlers" in *The Observer* on 31 March 1996. One of the first academic historians to praise the book, albeit with some reservations, was Volker R. Berghahn, of Brown University, writing in *The New York Times Book Review* on 14 April 1996. Very much more critical was Professor Omer Bartov's review "Ordinary Monsters" in *The New Republic*, 29 April 1996. One of the first considered – and distinctly reserved – British responses from an expert in German history was penned by Professor Peter Pulzer, of Oxford University, in *The London Review of Books*, 23 January 1997. The German weekly *Die Zeit* commissioned a number of reviews from German and American historians (including Christopher R. Browning and Gordon Craig) which – alongside other major German reviews – have been usefully collected together, for those who read German, by Julius H. Schoeps in *Ein Volk von Mördern? Die Dokumentation zur Goldhagen-Kontroverse und die Rolle der Deutschen im Holocaust* (Hamburg: Campe Paperback, 1996). One of the fullest and most balanced German responses, by the eminent historian Hans-Ulrich Wehler, has been translated into English and has now appeared under the title "The Goldhagen controversy: agonizing problems, scholarly failure and the political dimension", in *German History. The Journal of the German History Society* **15**(1), pp. 80–91, 1997. Goldhagen has defended himself against his numerous critics in a lengthy riposte entitled "Motives, Causes, and Alibis: A Reply to my Critics", in *The New Republic*, pp. 37–45, 23 December 1996. Nevertheless, it is clear that the more time the historical experts have had to evaluate the quality of Goldhagen's scholarship, the more critical they have become. In what is perhaps the most careful and detailed investigation into his research methods to date, the renowned scholar Ruth Bettina Birn, Chief Historian of the War Crimes and Crimes against Humanity Section of the Canadian Department of Justice, has accused Goldhagen of deploying his evidence selectively to underpin a preconceived theory and expressed her deep concern at the manner in which, in her view, aggressive advertising and mass marketing have in this case dictated the historical agenda. Her review article "Revising the Holocaust" is printed in *The Historical Journal* **40**(I), pp. 195–215, 1997. The German Holocaust expert Dieter Pohl has just published a similar lengthy and sharply critical analysis in the *Vierteljahrshefte für Zeitgeschichte* (Stuttgart: Deutsche Verlags-Anstalt, 1953). Important new criticism is also contained in the chapter entitled "The realm of shadows: recent writing on the Holocaust" of the forthcoming book *Ethics and Extermination: Essays on Nazi Genocide* by the distinguished British historian, Michael Burleigh (Cambridge: Cambridge University Press, 1997). The controversy continues.

21

Chapter Three

ᕫᔆ

Unreliable memories? The use and abuse of oral history

Alistair Thomson

Among the most obvious sources for contemporary history are the memories of people who have lived through past events. In the second half of the twentieth century "oral history" – the interviewing of eyewitness participants in past events for the purposes of historical interpretation and reconstruction – has had a significant impact upon contemporary history as practised in many countries. Yet oral historians have been plagued by criticisms about "unreliable memories". In this article I outline the arguments for oral history and the basis of such criticisms, and then use examples from my own interviews with Australian war veterans to show that the so-called "unreliability" of memory can be a resource rather than a problem for historical research.

The voice of the past

The social historian Paul Thompson has charted the pre-history of the modern oral history movement, explaining that historians from ancient times relied upon eyewitness accounts of significant events. For example, the Greek historian Thucydides used information from interviews with participants in writing the *History of the Peloponnesian War*, and Jules Michelet, author of the important mid-nineteenth century *History of the French Revolution*, used the "oral tradition" of participant accounts to counterbalance the version of official documents:

> When I say *oral* tradition I mean *national* tradition, which remained generally scattered in the mouths of the people, which everybody said and repeated, peasants, townsfolk, old men, women, even children; which you can hear if you enter of an evening into a village tavern;

which you may gather if, finding on the road a passer-by at rest, you begin to converse with him about the rain, the season, then the high price of victuals, then the times of the Emperor, then the times of the Revolution.

Yet, within a century, history professor James Westfall Thompson wrote of Michelet's work that "this may seem a strange way of collecting historical data". The late-nineteenth-century development of a professional history discipline based in universities led to the institutionalization of historical procedures and training inspired by the work of German historian Leopold von Ranke. The primary concern of the new professional historian was to discover "what really happened" in the past, and the most reliable sources were documents which could be preserved in archives and checked by other researchers. Oral evidence was regarded as unreliable folk tales and treated with disdain by academic historians. As most historical research at this time concerned the history of political and military elites who were likely to have produced and saved documentary evidence of their activities, the topics and the methods of professional history were mutually reinforcing.

After the Second World War, the increasing availability of portable tape recorders, which meant that interviews were recorded and transcribed and could be used and checked by other researchers, underpinned a revival of oral history. The timing and pattern of this revival differed markedly around the world. For example, the first organized oral history project, initiated by Allan Nevins at Columbia University in New York in 1948, sought to record the memories of civic leaders who had not got around to writing their memoirs. This emphasis on archival recordings with white male elites was representative of early oral history activity in the United States, although by the 1970s books like *Hard Times*, an oral history of the Great Depression by Studs Terkel, and Alex Haley's extraordinary account of the *Roots* of his African–American family, had spurred a growing popular and academic interest in oral history. British oral history pioneers of the 1950s and 1960s were particularly interested in recording the experiences of so-called "ordinary" working people – George Ewart Evans, for example, determined to "ask the fellows who cut the hay" about their life and times – and this interest fused with the commitment to "people's history" amongst social historians. By the mid-1970s, oral history was well established in archival projects and amongst academic and community historians in many parts of the world.

What have been the aims and aspirations of the oral history movement? While interviews with members of social and political elites have complemented existing documentary sources, the most distinctive contribution of oral history has been to include within the historical record the experiences and perspectives of groups of people who might otherwise have been neglected, perhaps written about by social observers or in official documents such as court records, but only rarely preserved in scraps of autobiographical writing. Through oral history interviews working-class men and women, indigenous peoples or members of cultural minorities, amongst others, have inscribed their experiences on the historical record and offered their own interpretations of history.

The political movements of emergent social groups have often used oral history as a significant historical and political resource. Thus in the 1970s activists in the women's movement recognised that oral interviews could uncover the experiences of the half of the population which had been, in Sheila Rowbotham's telling phrase, "hidden from history", and in recent years gay and lesbian historians, and members of the disability rights movement, have found strength and understanding through exploration of their collective memories. Indigenous peoples such as Native Americans and Australia's Aborigines have used oral testimony to support their struggles for cultural respect and land rights.

Oral history interviews have also enabled historians to recover and explore particular aspects of historical experience which are rarely recorded in documentary sources, such as personal relationships and domestic life, or the nature of clandestine organisations ranging from wartime resistance movements to the Ku Klux Klan. While memories can help fill in gaps in our historical understanding about past events and organizations, they are particularly valuable because, like autobiographical writing, they can convey the subjective or personal meanings of lived experience; what it *felt* like to get married, to be under fire, to face death in a concentration camp.

Because oral history is predicated on an active human relationship between historians and their sources, it can transform the practice of history in other ways. Recorded oral testimony is not just an historical source to be mined for information and subjected to historical interpretation by the interviewer and other historians. In an interview the narrator not only recalls the past; they also offer an interpretation of that past. In effect, oral history can challenge the special status of the historian and democratize the practice of history. Oral history projects in schools and museums have shown that people of all ages and with different skills and abilities can work together as historians. In participatory oral history projects members of community groups make their own histories, becoming the subjects of their own accounts rather than the objects of professional historians. For example, the slogan of the Brighton community history and publishing group QueenSpark Books is that "everyone has a history and anyone can be a writer", and members from all walks of life produce and publish a series of local best-sellers based on oral history interviews and autobiographical writing. For some practitioners, oral history has not just been about making histories. Perhaps the most significant spin-off from oral history has been the development of reminiscence work (or life review, as it is called in North America), a social movement which has linked academic oral historians, community publishing and reminiscence or life review workers in care settings. Changes in the psychology of old age in the 1960s and 1970s challenged an orthodoxy that reminiscence was an abnormal or patholog-ical activity, something to be discouraged, and sparked a crucial recognition that remembering could be a therapeutic and affirming process for older adults. In the 1980s, in Britain, North America and Australasia, there was an explosion of interest in reminiscence work with older people in residential homes and hospitals, and through adult education and self-help groups. Over time reminiscence work came to embrace other groups, such as people with mental health problems or adults with learning difficulties. In all of these projects the primary aim has been the empowerment of individuals or social groups through the process of remembering and reinterpreting the past, with an emphasis on the value of the process for the person re-membering as much as on any historical outcomes.

In fact, oral history and reminiscence work are really two sides of the same coin, with slightly different aims and outcomes, but a shared commit-ment to the value of remembering. Reminiscence work has encouraged oral historians to consider the significance of remembering for their interviewees. Several of the war veterans I interviewed commented that, although the process of remembering a painful past was sometimes difficult, they valued the opportunity to talk through events and feelings that they had never shared before. In turn, I have had to consider the risks of remembering and the limits of an interview.

"Old men forget"

The methods and politics of oral history sparked serious challenges in the early days of this emerging movement, ranging from fierce criticisms by traditional documentary historians to sophisticated re-evaluations of aims and approaches from within the emergent field. The main thrust of the criticism of oral history in the 1970s was that memory was unreliable as an historical source. It was, according to critics, distorted by physical deteri-oration and nostalgia in old age, by the personal bias of both interviewer and interviewee, and by the influence of collective and retrospective ver-sions of the past. For example, the Australian historian Patrick O'Farrell wrote in 1979 that oral history was moving into "the world of image, select-ive memory, later overlays and utter subjectivity . . . And where will it lead us? Not into history, but into myth." In 1981, British Tory politician and historian Enoch Powell cautioned that "old men forget", and A. J. P. Taylor argued that "memoirs of years ago are useless except for atmosphere . . . old men drooling about their youth – No." Underlying criticisms of memory was concern about the democratization of the historians' craft – O'Farrell derided oral history's "ideological base in the cult of the common man" – and a disparagement of oral history's apparent "discrimination" in favour of women, workers and minority groups. Goaded by the taunts of documentary historians, early oral historians developed their own handbook guidelines to assess the reliability of oral memory (while shrewdly reminding the traditionalists that documentary sources were no less selective and biased). From social psychology and anthropology they showed how to determine the bias and fabulation of memory, the significance of retrospection and the effects of the interviewer upon remembering. From sociology they adopted methods of representative sampling, and from documentary history they brought rules for checking the reliability and internal consistency of their source. These guidelines provided useful signposts for reading memories and for combining them with other historical sources to find out what happened in the past. However, the tendency to defend and use oral history as just another historical source to discover "how it really was" led to the neglect of other aspects and values of oral testimony. In their efforts to correct bias and fabulation – to iron out the glitches in memory – some practitioners lost sight of the reasons why individuals construct their memories in particular ways, and did not see how the process of remembering could be a key to exploring the personal or "subjective" meanings of lived experience and the nature of individual and social memory. By seeking to discover a single, fixed and recoverable history, some oral historians neglected the complex layering of individual memory and the plurality of versions of the past provided by different speakers. They did not see that the "distortions" of memory could be a resource as much as a problem.

From the late 1970s a number of oral historians began to reconsider "the peculiarities of oral history" and to see them as a strength rather than a weakness. For example, Luisa Passerini analyzed the silences and inconsistencies in Italian working-class memories of Mussolini's inter-war fascist regime to show how fascist ideology had become deeply entangled in everyday life and personal identity, and to explore the difficulties of remembering involvement in a discredited regime. Another Italian, Alessandro Portelli noticed that interviewees in the factory town of Terni "misremembered" the date of the death of the worker Luigi Trastulli. Trastulli had died during a small anti-NATO demonstration in 1949, but local people remembered his death as a martyrdom during the course of a catastrophic strike and lockout in 1953 which had involved the whole town and led to defeat for the union and the end of work security. Portelli argued that the mistaken memory was a vital clue to understanding the *meanings* of these events for individuals and for the working-class community, as they happened and as they lived on in memory.

The work of Passerini, Portelli and others showed oral historians that interview testimony could be used in many ways, and not only to find out what happened in the past. By working with memories we can explore the impact of past experiences upon people's lives and identities. What did these events mean for participants at the time, and how have their meaning

27

and significance changed over time right up to the present day? We can see how collective or social memories have developed and, in turn, we can consider the impact of public versions of the past – as represented in books and films, in political rhetoric or folk stories, and so on – upon individual remembering. How do powerful public memories shape how we remember and recall our lives, perhaps providing ways of making sense of the past, perhaps silencing memories which do not fit?

In short, oral history is not simply "the voice of the past"; it is a living record of the complex interaction between past and present within each individual and in society. And if history is not just concerned with finding out about the past, but is also about the significance of the past in the present, then oral history provides a key with which to unlock that relationship. As the North American historian Michael Frisch writes, oral history is:

> a powerful tool for discovering, exploring, and evaluating the nature of the process of historical memory – how people make sense of their past, how they connect individual experience and its social context, how the past becomes part of the present, and how people use it to interpret their lives and the world around them.

Anzac memories: gone for a soldier

I will illustrate this approach to oral history with examples from interviews with Australian working-class veterans of the Great War of 1914–18 which I conducted in the 1980s. The two extracts I reproduce focus on memories of enlistment, on how and why two young Australians joined the army and went overseas to fight on the European Western Front. In the memories of many of the old men I interviewed the story of enlistment is highly significant and fraught with anxiety and contradiction. It reveals a struggle to make sense of a decision that may have been difficult at the time, that sometimes had disastrous consequences, for which public regard has varied dramatically – from patriotic enthusiasm and admiration through to doubt and even opposition to participation in "a European war" – and that could be remembered with either pride or regret. In short, enlistment is an emotional minefield in the memory of many veterans.

Percy Bird volunteered for the Australian Imperial Force (AIF) midway through 1915, about a year after the outbreak of war. At 26 years of age he had been working as a clerk with the Victorian railways, and he was engaged to be married. To make sense of Percy's account of his enlistment and wartime experience you really need to hear the tape and to know about Percy Bird as a storyteller. The ways in which people remember their lives and the forms of the narrative are often as revealing about the meaning of the account as what is actually said. Percy Bird was a performer, a singer and a great storyteller, with an anecdotal style akin to that of a stand-up comedian. He had developed his singing and storytelling abilities at wartime concert parties and amongst his mates in the trenches, and even in old age he loved to spin a yarn for the other residents of his retirement home. Percy's performance drew upon a fixed repertoire of short, discrete anecdotes, loosely arranged in approximate chronological order but also prompted by cue words in a previous story or a question, or by the established sequence of the story. Each story had a punch line or "tag" which had helped to fix it in Percy's memory, and which gave it a purposeful theme and made it a "good" story.

The main themes through which Percy articulated his war memory were the humour of trench life, lucky escapes from enemy shells, his successful participation in army concerts, and the impressive abilities of the Australian soldiers (who shared the "Anzac" nickname with the New Zealanders). In Percy's remembering the war was never horrifying or disillusioning, and he avoided talking about his experiences in the line and under fire. When I met Percy for our first interview he presented me with a twelve-page set of these stories, entitled "The 5th Battalion, 1916 and 1917, France", and then proceeded to retell these same stories with great glee and with little regard for my questions. I realised that over the years Percy Bird had composed an account of his war years that was popular with a variety of audiences, and that provided him with a relatively safe and comfortable way of remembering the war.

This is how Percy Bird responded to my questions about his enlistment.

Can you remember where you were when the war broke out, and your response to the war?

Oh well, oh yes, I was here. I was in Melbourne on the 4th August 1914, and in the train from Williamstown going to Melbourne. A number of us got in the same carriage and we saw a boat going down the river, the Yarra. "Hello. Look at that." It was the *Holtz*, I think they named it. A German boat trying to get out, and they were, the artillery fired to stop them. He had to fire two or three shots to stop them. So they grabbed them.

What was your initial response to the war?

Oh well, nothing particular. But I was going to join up somewhere about February, 1915, but my father was put into hospital seriously ill, and my mother said, "Don't do anything until we see how Dad gets on." So I enlisted on the, somewhere early in July 1915, because they had time to operate on my father, but his heart wouldn't take it, so they said, "Well, we'll let him have another twelve months." You see, so he died on the 4th of March, no the 4th of April, 1916.

Why did you want to enlist?

Oh (awkward laugh). Be like all the others (awkward laugh). I wanted to enlist like all the others, you know. Well, like lots of the others, I should say, because I thought I was . . . well, I was . . . should enlist. Being a member of . . . being an Australian. So then, when I did go on the boat going over. . . .

The story about the German ship the *Holtz* that Percy told me when I first asked him about the outbreak of war was a typical Percy Bird story. It offered a useful hook to remember the start of the war, and linked Percy to an historical public event which would be of interest to his listeners. In fact, the geography of Melbourne's river system and railways makes it unlikely that Percy could have seen *Holtz* from his railway carriage. He may have heard the explosions or read about the event in the newspaper, and in time the story became his own with Percy very much in the picture.

Though Percy was happy to talk about the start of the war, he would have preferred to skip the details of his own enlistment and move straight into stories about the trip overseas with reinforcements for the 5th Battalion. The first eighteen months of the war was a difficult time for Percy. On the one hand, there was enormous pressure on eligible young men to join up, and as a one-time member of the Boy's Naval Brigade, Percy had a strong sense of patriotism and military duty. On the other hand, the family trauma of his father's illness and the commitment to a new fiancée were countervailing pressures that made enlistment difficult. In effect, enlistment represented a choice between two different masculinities, between the family man and the independent soldier adventurer. After an awkward period of delay, the pressures to join up and be a soldiering man won out.

Yet enlistment never became one of Percy's favoured war stories, because it had been a difficult choice at the time, and because he was later troubled by people who challenged the worth of Australian participation in a European war. Though Percy did return from the war to marry his fiancée, he may also have been wary of talking about leaving her in the first place. When pressed by my questioning, Percy breaks into an awkward laugh and stumbles through an explanation which justifies the decision in terms of duty, patriotism and mateship. Being "like all the others" and "being an Australian" were certainly part of the reason why Percy Bird went to war, though in 1915 membership of the Empire meant more to many young recruits than an Australian identity that was strengthened in the course of the war, and that may have been added to the story with hindsight. The silences and awkwardness of Percy's account hint at other influential factors and at the difficulty of recall. As historians we can use Percy's account – with all its gaps and inconsistencies – as rich evidence about the complex experience of joining up, and to illuminate the meanings of enlistment for Percy and other Australians, during and after the war and up to the present day.

Fred Farrall remembered the war and his life in a very different way. Fred's life story is deliberate, detailed and sequential, a well-rehearsed unfolding of the transformations of his life, often superbly told through tensions and twists towards climactic punch lines. Most importantly, Fred's stories compose a particular meaning in which his war and his life is a process of conversion. Stripped to essentials, Fred's narrative is as follows. The naive and patriotic farm boy goes to war as a willing recruit but unwitting sacrificial lamb. He becomes a frightened, inadequate and disillusioned soldier on the Western Front, and a confused and traumatised veteran upon his return to Australia. After several years in a personal wilderness he discovers in the labour movement supportive comrades and a new, socialist way of understanding his life and the world, and regains his self-esteem as a man. He articulates his disillusionment about the war in political terms and thus redefines the war as one stage on the way to his enlightenment. Many of Fred's stories are framed in terms of this movement towards conversion. The narrative is often interrupted and explained by an ironic reflection which situates a particular incident within the larger pattern which he has made of his life. Fred's enlistment story shows how his remembering worked in this way and conveys his skill and style as a storyteller.

The war broke out in 1914. Well of course in August 1914 I was then actually fifteen years of age, and as I'd wanted to be a jockey I wasn't very robust, in fact I was very small. So my father then began to make some changes, politically speaking, because the Labor Party were not very enthusiastic about the war. Although there was a Labor government, Andrew Fisher, who pledged Australia's support to the last man and the last shilling, as politicians can easily do. But there was a fair bit of opposition from other sections of the Labor Party and my father became a staunch supporter for the war. When the landing was made in Gallipoli, of course, we all had to have it read to us from the papers after tea at night. It was sort of . . . almost something like a religious service and we listened to it and we believed it.

The war went on and 1915, in September 1915, I'd reached the age of eighteen. What did I say? Did I say earlier that I was fifteen when the war . . . I was sixteen when the war broke out. In another month's time I was seventeen then, so I'd reached the age of eighteen and having given away the idea of being a jockey I began to build up my physique somewhat. Previous to that I'd, you know, endeavoured to keep my weight down, but after that denial on the part of my father to do what I wanted to do I just sort of grew up more. The physical standard for joining the army in 1914 and early 1915 was very, very high and I had no hope anyway at being able to measure up to that sort of thing, that standard. But after Gallipoli, or while Gallipoli was on, and they'd suffered a lot of casualties, they lowered the standard considerably here.

When we were in the harvest field in November 1915, we were haymaking and dad had one or two or three men working for him in the harvest as we used to have. They would be swagmen that would be picked up in Ganmain and brought out to do some work, you see. So I was working with one of them, Bill Fraser, and I said to Bill one day, "I'm thinking about going to the war, Bill." Well he was an Irishman and he gave me some pretty good advice and a bit of a lecture while we were picking up sheaves of hay and putting them in stooks where they belonged. He told me that I should stay on the farm. He said, "You should remember", he said, "that next to your life the most valuable thing you've got is your health. You stay here on the farm and look after it because it's worthwhile keeping." And finished his advice by saying "Let the rich men fight their own wars." Well, I didn't take Bill's advice. I had listened to the Prime Minister and his "last man and last shilling to defend the Empire", the Premier of New South Wales, the Archbishop. I did what they said to do. I enlisted.

This excerpt is a typical example of Fred's story-telling technique. The listener's interest is sustained by the tensions between different characters and courses of action. The narrative works as a story precisely because it is framed by Fred's retrospective vision of his life. The ironies are resonant because we know, as Fred now knows, the consequences of his enlistment, and that Fred should have listened to Bill Fraser's advice. That doesn't mean that the details about how Fred felt and acted at the time are invented, merely that the way in which he has composed his story of enlistment causes him to highlight certain experiences and make sense of them in particular ways.

For example, Fred mentions that his father stopped him from becoming a jockey. Fred hated farm life and desperately wanted to leave the farm, and when a "Kangaroo" recruiting march came to a nearby town he jumped at the chance to join up. But he does not refer to his distaste for farm life and the desire to escape as a personal motivation for enlistment. Fred prefers to emphasise his patriotic enthusiasm, and to suggest that like other AIF recruits he was duped by patriotic rhetoric. That explanation fits more neatly into his political story of a conversion from patriotism to disillusionment. By contrast, the motivations of escape and adventure are less appealing to Fred the political activist who prefers to emphasise serious and principled motivations, even if they were mistaken. Fred's story draws upon a radical understanding of the war which was developed by socialists and pacifists between the wars, but which was eventually silenced by an "Anzac legend" which celebrated the achievements of the Australian soldiers through war memorials, commemoration ceremonies and official histories. As an old man Fred still resisted the Anzac legend, and yet, ironically, by continuing to make sense of the war in radical terms he suppressed significant aspects of his own experience.

Fred Farrall's enlistment story, like that of Percy Bird, can be used in several ways. By listening to these stories and reading between the lines of memory, we can see that enlistment was motivated by a complicated mix of factors. The Anzac legend simplifies the historical picture by depicting enlistment primarily in terms of patriotism and adventure. For example, in 1990 publicity for a 75th Anniversary Anzac Commemorative Coin eulogized Australian Great War recruits in the following terms: "They fought for what they believed in. They fought for freedom. They fought for their country. They fought for us. They fought for our children." Soldiers' memories suggest a much more complex and nuanced historical understanding of these men's response to the outbreak of war. More than that, veterans' memories provide clues about the continuing significance of the war for participants and other Australians. Percy and Fred's efforts to explain their enlistment and to make sense of the war offer rich evidence about the changing and contested meanings of the Great War, and about the significance of that past in Australian society.

As historians we want to know about what happened in the past; but we also want to explore how past events have impacted upon individuals and societies, at the time and over the years. Through working with memories – both "reliable" and "unreliable" – oral history allows us to explore these relationships between past and present. It reminds us that memory is a battlefield, and that historians cannot help but enter the fray.

Suggestions for further reading

The standard text on the history and achievements of oral history is P. Thompson, *The voice of the past: oral history* (Oxford: Oxford University Press, 1988 – see pp. 22–3 for the quotes from Jules Michelet and James Westfall Thompson). The seminal works of three pioneering oral historians are: G. E. Evans, *Ask the fellows who cut the hay* (London: Faber, 1956); S. Terkel, *Hard times: an oral history of the Great Depression* (New York: Pantheon Books, 1970); A. Haley, *Roots: the saga of an American family* (London: Hutchinson, 1977). Three recent anthologies include some of the best writings about the theory and practice of oral history: D. K. Dunaway, & W. K. Baum (eds), *Oral history: an interdisciplinary anthology*, 2nd edn (Walnut Creek: Altamira Press, 1996); Gluck Berger, S. & D. Patai (eds), *Women's words: the feminist practice of oral history* (New York and London: Routledge, 1991); R. Perks, & A. Thomson (eds). *The oral history reader* (London and New York: Routledge, 1998). Other writings about oral history can be found in the various national journals, incuding, among others: *Oral History* (Great Britain), *Oral History Review* (United States), and the *Oral History Association of Australia Journal*. Among early critics of oral history were: B. Tuchman, Distinguishing the significant from the insignificant. *Radcliffe Quarterly* 56, pp. 9–10, 1972; E. Powell, "Old men forget", *The Times*, 5 November 1981; P. O'Farrell, Oral history: facts and fiction, *Oral History Association of Australia Journal* **5**, pp. 3–9, 1982–3. The reference to A. J. P. Taylor's comments is in B. Harrison, Oral history and recent political history, *Oral History* **1**(3), pp. 30–48, 1972. For the inspirational oral histories of Luisa Passerini and Alessandro Portelli, see L. Passerini, *Fascism in popular memory: the cultural experience of the Turin working class* (Cambridge: Cambridge University Press, 1987) and A. Portelli, *The death of Luigi Trastulli and other stories: form and meaning in oral history* (Albany: State University of New York Press, 1991). The quote from Michael Frisch is from his thoughtful collection of essays: see page 188, M. Frisch, *A shared authority: essays on the craft and meaning of oral and public history* (Albany: State University of New York Press, 1990). For the ideas of another important North American oral historian, see R. Grele, *Envelopes of sound: the art of oral history*, 2nd edn, revised and enlarged (New York: Praeger, 1991). On reminiscence work see J. Bornat (ed.). *Reminiscence reviewed: achievements, evaluations, perspectives* (Buckingham: Open University Press, 1993). For a more detailed account of my own oral history of Australian soldiers of the First World War, see A. Thomson, *Anzac memories: living with the legend* (Melbourne: Oxford University Press, 1994).

Chapter Four

ふる

The English reputations of Oliver Cromwell 1660–1900

Blair Worden

From his century to ours, Oliver Cromwell has been the most controversial figure of English history. The civil wars and Interregnum, the period which he came to dominate, were a time of revolutionary violence unique in our history. Its passions and divisions have never gone away. If they have exerted less power in the twentieth century than in its predecessors, that is because in modern times the past has lost something of its hold on the political consciousness of the present. In earlier centuries, the centuries covered by this essay, the arguments between Cavaliers and Roundheads were time and again recalled, even relived, by the heirs of those parties: by Tories on the one hand, by Whigs and then Liberals on the other.

Cromwell's stature in our history reflects the uniqueness not only of his times but of the man. For two centuries after his death, even writers who condemned him wondered at the exploits of that "wonderful" or "extraordinary" figure. They marvelled at the meteoric rise that had taken him, in middle age, from provincial obscurity and from the backbenches of the Commons to the conquest and sovereignty of Britain. With his army at his back he crushed the royalists in the 1640s. In 1649 he carried through the trial and execution of Charles I and the abolition of monarchy. In 1649-51 he overcame Ireland and Scotland and subjected them, with England, to Puritan rule. Friends were crushed as well as foes. The more conservative and cautious of his fellow Roundheads were outmanoeuvered by him during the civil wars and driven from power by the regicide. In 1653 his army forcibly expelled the Long Parliament, of which it had ostensibly been the servant. Later in that year it installed him as Lord Protector, the position he would hold until his death in 1658. Each of his coups swelled the ranks of former allies whom he had reduced to impotent outrage. Supreme at home, he was courted by the great rival monarchies abroad, France and

Spain. England, which before the civil wars had cut a shameful figure on the continent, was now a great power.

Wonder at Cromwell's achievements produced, in the decades and centuries following his lifetime, some retrospective exaggerations of them. His military dominance, which properly begins in 1648 in the second civil war, was projected back into the first, of 1642–6. In popular mythology he came to have fought in as many places as Queen Elizabeth has slept. He was likewise believed to have demolished countless religious buildings or ornaments, the responsibility for whose destruction had in fact lain either with other armies of the civil wars or with the Reformation in the time of Thomas Cromwell, a figure with whose deeds Oliver's were often conflated. Oliver's political dominance was also overstated, particularly in accounts of his career down to 1653. From the eighteenth century onwards, it is true, historians would occasionally try to cut Cromwell down to size, to show that in his actions and character, whether they were viewed as good or evil, there was nothing to astonish. Yet, for most of his posthumous life, he has towered above his age. Time and again he has seemed England's equivalent to Julius Caesar or, from the early nineteenth century, to Napoleon. Yet what kind of person had he been? What motives had impelled his ascent? No one in the earlier stages of the revolution anticipated or wanted his rule. In the 1640s he fought for a parliament which was pledged to restore the king once the wars were over. Then, in 1649, he pledged himself to support parliamentary rule without a single ruler. How, four years later, could he justify his own elevation as single ruler, as in effect the successor to the Stuarts? Had he, as his enemies alleged, planned it all along? Had he been a master of dissimulation and hypocrisy, winning the trust of his parliamentary allies, and mouthing their Puritan language, while nursing a secret and ungodly ambition to usurp the throne? Or had he had nobler or at least more reputable motives? Might not the destruction first of the king, then of the Long Parliament, have been their fault rather than his? By what other means could he have prevented the restoration of Stuart tyranny in the first instance and the descent of the nation into anarchy in the second? Might not the arbitrary features of his rule as Protector, of which his resort to military rule and to non-parliamentary taxation in 1655 was the most conspicuous, have been born of emergency and necessity? Might not their purpose have been, not to extinguish constitutional liberties, but to preserve, in an unsettled and bitterly divided land, the public order without which the restoration of those liberties was unattainable?

Amidst those arguments, which have crossed the centuries, assessments of Cromwell's achievements have taken second place to judgements of his motives and character. Was he good or bad, sincere or insincere? We simplify, but do not over-simplify, if we say that historians were predominantly unsympathetic to Cromwell until around the middle of the nineteenth century and have been predominantly sympathetic to him since. Yet historical writing does not necessarily reflect public sentiment or even do much to affect it. Many historians and biographers have admitted that their views were at odds with opinion around them. This was particularly true of the early stage of Cromwell's posthumous standing, the reign of Charles II. Writers critical of Cromwell complained of the "many vulgar errors" of contemporaries, whom they had heard comparing the present reign unfavourably with Cromwell's rule and "venerating" or "idolizing" or "adoring" the protector's memory. A century and more later, similar anxieties were at work. In 1796 John Thelwall was dismayed to observe that Cromwell had, "even at this day, many enthusiastic admirers, who do not scruple to admire him as the greatest champion that liberty ever had in this country". In 1828 William Godwin remarked that a "favourable" impression of the protectorate had "fixed the attention of mankind", an impression he was eager to correct. It was in the same year that the young Macaulay, who was more friendly to Cromwell, asserted that Oliver had "always continued popular with the great body of his countrymen". Yet public opinion can be hard to gauge. In 1721 *Cato's Letters* reported that Cromwell "is scarce ever mentioned but with detestation, or thought of but as a monster". Glimpses of conversations about Cromwell later in the eighteenth century indicate the prevalence of the epithet "monster".

From the middle of the nineteenth century, when more favourable writing on Cromwell came to the fore, those who wrote admiringly of him likewise knew that they did not necessarily speak for the body of their compatriots. They thought of themselves as representing the "educated" or "sober" portion of mankind, which had distanced itself from "the old Tory and fox-hunting style of talking about him". Down to this century Cromwell retained a status in folklore, especially in some rural areas, as a demon or archetypal villain. Within living memory attempts to name colleges or roads after him were thwarted by irate resistance.

Historians have sometimes demonized him too. Yet from the later seventeenth century his historical critics, even at their most vituperative, have generally recognised merits in him. He could not have risen and triumphed as he did, they have acknowledged, without surpassing qualities: valour, resolution, vigilance, sagacity, dexterity, decisiveness, insight into human nature. Alongside those practical virtues they acknowledged the presence in him of greatness of heart and generosity of soul. The most influential of royalist histories, the *History of the Rebellion* by Charles I's adviser and Charles II's Lord Chancellor Edward Hyde, Earl of Clarendon, paid tribute to the "great heart" of Cromwell, that "brave bad man" who, as "he had all the wickednesses . . . for which hell-fire is prepared, so he had some virtues which have caused the memory of some men in all ages to be celebrated". Thereafter most of Cromwell's critics recognized a two-sidedness to him. Tobias Smollett's description of Cromwell in 1758 as "the strangest compound of villainy and virtue, baseness and magnanimity, absurdity and good sense, that we find upon record in the annals of mankind" echoes many an earlier assessment. The ambivalence of Cromwell's character sustained his fascination. In 1739 his biographer John Banks had "often heard Oliver Cromwell applauded and condemned by the same gentlemen, almost in the same breath." "How to reconcile" the good and bad in Cromwell, observed Thomas Price a century later, "has perplexed all candid men".

The fiercest denunciations of Cromwell belong to the Restoration period. From 1660, when his body was exhumed from Westminster Abbey and strung up at Tyburn, royalists queued to portray the regicide, which Cromwell had engineered, as an act not merely of treason and murder but of blasphemy, carried out at least metaphorically, and perhaps literally, in league with the devil. In *The Loyall Martyrologie* of 1665 Cromwell was "this wicked monster", "the centre of mischief, a shame to the British chronicle, a blot to gentility, a pattern for tyranny, whose horrid treasons will scarce gain credit with posterity, whose bloody tyranny will quite drown the names of Nero, Domitian, Caligula, etc". James Heath's widely read biography of the same year, *Flagellum*, established the stock charges of hypocrisy, dissimulation and ruthless ambition that would persist down the centuries. Heath's colourfully inventive account of Cromwell's misspent youth would likewise endure.

Yet the vilification of Cromwell in the later seventeenth century was not an exclusively royalist achievement. His memory had republican enemies too. Royalists might underline the wickedness of the regicide, but there was a limit to the indignation they could mount against Cromwell's subsequent coups and purges, which had been directed at his fellow Roundhead criminals. To republicans, by contrast, Cromwell's usurpations of the 1650s had betrayed the cause of liberty. Republican accounts of the protectorate lack the magnanimity, the acknowledgement of the man's greatness, that can soften royalist attacks on him. There survive two republican accounts of Cromwell's rule written during the 1660s, one by the London merchant Slingsby Bethel, the other by Bethel's friend the exiled regicide Edmund Ludlow. In the long term those writings would prove at least as influential in shaping unfriendly images of Cromwell as the royalist accounts published in the same decade. That was partly because republicans, who had been at or close to the centre of power before and after the protectorate, were better informed about the 1650s than royalists. It was partly, too, because the successes of republican rule from 1649 to 1653 supplied an additional perspective from which the protectorate could be condemned.

Republican no less than royalist writing on Cromwell was intended to counter his enduring appeal. The principal explanation of the "idolatry" of him that was noticed both by royalist and by republican writers of the Restoration lay in England's return to diplomatic impotence under Charles II, in the neglect and corruption of the royal navy, and in the effeminate decadence of the restored court. As the honeymoon of the Restoration faded, so nostalgia emerged for the frugality of Cromwell's rule and for its military and naval might. In 1667, after the Dutch navy had humiliated England in the Medway, Samuel Pepys recorded that "everybody doth nowadays reflect upon Oliver and commend him, so brave things he did and made all the neighbour princes fear him".

Here is a persistent theme among the historical images of Cromwell. His exploits abroad have frequently won respect even from critics of his conduct at home. They have been remembered particularly at moments of diplomatic weakness or crisis. In the eighteenth century, especially in the era of Walpole, failures of the government to stand up to foreign navies or to eliminate piracy provoked numerous appeals to the example of Cromwell's naval vigour and of the triumphs of his naval commander Robert Blake. For if, in domestic politics, Cromwell had led a party, abroad he had led a country. Eighteenth-century histories which condemned his domestic policies were proud to recall the exploits of "English" soldiers and sailors under his rule. The same pattern can be witnessed, if less frequently, in the nineteenth century. One of the most electric moments of twentieth-century parliamentary history occurred in the debate that produced the fall of Neville Chamberlain, when an MP quoted words of Cromwell in order to arraign the appeasement of Hitler.

Cromwell's republican critics, in and after the seventeenth century, were galled by public approbation of his foreign achievements. The years of England's military and naval greatness, they maintained, had been those of 1649-53, when England had had no single ruler. Her subsequent decline had begun not in 1660 but under Cromwell, who had weakened the nation's trade and finances. He was also alleged to have committed a series of diplomatic blunders, the gravest of which was his decision to ally with France against its weaker rival, Spain. That move, it was claimed, had destroyed the balance of power in Europe, which it was in England's interest to preserve, and had left her exposed to the might of Louis XIV after the Restoration. Those charges were levelled in Slingsby Bethel's *The World's Mistake in Oliver Cromwell* in 1668. England's subsequent wars with France, lasting into the nineteenth century, gave enduring credence to Bethel's judgement, which writers sympathetic to Cromwell have always felt the need to address. Bethel also made a number of charges of tyranny in the protector's domestic administration. His purpose in writing was to convert the mistaken public admiration for Cromwell into an appetite for the restoration of the Commonwealth of 1649-53. It was a doomed hope. Instead, his accusations were rapidly and silently appropriated by royalist writers, in whose accounts they jostled with more respectful judgements of the protector's foreign policy.

The second republican writing of the 1660s to attack Cromwell, Edmund Ludlow's manuscript autobiography *A Voyce from the Watch Tower*, was published posthumously, in 1698, as *Ludlow's Memoirs*, where his words were heavily edited with an eye to the political controversies of William III's reign. The *Memoirs* repeated Bethel's charges and added to them. They portrayed Cromwell as a hypocrite who had duped his public-spirited allies and had sacrificed the revolution to "the idol of his own ambition". They also represented his rule as the origin of the threat posed to English liberty by a standing army, an anxiety which was at the front of the public mind when the *Memoirs* appeared and which would persist both in public debate and in accounts of Cromwell through the eighteenth century. Even historians who rejected the arguments of the *Memoirs* were impressed by their vivid narrative of the 1650s. Accusations which were made against Cromwell in the *Memoirs*, but for which there is no independent evidence, would long figure in standard accounts, even sympathetic ones, of the Interregnum. Most of those charges concerned Cromwell's alleged aim to be made king and the thwarting of that ambition.

Yet the republican version, like the royalist one, did not go unchallenged. The eighteenth century produced a series of histories and biographies which, while conceding that Cromwell's character had contained elements of ambition and dissimulation, presented those characteristics less as evidence of diabolism than as customary and necessary adjuncts of sovereignty, which in Cromwell's case had been combined, even if they had sometimes conflicted, with a concern for the public good. Three broadly sympathetic and widely read biographies, those of Isaac Kimber in 1724, John Banks in 1739, and William Harris in 1762, encouraged that interpretation. The balance of eighteenth-century writing still gave more weight to Cromwell's vices than to his virtues. Yet even writers with Tory sympathies were willing to list healthy achievements alongside the catalogue of his infamies. He was credited not only with triumphs abroad but with efficacious domestic reforms, above all with measures to secure the just and able administration of the legal system.

Three developments combined to produce this more subtle and complex picture. First, there was the passage of time. Though the passions of the civil war were sedulously preserved by polemicists, who were ingenious in identifying parallels between past and present, they could never be felt quite so keenly as by the generation that had lived through the revolution. By the 1690s the popular historian Nathaniel Crouch could produce a biography of Cromwell that was almost detached in tone, written as it was to gratify public curiosity rather than to score political points. The further the revolution receded into the past, the less ready were sophisticated writers to subscribe to inflexible partisanship, whether Cavalier or Roundhead. In 1764 Horace Walpole explained that when he thought about the civil wars he had no instinctive preference for either Charles I or Cromwell, and that "if I sometimes commend, sometimes blame them, it is not from being inconsistent, but from considering them" in relation to the particular issue in his mind at the time.

Secondly, there was the publication of source material. Historical opinion is often portrayed, as it is in this essay, as a reflection of the times that produced it. Yet it is also shaped by the availability and the scholarly use of documents. Under Charles II collections of documents from the revolution had been published for party political purposes. In the eighteenth century the force behind such compilations was less often political than antiquarian. The 1740s and 1750s produced fat volumes of hitherto mainly unknown tracts and manuscripts from the mid-seventeenth century: above all the *Thurloe State Papers*, the *Harleian Miscellany*, the *Somers Tracts*. The influence of those publications, it is true, was fitful and uneven. A striking feature of biographies of Cromwell down to the nineteenth century is the readiness of some authors to reproduce, without acknowledgement, arguments and often words of much earlier writers, and to ignore discoveries made in the interim. Yet other biographers were more conscientious. Simple or brutal generalizations about Cromwell which gained currency in the later seventeenth and earlier eighteenth century were tested against new evidence and found wanting.

Thirdly, there was the Revolution of 1688. If Cromwell had had his failings, then so, it was now widely agreed, had his Stuart predecessors and successors. It became possible to portray the protectorate less as an interruption of seventeenth-century monarchical rule than as an admittedly irregular example of it. Comparisons between Cromwellian and Stuart government had at worst a neutral and at best an elevating effect on his standing. Even if his power had been unjustly gained, he was now acknowledged by many writers to have used it no worse, and by some to have used it better, than the Stuarts had used theirs. His reign, it was pointed out, had been more frugal, more efficient, and less corrupt than those of his royal predecessors and successors. Besides, Cromwell had fought against absolutism, a principle which the earlier and later Stuarts followed but which 1688 repudiated. Thenceforth many writers, even if they thought of the regicide as a crime, regarded the impulse behind it as no more wicked than that behind the personal rule of Charles I.

Of course the ascendant Whigs of the eighteenth century, who took their stand on constitutionalism, could not comfortably endorse Cromwell's military assaults on parliaments. They were usually readier to praise the heroes of the early stages of the Long Parliament, John Pym and John Hampden, whose methods had been more constitutional, than to think of Cromwell as a friend to liberty. Yet there was an increasing willingness to believe that Cromwell, however mixed his motives, had preferred constitutional to military methods and, in resorting to the latter, had deployed the only available means to defeat Stuart tyranny in the 1640s and to prevent its return in the 1650s.

By the later eighteenth century even writers with republican sympathies were ready to align Cromwell with Pym and Hampden among the heroes of the revolution. Admittedly Catherine Macaulay, whose diatribes against Cromwell around 1770 repeated the case of Bethel and Ludlow a century earlier, stood aside from that trend. Yet perspectives had emerged from which Cromwell's acts of violence against parliaments could seem not invasions of liberty but defences of it. For beside the Whig constitutionalism of the eighteenth century there existed, sometimes in the same minds, that country–party sentiment which, while it looked to parliamentary rule as an ideal, was as shocked by the parliamentary corruption of the present as by the monarchical corruption of the past. Cromwell's rule was sometimes compared favourably, in its frugality and fiscal propriety, with the corrupt regimes of Walpole and of Walpole's successors. It now seemed that Cromwell, in expelling the Long Parliament, had broken a factious oligarchy of a kind all too familiar to critics of the septennial parliaments whom Hanoverian statesmen had learned to pack with placemen. In its later stages the leaders of that parliament, no less than the ministers who dominated its eighteenth-century successors, had monopolized the distribution of offices and had grown ever more distant from the electorate they claimed to represent. Cromwell's impatience with parliamentary corruption earned him eighteenth-century credit on another front too. The protectoral constitution of 1653, the Instrument of Government, provided not only for triennial elections but for an overhaul of the electoral system. The inequitable distribution of seats was ended and the rotten boroughs were swept away. Those reforms died with Cromwell. In the eighteenth century they were often remembered and commended. In the words of Cromwell's biographer John Banks, they had reduced the "possibility of corruption and ministerial influence".

As we move from the eighteenth century into the nineteenth, so we find Cromwell the reformer and scourge of parliament winning applause from a different direction. His overhaul of the electoral system was now praised not only as a challenge to ministerial influence but for anticipating the principles of representation that were championed by the popular movement for parliamentary reform. In 1831, during the crisis of parliamentary reform, there was a call for a "second Oliver" to expel the unreformed parliament, just as Cromwell had expelled the unreformed parliament of 1653. The cry for a "second Oliver", whose sword would break the established order, also arose during times of hardship in the first half of the nineteenth century. There seems to have been a widespread belief that the protectorate had been a period of popular prosperity which the restoration of monarchical and aristocratic privilege in 1660 had ended.

Popular radicals, it is true, were never of one mind about Cromwell. Some thought of him as a usurper of liberty and as the imposer of heavy and illegal taxes. Yet by the middle of the nineteenth century it was often said that Cromwell had spoken for "the middle and lower classes" against the privileged aristocracy. That development was aided by the influence of

Macaulay, who had declared that "no sovereign ever carried to the throne so large a portion of the best qualities of the middling orders, so strong a sympathy with the feelings and interests of the people". There were limits to the radicalism of Macaulay and of those after him who likewise stressed Cromwell's middle-class and popular credentials. They wanted reform, not revolution. They were no advocates of a universal franchise. Yet in historical writing Cromwell had become, in however loose a sense, the people's friend. His bad press since the seventeenth century, it was explained in 1848, had originated not in the regicide, the ostensible ground of his condemnation, but in the resentment of an aristocracy for whose tastes and opinions historians had too often catered.

Such views flourished among the debating societies and Mechanics Institutes whose middle-class and respectable working-class memberships swelled in the middle decades of the nineteenth century. Edmund Clarke, addressing the Manchester Mechanics Institute in 1846, declared that before the Puritan Revolution "the world knew nothing of freedom" beyond the "peculiar privileges and immunities" of the aristocracy, and that Cromwell had "infused the loftiest energy into the common people, and showed that there was a soul in the plebeian, and a might in his arm, before which the aristocrat and his retainers were as dry twigs before the blast". While recruiting and disciplining his troops, it now appeared, Cromwell had discovered, in the principle of conscience, an alternative to the delusory values of chivalry and honour espoused by aristocratic royalist leaders. Oliver was finding a new constituency. In 1852 the Watlington Mutual Improvement Society resolved, after seven nights' discussion and a ballot vote, "that a better Christian, a more noble-minded spirit, a greater warrior, a more constant man has scarcely ever appeared on the face of the earth".

More dispassionate nineteenth-century voices concurred in describing Cromwell as the agent of a social challenge. The French statesman Francois Guizot, whose detailed studies of the Puritan Revolution appeared in English translations in the middle of the century, saw the civil war as a "social" conflict between old and new classes. That perception had come to stay, at least until very recent times. At the century's end S. R. Gardiner, the most respected of all historians of the Puritan Revolution, explained that Cromwell had been the "mouthpiece" of a new "class". C. H. Firth, in the biography of Cromwell which appeared in 1900, called him "the persistent champion of the rights of the peasants and freeholders" in East Anglia. G. M. Trevelyan, whose *England under the Stuarts*, first published in 1904, may be the most widely read account of the seventeenth century ever to have been published, endorsed Firth's view. The political, social and economic changes of the nineteenth century had had a profound effect on perceptions of Cromwell. Victorians often hailed him – implausibly to later eyes – as the champion of free trade and as the improver of national communications (that essential ally, in nineteenth-century thinking, of liberty and progress) through better roads and a new postal system, an interpretation perhaps most amply advanced in F. A. Inderwick's book on the Interregnum in 1891.

Yet the improvement of Cromwell's standing in the nineteenth century cannot be explained solely in terms of changes in Victorian society and values. It was also the product of by far the most influential book ever to have been written on Cromwell, the edition by Thomas Carlyle of the *Letters and Speeches of Oliver Cromwell*, a work first published in 1845. Carlyle had already caught the public imagination with a lecture on Cromwell in the series *On Heroes and Hero-Worship* which he delivered and published in 1840–41. He intended to write a biography of Cromwell, but abandoned the project in favour of an edition, the first to have been produced, of Cromwell's words. This was a less revolutionary accomplishment than he liked to imply. Most of the documents he brought together had already been published, if in scattered places. Though he was contemptuous of previous editors, he owed much to their labours. Carlyle was not really a historian. He knew very little about English history before or after the Puritan Revolution. He knew little more about the revolution itself, save as it showed forth the genius of his hero. True heroes, he thought, transcended history. In Carlyle's sulphurous mind, the Scottish Calvinism of his upbringing interacted with German Romanticism and pantheism. His aim was to recover, from two centuries of darkness and cant and contumely, the wild beauty and nobility of Cromwell's soul.

Fortunately the essence of Carlyle's contribution did not lie in his philosophy. His achievement was to demonstrate, to the satisfaction of most of his readers, the thread of sincere religious conviction running through Cromwell's life and mind. No-one who struggled to understand Oliver's words and to recover their inner meaning, Carlyle contended, could accept the slurs of hypocrisy and dissimulation that, since his own time, had been cast on his memory. Although Carlyle did not persuade everyone, the overwhelming response to his publication in the years and decades that followed it was one of grateful recognition. Cromwell had at last become a knowable human being. Traditional accounts, which had offered an incongruous mixture of merits and wickedness, now looked superficial and implausible. Before Carlyle's publication, the dominant testimony about Cromwell had been the evidence bequeathed by his enemies. Henceforth the principal source would be Oliver's own words. Soon it became a commonplace that Carlyle had transformed Cromwell's standing. Around half a century after the appearance of the *Letters and Speeches*, Gardiner and Firth wrote the monumental narratives of the Puritan Revolution on which modern scholarship rests. Supplying the careful reconstruction of events that Carlyle had not provided, they revolutionized the study of Cromwell's times. But they did not revolutionise perceptions of the man. As G. M. Young would remark, "the Cromwell of Gardiner and Firth is in essence the Cromwell of Carlyle". Profound as Carlyle's contribution was, the mid-nineteenth-century alteration in perceptions of him was not his work alone. As he acknowledged, it had been under way before he published. Macaulay's generally sympathetic account of Cromwell played its part. There was a cluster of favourable interpretations of Cromwell in the late 1830s. The extent of public admiration for him became evident in 1845, while Carlyle's edition was at the printer's. Controversy flared, both in the national and in the provincial press, over a proposal to include a statue of Cromwell in the row of England's monarchs in the new Houses of Parliament. Though the scheme was defeated, the sentiments voiced in its favour reveal the existence of an audience which Carlyle's edition would confirm in, rather than convert to, Cromwellianism.

The enthusiastic response to the *Letters and Speeches* had two bases of public opinion, which sometimes overlapped. First, the work appealed to that feeling of hostility to the established order which continued to remember Cromwell as the champion of the poor and as the destroyer of the factious and oligarchical Long Parliament. Eloquent on behalf of the oppressed, Carlyle despised parliaments, whether of the nineteenth century or of the seventeenth. They governed, he thought, in their own class interests. Their members were men of puny stature. To such "constitutional patriots" as Pym and Hampden he did allow a certain credit. Yet those "smooth-shaven respectabilities" had defied Charles I over taxation, a material rather than a spiritual grievance, a cause unworthy of a Cromwell, of that "rugged outcast", "coarse", "drossy", "shaggy", "unkempt", who had stood above the constitutional wrangles of his age and had "grappled, heart to heart, with the naked truth of things". Carlyle acknowledged that, on a first reading, Cromwell's speeches to his parliaments can be hard to follow. Earlier writers had made much of their incoherence, attributing it mainly to a wish on the protector's part to confuse or dupe his audiences. To Carlyle, Cromwell's moments of inarticulacy were marks of spiritual authenticity. Instead of the classical rotundities which Carlyle associated with parliamentary proceedings, Cromwell had offered his hearers "the free outpouring utterances of what is in the heart".

Secondly, the *Letters and Speeches* touched the pulse of Victorian Nonconformity in its era of emancipation and self-realization. From the time of its origins in the Restoration, the Nonconformist tradition had been the target of royalist and Tory criticism and abuse. The charges of hypocrisy that were aimed at Cromwell's memory were directed at Dissent too. Now Carlyle, in vindicating Cromwell, vindicated Puritanism and, with it, its Nonconformist inheritance. As a Puritan, explained Carlyle, Cromwell was "the Pattern man", for the present no less than for the past.

Nonconformist admiration for Cromwell was not new. Favourable images of him in the eighteenth and earlier nineteenth century had owed much to writers from Dissenting backgrounds. Yet sympathisers with Cromwell's Puritanism had generally been embarrassed by what had come to seem its excesses. They distanced themselves from his "enthusiasm", from his "fanaticism", from his Old Testament providentialism, from his readiness to invoke God's will as a sanction for violence and illegality. Carlyle swept such inhibitions aside. Though his own philosophy was distant from Nonconformity, he heartened Nonconformists by recognising in seventeenth-century Puritanism "the last of all our heroisms", a standard of conduct and belief from which, lamentably, the modern world had fallen away. "Godlike" Cromwell, he declared, had been "heaven's lightning". Oliver "knew in every fibre, and with heroic daring laid to heart, that an Almighty Justice does rule the world; that it is good to fight on God's side, and bad to fight on the Devil's".

Carlyle had no interest in Whiggish theories of constitutional liberty. In ignoring them he appealed to a nascent militancy within Nonconformity. That emerging spirit challenged the tradition of political quietude, and the habit of subordination to the Whig party, which had permeated Dissent since the later seventeenth century. The bolder Nonconformists now wished to emulate seventeenth-century Puritanism in its era not of subordination but of power: in the era, as Carlyle put it, when Cromwell had striven to establish a "theocracy", "a real reign of God", and when "Puritan England" had recognised "that this Oliver was their captain; and in heart could not but say, long life to him; as we do now". In 1873 the Nonconformist magazine *The Congregationalist* looked back beyond "two centuries of humiliation and subordination to the time when our forefathers held sway in England". No less than Whigs, it observed, Nonconformists had their "traditions. If we have served under Somers, Walpole, Fox, Grey, and Russell, we have reigned with Cromwell". In the decades around 1800 sympathisers with Cromwell had shared the secular perspective of the Whigs. They had emphasized the Roundhead struggle for constitutional and natural rights. Almost from the moment of Carlyle's publication, Nonconformist writers and lecturers drew on it to bring a biblical and spiritual dimension to their accounts of the Puritan Revolution.

Carlyle appealed too to the anti-Catholic strain in Nonconformity, which viewed apprehensively the ultramontane ambitions of the papacy abroad and the successes of the Oxford Movement at home. He struck a Nonconformist chord in commending Cromwell's aim "to unite the Protestant world of struggling light against the papal world of potent darkness". Earlier sympathisers with Cromwell had been troubled by the apparent cruelty, which they could only half-excuse, of his slaughters of Irish Catholics in 1649. To Carlyle those massacres had been not "murder" but "surgery", a necessary assertion of the claims of heaven over those of hell. Once Carlyle had published, unqualified approval of Cromwell's conduct in Ireland became acceptable for the first time since the revolution itself.

Yet there was also a less militant and more deferential strand in Victorian Nonconfomity, a strand which also made use of Carlyle but which eschewed the more intemperate passages of his commentary. Those gentler spirits, instead of contrasting, as their more militant colleagues did, the blessings of Cromwellian rule with the centuries of oppression that had succeeded it, endorsed the position of Macaulay (himself of Dissenting origin), who had applauded the progress of constitutional order and religious liberty from the seventeenth century to the nineteenth. S. R. Gardiner (likewise of Nonconformist affiliation) maintained that the true gifts of Puritanism to English culture, its high seriousness and demanding morality and loveliness of spirit, had been bestowed after rather than during its period of rule, in its time of influence rather than of power. To Gardiner and others Cromwell's great achievement was the establishment not of Puritan government but of religious toleration, a principle which the persecution that had been inflicted in the Restoration era had never quite succeeded in eliminating and which had at last borne fruit in the nineteenth century. Toleration was an ideal of limited appeal to Carlyle, who preferred to commend Cromwell's brisk measures against "godless detestable persons". Where Carlyle welcomed Cromwell's anti-Catholicism and mocked the Oxford Movement, moderate Nonconformists were troubled by the limits of Cromwell's tolerance, which had not extended to Catholics or Anglicans – although that shortcoming could be explained, they suggested, partly by the political pressures of the time and partly by the seventeenth century's failure to grasp those broader principles of toleration which had found acceptance only in the nineteenth.

Yet Cromwell's politics did not go away. On the contrary they occupied a critical place in Victorian public controversy. Politicians addressing the new electorates created by the Reform Acts of 1832 and 1867 discovered the powerful appeal of references to Cromwell, whether friendly or unfriendly. The Liberal Party, which had succeeded the Whigs as the political patron of Nonconformity, smiled on Cromwell's memory (at times somewhat hesitantly). Cromwell, it emerged, had championed the essential Liberal virtues of free trade and free worship. Liberals supported, amidst noisy contention and against Tory opposition, the erection of a statue to Cromwell in Manchester, the capital of Liberal Nonconformity, in 1875, and of another at Westminster in 1899, the tercentenary of his birth. In those controversies all the old arguments about Cromwell's sincerity or hypocrisy, about his taste for violence or his respect for constitutional means, flared into fresh life.

By the end of the century, admittedly, the heyday of Nonconformity had passed. Yet Carlyle's hero-worship had won admirers for Cromwell in other quarters too. Whereas the eighteenth century had most liked "disinterested" politicians, who rose above the corruptions and temptations of power, the nineteenth century acquired a taste for great leaders and organisers, men of will and decisiveness, creators and preservers of order and stability. Cromwell was increasingly commended for having restored order to England in 1653. In 1856 Cromwell's critic Andrew Bisset complained that "constantly . . . well-informed writers" were "asserting that a Cromwell or a Napoleon is needed to prevent anarchy". From the publication of Carlyle's *Letters and Speeches* to the rise of the dictators of the 1930s we find occasional shudders of unease at what was held to be a Germanic tendency, to be blamed on Carlyle, for writers on Cromwell to equate might with right.

Often approving of Cromwell's strength at home, the late Victorian era also praised his strength abroad. He was lauded, particularly during the Boer War, as one of the principal founders of the British Empire. The modern preoccupation with Cromwell's skills of military strategy and tactics derives from the same period. Yet the late nineteenth century also subjected him to a new form of criticism. Hitherto the friend of the oppressed, Cromwell now became their enemy. To the Labour movement Cromwell was "bourgeois". His appeal to Nonconformists did him no favours among socialists who saw Nonconformity as the pious face of industrial exploitation. His suppression of the Levellers in 1647 and 1649, which had worried few earlier writers, now counted against him.

With that voice from the Left we enter the twentieth century, which has often echoed it. Yet Cromwell has never been quite so divisive a figure as he was from 1660 to 1900. The professionalization of the study of history, the growing conviction that the historian's job is to describe and explain rather than to judge, and the respect increasingly paid to long-term historical forces beyond the control of any individual, have reduced the contentiousness of historical biography. The tercentenary of 1899, which marks the summit of interest in Cromwell, inflamed public opinion. The quartercentenary, even if it does the same, is unlikely to do so on a comparable scale.

Suggestions for further reading

The essential guide to publications on Cromwell (though not, alas, a wholly dependable one) is W. C. Abbott, *A Bibliography of Oliver Cromwell* (Cambridge, Mass: 1929). R. C. Richardson (ed.), *Images of Oliver Cromwell. Essays for and by Roger Howell, Jr.* (Manchester: Manchester University Press, 1993) is a valuable collection on Cromwell's posthumous reputation. T. W. Mason, Nineteenth-Century Cromwell, *Past and Present* 40, 1968, described a substantial exercise in scholarly collaboration which was concerned to reconstruct images and judgements of Cromwell. The fruits of that venture have mostly remained unpublished, and I am grateful to have seen unpublished material produced by it. Alan Smith writes on The Image of Cromwell in Folklore and Tradition, *Folklore* 79, 1968. For the composition of Carlyle's edition see C. H. Firth's introduction to the version of the *Letters and Speeches of Oliver Cromwell* edited by S. C. Lomas, 3 vols (London: 1904). For recent thinking on Cromwell see John Morrill (ed.), *Oliver Cromwell and the English Revolution* (Harlow, England: Longman, 1990).

Chapter Five

৵

Histories of the welfare state

Pat Thane

All modern states are now "welfare states". In all of them a high proportion of government expenditure is devoted to such items as old age pensions, health care, education, social services and provision for the unemployed, although different states make these provisions in different ways. In all such countries, including Britain, at the end of the twentieth century the level, characteristics and objectives of such social expenditure are central to political debate – in determining the outcomes of elections, for example. At the beginning of the century this was not so and levels of government social expenditure were much lower. In 1900 less than three per cent of the Gross Domestic Product (GDP) of Great Britain was devoted to publicly funded social services. In 1993 education, health and social security took almost 25 per cent. Historians disagree about how and why these changes have come about, and also about their social, economic and political implications.

"Whig Histories?"

Historians of twentieth-century welfare states who emphasize this growth in state welfare activity over time are sometimes described as writing "Whig" histories. By this is meant that they assume that the histories of welfare states are histories of steady improvement in the quality of public social provision and of the increasing beneficence of the state.

This was broadly true of histories written in Britain before the early 1970s, in particular those written after 1945. There was good reason for this: publicly funded provision for "welfare", that is measures to improve the living conditions of poorer people, expanded and improved in most developed countries, even amid the economic depression of the 1930s and especially in the international economic boom of the years after the Second

World War, though the form and pace of change was not identical everywhere. Between 1945 and *c*. 1973 world poverty was really on the retreat, although this was at least as much (but almost certainly more) the result of increasing levels of world trade as of social welfare policies. Everywhere there was a reciprocal relationship between prosperity and levels of state welfare; each reinforced the other.

Histories of welfare states written during this period tended to attribute improvement in social conditions and extensions of state welfare from the beginning of the century to increasing prosperity and the encouragement it gave to greater benevolence among the "haves", whilst it increased their capacity to pay higher taxes to fund state welfare; and to the increased political influence of deprived (or in the political language of the 1990s "excluded") people themselves as they obtained the vote for the first time and became involved in Labour, socialist and trade union movements.

The "oil shock" of 1973 raised prices and deflated demand internationally, bringing a return of economic instability and unemployment which was quite unforeseen in the post-war "golden age" which preceded it. One outcome was that state welfare faced almost universal criticism for absorbing public and private expenditure which might, some thought, be better spent on investment or consumption to boost economic growth. In this climate, which has persisted to the late 1990s, it was more difficult to see the histories of welfare states as accounts of continuing improvement of provision or of outcome in terms of social conditions. In some parts of the world, notably sub-Saharan Africa, severe poverty returned and in Britain there was strong evidence of a large and growing gap between rich and poor.

At the same time, the 1970s saw a more critical tone emerging in the social sciences. Post-war social science research in Britain was broadly, though not universally, supportive of a growing state which engaged actively with improving conditions for the more deprived sectors of society. How effectively the British welfare state was in fact doing so was called in question by social scientists sympathetic to the project at least from the mid-1950s. The aim of these critics was to bring about more and better state welfare. By the end of the 1960s criticism was more widespread and not always so sympathetic. A somewhat vulgarized "Marxism" entered the debate. It viewed the state as normally an expression of the interests of the capitalist class and effectively incapable of seeking genuine improvements in the conditions of "the poor and the poorest".

Among historians this debate encouraged a search for a more complex approach, an awareness of the multiple motivations behind state welfare policies, influenced by ideas drawn from anthropology and sociology. New work pointed out the role of the self-interest of elites, as well as their benevolence: that they were influenced by the recognition that improving the conditions of poor people might not simply improve their lives, but also discourage them from becoming politically organized or a threat to public order; that a fitter, better-fed people was not just desirable in itself but would create a nation of stronger, more effective, mothers, workers and soldiers. It was realized that, far from state social welfare creating social and economic equality, it might serve to reinforce old inequalities.

Research indicated that from the beginning of the century in Britain conservative politicians, employers and other influential groups recognized the role of welfare policies in undermining the appeal of left-wing parties – if the right could offer welfare, why should workers vote for the uncertainties of left-wing politics? It also indicated that they recognized its importance in maximizing economic growth and military competitiveness. Social surveys and military recruitment experience at the beginning of the century showed how many men were unfit for efficient work or military service. At the same time, concern about the declining birthrate also encouraged the development of policies designed to improve the survival rates and fitness of infants. The certainties of mid-Victorian Britain were under threat by the end of the century, above all through increasing international economic and military competition and the growing assertiveness of excluded men and women. State welfare appeared to provide some answers to these problems.

The concept of "social control", borrowed, sometimes a little uncritically from the social sciences, had a brief vogue as an analytical tool. "Social control" was taken to encapsulate the many ways in which social policies sought to regulate the lives of the poor. This was clearly so. Most social services and cash payments were conditional upon conformity with certain norms of behaviour, as they always had been. The social policies of any state express the value system of that state. Poor relief under the Old and the New Poor Laws had generally been paid on condition of respectable behaviour. So also were many benefits provided through the new state welfare structures of the twentieth century. The first old age pensions, in 1908, excluded people with records of drunkenness, criminality or "habitual failure to work". "Social control" usefully drew attention to the reality that the intentions behind state welfare were not unremittingly benign. This had been insufficiently recognized in the earlier historiography. There was a danger, however, of seeing "social control" as the only perspective on social policy, rather than as one of many.

The later 1970s produced a wider-ranging, more complex analysis of why and how the great twentieth-century expansion of state welfare had come about, which related it to broader social, economic and political change, nationally and internationally. The studies which resulted were far from being the pedestrian administrative histories with which this field is often identified. They all sought to analyze why the welfare role of the state, or some aspects of it, had grown so dramatically, as they unmistakeably had. They did not assume that growth was synonymous with improvement, or that it had taken place in the most beneficial ways. The bulk of the studies of the history of social welfare written since the mid-1970s cannot usefully be described as "Whig" histories.

From "welfare state" to "welfare system"

In other respects the writing of the histories of welfare states was affected by the political and ideological changes of the 1970s and after. The growing emphasis of Conservative government policy after 1979 upon the role of non-governmental agencies in the provision of welfare services reminded historians that the state had never been the sole provider. An implicit assumption of histories written after 1945 was that the state was the natural provider of welfare and that such historically important actors as families and charities were destined for the dustbin of history. Later histories showed increasing awareness of their continuing importance. The focus shifted from "welfare states" to "welfare systems", acknowledging that the great variety of situations in which individuals needed support from others were accommodated by a variety of responses; that the role of the state was complemented by voluntary action and by support within the family, as well as by the private commercial sector and, more rarely, by employers. There was what social scientists called a "mixed economy of welfare". Older forms of provision were not "crowded out", some economists had believed, by the growth of welfare states.

In consequence, historians paid more attention, in particular, to occupational welfare, and to charity. The latter had long been accepted as an important feature of medieval and early modern life, but for the nineteenth century it had for some time been treated primarily as a channel for upper- and middle-class exertion of authority over the poor, whereas for the twentieth century it was treated as being of marginal significance. Historians increasingly stressed the complexity of the motives of nineteenth-century philanthropists and the innovative character of much of their work, which was often later adopted by the state for example, the introduction of health visitors and a range of maternal and infant welfare services, support for blind and disabled people and much else. They also stressed the fact that working-class people gave to charity as well as received from it. It also became clear that voluntary effort continued to play an important role in British society in the twentieth century. Voluntary institutions either worked closely with the state, especially with local government, or they continued their innovative role of bringing social problems to public notice and devising new forms of action.

Historians of nineteenth-century household structure described the role of the family in caring – for example, for older people. Social surveys from 1945 onwards noted, initially with great surprise, that families still had a central role in such care – quite contrary to the then accepted sociological assumption that footloose modern urban industrial society had destroyed the functioning extended family. They continued to discover this in the 1990s. In the mid-1980s it was estimated that unpaid family services were saving the social services budget *c*. £23 billion per annum, when the cost of statutory personal social services was £3.4 billion. Cross-national studies also revealed the continuing importance of the family in the care of older people in advanced welfare states.

The "economy" of welfare has been "mixed" throughout history; the surprise was the degree to which it remained so despite the growth of state welfare in the twentieth century.

Women and welfare

Another important social and ideological shift from the late-1960s was the renewed prominence of the women's movement. This affected most areas of academic study as profoundly as it affected the rest of society.

It is possible to read histories of social policy written before the 1970s and to emerge quite unaware that, throughout history, females have been more likely than males to suffer poverty; and that women have played some part in bringing about remedies for poverty. By the 1990s the picture was transformed.

Initially, studies, as in other areas of feminist scholarship, took the form of "retrieval", seeking to place women at last within histories which had been distorted by leaving them out. Under similar influences social policy specialists began to notice how very many poor people were female and they spoke of a "feminization of poverty" as though they were detecting something new. Historians pointed out that poverty had always been female, for the obvious reasons that for centuries women had outlived men, leaving many of them as widows with children to support – the single mother is no innovation of the late twentieth century, although the causes have changed from the death of the husband to divorce and separation; or being left alone to survive into old age. With or without children, women have had few opportunities to support themselves in most countries through the centuries and, unavoidably, they have always been vulnerable to hardship.

There was a tendency for this initial work to present women as victims with a limited capacity to influence policy in their own interests. The revival of interest in philanthropy led to the recognition of the important and innovative role played by women in voluntary organizations, especially during the great expansion of philanthropy in the nineteenth century. They were shown to be no mere, patronizing Ladies Bountiful, but hardworking, though largely unpaid, professionals, often working in appalling conditions, busy devising new strategies for social policy especially in the interests of women and children.

In the twentieth century the gradual increase in access to paid work for middle-class women reduced the supply of voluntary workers. Women were paid – generally relatively poorly – for many of the social service roles they once performed as volunteers. But women, and a good many men, still work as unpaid carers in the 1990s, in voluntary agencies, in the family and among friends and neighbours.

Have welfare states delivered only minimal "benefits" and low-paid social service jobs to women? Some argue that welfare states are irredeemably "patriarchal", created largely by men and protective of their interests. Others have asked whether it is wholly coincidental that welfare states have come into being in Britain and elsewhere over the same time period, that is to say since the later nineteenth century, as the emergence of sustained women's movements? Many women who demanded the vote at the beginning of the century wanted it explicitly to remedy appalling social conditions which male electorates had tolerated for too long. The greater attention paid to the health care of women and children, to housing, education and other social issues during the twentieth century cannot wholly be attributed to the fact that in all developed countries women at last acquired a voice in politics and formed a majority of the electorates. The growth of male electorates to include more working men and similar influences upon policy discussed above were clearly important and it is difficult to disentangle the strands of influence. But in many areas women voters in local and central government made an important contribution to placing welfare firmly upon the agenda of British politics and to shaping the aspects which were given salience.

Some argue that, in doing so, women have merely increased their shackles; that the patriarchal welfare state has served to reinforce female dependence in the family, above all by assuming that the primary roles of women were as wives and mothers. Since state policies are necessarily expressions of the dominant culture, it is not surprising that a society in which gender inequality is pervasive produces social policies which replicate or reinforce that inequality. For much of the twentieth century British policy did tend to reinforce the domestic roles of women. Yet critics of the British welfare state argued from a different perspective in the 1980s and 1990s that it enabled too many women to be independent of men, bringing up children as lone mothers, funded by income support and housing benefit. It can, however, be argued just as plausibly that such benefits have enabled even very poor women to live independently of unsatisfactory men, though often in miserable conditions. Whether dependence upon the state is worse or better than dependence upon a man is an open question, and the answer must vary with individual experience; so also is the question of whether dependence is all the state can offer women in such a situation.

But for all its limitations dependence and reinforcement of conventional gender roles is not all that the welfare state has had to offer to women. Above all they have benefited immensely from health services and from an education system in which by the 1990s females were gaining more than males in terms of examination success. If the welfare state has not delivered all that many have hoped for women, it has not notably empowered poorer men. The gender implications of the welfare state – the relative inputs and outcomes for men and women, and its influence upon gender roles and relations – are important and were too long neglected. They are still far from being understood, but they are too complex to be usefully summed up by reference to a "patriarchal welfare state".

Welfare before the welfare state

Evidently, therefore, histories of the British welfare state written since the 1970s have delivered equivocal judgements upon the outcomes. Yet it has still been assumed that it has delivered social improvements beyond anything known in previous centuries. This view has been challenged by historians of early modern England and Wales (Scotland has a different history and was, of course, for long an independent country). It used to be taken for granted that the Old Poor Law, founded on the legislation of 1597 and 1601 was irredeemably punitive, offering minimal relief only to the "deserving" poor who could neither work nor support themselves in any way.

This account has been revised. Historians now stress, first, the deep roots of parish support for the poor in medieval practices which predate 1597 and secondly, the wide range and relative generosity of the Old Poor Law, which some have dubbed a "welfare state in miniature". It is claimed that although "the Old Poor Law did not constitute a modern welfare state . . . English men and women could count on the relief authorities to help them in a variety of well-defined situations: old age, widowhood, illness or disability". Research on the Poor Law through the seventeenth and eighteenth centuries shows it bestowing, out of funds raised from local taxation, not only relief in cash and kind, but medical care, nursing, housing, clothing, care of orphaned and abandoned children, indeed many of the services of the modern welfare state. One historian has argued that cash support for old people even in the early days of the New Poor Law (which was designed to be more punitive than the Old Poor Law) and by implication earlier, was at least as regular and possibly more generous than the old age pensions of the post-Second World War welfare state.

A third point made by historians of population and household structure to account for this apparent generosity is the predominance of the "nuclear family" in early modern England. Against an older picture of pre-industrial England as a relatively unchanging world in which most people lived in large multi-generational family groups in static communities, it has emerged since the 1970s that the English were, geographically, highly mobile over many centuries before industrialization, and that typically they lived in relatively small (fewer than five people) households consisting primarily of parents and dependent children.

It has been argued that such households could not easily, and were not expected to, provide for the needs of relatives outside the household, such as impoverished, ageing parents, a widowed sister or orphaned nieces or nephews. This phenomenon has been labelled "nuclear hardship". It is argued that the Poor Law provided what the family did not; that in English custom the local community (or collectivity in Peter Laslett's preferred term) took over the supportive role which in some societies is expected of families. This was possible in a relatively wealthy society such as much of early modern England was. English communities had resources available for distribution to the poorest; in contrast, for example, with seventeenth-century Scotland, where attempts to introduce legislation similar to the English Poor Law failed because communities were too poor to sustain them. Poor people starved in early modern Scotland on a scale unimaginable in England at the same period.

Early modern, like later modern, historians stress the variety of motives for the giving of poor relief: distaste for the indigent living and dying on the streets, fear that deprivation would provoke unrest, the desire to assert the social superiority of giver over receiver, and Christian charity. This reinterpretation of the Old Poor Law provides a salutary challenge to any-one who believes that history is a tale of unremitting progress. For the great majority of historians who do not, it provides an important reminder that publicly funded welfare provision is not an invention of the twentieth century. Studies of the relationship between welfare and household structure also remind us that at no time can the history of social welfare be separated from its wider social, economic and political context if we are to understand its making, its content and its outcomes.

However, it is possible to go too far in stressing the virtues of the Old Poor Law. At its best the Old and even the New Poor Law had the capacity to provide a wide range of services, but strictly for those who were quite destitute and could prove that they had access to no other resources, such as paid work, family, friends or charity. Even people in their eighties would be expected to earn what they could from paid work so long as they were thought able to do so. The overwhelming majority of those assisted were old people, widows and children – the recognized "deserving" poor. Fit, unemployed men got short shrift, except for a brief period at the end of the eighteenth century when the reality of their desitution was unmistakeable and variants of the "Speenhamland system" operated. Those who were not accepted members of a community could be excluded, indeed were excluded by law under the Settlement Acts (from 1662). These sanctioned the payment of relief only in the claimant's parish of "settlement", which was established by birth, by marriage for a woman, or by long residence and work in the parish.

The Old and the New Poor Laws were also highly variable in their practices from place to place and time to time. Under the Old Poor Law about 15,000 parishes, some of them tiny, had to meet local needs entirely from the yield of taxation from their own parish; the New Poor Law of 1834 grouped parishes into larger "Unions", but each Union had still to be self-financing for most purposes. Some had greater resources than others. But the variability in Poor Law practice cannot be explained only in terms of local resources. Some Yorkshire parishes in the seventeenth and eighteenth centuries gave almost no poor relief and gave any at all with the greatest reluctance, although there is no sign that they were poorer than more generous parishes. Most of our current understanding of the Poor Law derives from the study of rather too few parishes, most of them in southern England. We know all too little about just how variable Poor Law practice really was.

In consequence, references to the Old Poor Law as a "welfare state in miniature" or suggestions that its provisions may have equalled or outstripped those of the modern welfare state should be treated with caution. Whatever the virtues of the Old Poor Law (which could be considerable at their best), or the shortcomings of the modern welfare state (which can be considerable at their worst), there is a qualitative difference between a system which, for example, guarantees basic support to all at the age of 65 and one which gave relief only to a minority even of the very poor among the aged, on strict tests of need and with no guarantee of continuity. There is a real question as to whether the vastly richer Britain of the twentieth century is relatively more or less generous to its poor than the England of the seventeenth and eighteenth centuries. At present we do not have adequate data or techniques capable of making this comparison usefully in either a cultural or a quantitative dimension. Many historians confess themselves mystified as to how many very poor people did survive, given the manifest inadequacy of poor relief, even when they received it.

A possible answer is that families provided more support than the "nuclear hardship hypothesis" allows. This hypothesis is derived from observing whether households included needy people outside the nuclear family core. But it is possible to give substantial support to a relative without sharing a home with them. There is much evidence that, for example, old people were provided with food and other necessities and help about the house and garden – in effect, with the essentials for survival, by adult children and other relatives who lived in separate households nearby.

The extent and role of charity in early modern, and indeed modern England is also imperfectly understood. Certainly charity was an important component of early modern culture and large amounts were redistributed from rich to poor through formal or informal charitable institutions, from the large numbers of charitable almshouses for needy old people to casual giving to beggars on the street, or the ritualized begging system of many early modern communities where the poor would receive food left over from the meals of their neighbours. It is difficult to construct a clear picture of the dimensions of charity because so many charitable transactions were not systematically recorded.

There may be a tendency to overestimate the role of the Poor Law in the precarious economy of the very poor because it left behind the systematic records on which it is easiest for the historian to work, whereas charity and giving within families did not. In reality, until at least the early twentieth century and often well beyond most poor people in England and in very many other countries survived in what historians call an "economy of make-shifts", constantly patching together fragments of resources from paid work, family, friends, charity, growing their own food, making and remaking their own clothes and much else. The "mixed economy of welfare" has a very long history.

The persistence of the Poor Law

It is valuable to look at the modern welfare state in relation to the Old Poor Law, not in order to assess which was better or worse, because we do not have the techniques to do this, but in order to remind ourselves of the long existence of the Poor Law and of its underestimated, powerful, institutional and cultural legacy. The growth of a strongly centralized state in twentieth-century Britain has been an important change, but it has grown within a stable and long-established political culture, building upon firmly-entrenched institutions. It is conventional to stress how much was new about the post-1945 British welfare state, but this may be to underestimate the extent of continuity with the past.

This is evident in respect of social security. The range of benefits provided has grown over the century with the introduction, one by one, of old age pensions, widows' pensions and health, unemployment, disability and maternity benefits. The conditions on which they were granted were generally less rigorously selective than under the Poor Law (which was finally abolished only in 1948). But until 1978, when an income-related element was introduced for some benefits, they were all flat-rate, residual subsistence payments designed to keep destitution at bay rather than to provide income comparable with that received when in work. They were financed partly by contributions which were also flat-rate (all workers regardless of income paid the same amount each week) and therefore regressive, i.e. they took a higher proportion of the incomes of the lower than of the higher paid. The better off supported the system additionally as income tax payers. Beveridge's Social Insurance White Paper of 1942, which provided the blueprint for the post-war social security system, explicitly anticipated that need above the basic level would be provided, not by the state, but by individual saving through voluntary (e.g. trade unions or friendly societies) or commercial institutions – preferably, in his view, the former. It was a system with a very limited capacity for redistribution.

This contrasts with the social security systems developed in other countries in the post-war years, building on different cultural and institutional legacies. Both France and Germany developed income – related social security payments intended to provide income replacement at a certain level of comfort in times of crisis or dependence, rather than bare subsistence – for which the better-paid contributed relatively more, the poorer relatively less. By the 1970s and 1980s the outcome was state benefits considerably more generous than those available in Britain. Such an approach was not seriously considered in Britain earlier than the mid-1950s, when the relative shortcomings of the British social security system were becoming obvious.

Minimal, residual state-administered provision combined with self-help, which was fundamental to the Poor Law tradition, remained the dominant approach to social security in Britain long after the inauguration of the postwar "welfare state". This profound and largely unconscious conservatism in British thinking about social welfare made it easier for governments from the 1980s to "roll back" the more generous manifestations of the welfare state. On the other hand, it proved difficult to destroy the residual core with its deep Poor Law roots. That the collectivity should provide, at a certain basic level, for the old, sick and unemployed, for health care and education among other things has never been universally held, but its tenacity in British culture was evident through the 1980s and 1990s, notably in influencing the landslide Labour Party victory in the election of 1997.

"Consensus" in "the best welfare state in the world"

But the Poor Law legacy has ensured that although the British favour a "welfare state", they have fairly low expectations of what it should do. They also long believed that the British welfare system as established in the late 1940s was unique, and more effective, in providing for need in comparison with neighbouring countries than was actually the case. It is commonly believed in the 1990s that the Beveridge system provided adequately for the needs of the 1940s, when full employment and stable marriages were the norm, and that it has become outdated only recently, due to social and economic change bringing insecure employment and changing household patterns.

But even in its early days the post-war social security system was so minimal that by 1954 1.8 million people received means–tested supplements to their national insurance benefits because they could not live on them alone and could not afford to provide any addition for themselves. Beveridge did not succeed in his long-held aim of abolishing the means test and providing full subsistence benefits as a right to all. This was partly because the post-war Labour government did not fully implement his proposals, but the proposals themselves were strictly limited.

That a welfare state brought into being in the aftermath of an exhausting and expensive war, in an economy wrestling with revival not only after the war but following the long Depression of the 1920s and 1930s, was limited, is not surprising. Where the experience of the British welfare state differs from that of other countries of western Europe and elsewhere is that it improved relatively slowly in the 1950s and 1960s. The period from 1945 to c. 1973 is often described as one of "consensus" in British politics, in which Conservative and Labour governments broadly agreed on principles of economic and social policy. Throughout this period Labour was committed to improving the basic system which they had established after the war and trying to break out of the Poor Law straitjacket. But the Conservatives who were in office for 17 of the 28 years between 1945 and 1973 (while Labour governed with a secure majority for only nine) was from the outset opposed to a universalistic system of services financed from taxation and preferred in principle the established model of residual, targeted benefits supplemented by private provision. They did not cut back on the system they took over when they won the election of 1951 largely because they did not need to; it strayed very little outside their principles. But neither did they significantly improve it. Social security payments remained minimal and flat-rate, and for many supplemented by means-tested benefits, whilst Labour in opposition was moving towards supporting a more redistributive, income-related system of the kind that was being implemented in other European countries.

The Conservatives did more to improve the National Health Service. They hoped initially to cut it, but it was popular with voters and both provision and demand for private health care were weak before the 1980s when the Thatcher governments began a sustained attempt to encourage it. By then they believed that a more prosperous middle class could afford to pay for their own welfare, as few of them had been able to do in the 1940s. Awareness that the middle classes as well as the working classes needed the welfare state and certainly made use of health and education services in particular had restrained Conservative resistance to it through the post-war years. The belief that the post-war welfare state was redistributive and significantly reduced poverty overlooks the degree to which the middle classes were its beneficiaries. They gained access to free education, health care and subsidized social security payments which had been available, at lower levels only, to working-class people before 1945, and which they had difficulty in affording for themselves. This middle-class gain is sometimes seen as an "unintended consequence" of Labour's welfare policies. In fact, it was intended, by building in the support of middle-class taxpayers for the new welfare system, to prevent its erosion, and was an unsuccessful attempt by Labour to hold the middle-class vote they gained in 1945.

There are clear continuities in Conservative thinking on welfare from the 1940s to the 1990s, which were far from "consensual" with those of Labour. Their governments from 1951–97 were marked by successive attempts to cut back the welfare state, which were persistently restrained by the electorate.

Welfare spending and the economy

If the British welfare state has always been more limited than is often thought, it might be wondered why some argue that welfare spending has been the source of our postwar economic difficulties. Especially, as we have seen already, when at the beginning of the century welfare spending was thought to be conducive to economic success.

The most sustained attempt to blame Britain's economic decline on the costly welfare state have been the two books of Correlli Barnett *The Audit of War* (London, 1986) and *The Lost Victory* (London, 1995). Barnett perceives a conspiracy of socialists, naive Christians and philanthropists, driven on by William Beveridge, beguiling Britain into accepting an impossibly costly welfare state, a "New Jerusalem" which diverted resources from the necessary investment and restructuring of the post-war economy. Barnett's experience is as a military historian and he has a limited capacity for social, economic or political history. His use of sources is extensive but selective and uncritical. There are a number of difficulties with his account. First, it underestimates the degree to which the post-1945 Labour government did, successfully, encourage restructuring and investment in export-earning industries and held back welfare expenditure, e.g. on house-building to do so. Secondly, it assumes that the British state spent more on welfare than her more economically successful competitors, such as Germany. In fact, even by 1950, when continental western Europe was barely emerging from the devastation of the war, Britain was spending a lower percentage of GDP on welfare than West Germany, Austria or Belgium. By 1952 British social security expenditure was lower than that of France and Denmark. By 1957 Britain had also fallen behind Italy, Sweden and the Netherlands. Until the 1980s Britain consistently devoted a lower proportion of GDP to social security than any West European country with the exception of Switzerland. The pattern is similar for other areas of social policy. Barnett also overlooks the fact that the much greater gulf between Britain and her competitors was in defence expenditure, which in Britain was markedly higher and comparable by 1950 with social expenditure. Germany, by contrast, had the great advantage of being prohibited after the war from spending on defence.

It would be easy to forget, reading Barnett, that up to the 1960s Britain was the second largest industrial economy in the world (after the USA) with

61

comparable levels of technological innovation with Germany. The British economy has been in more evident trouble since the 1970s when there have been serious, if generally unsuccessful, attempts to cut welfare spending. It is not self-evident that the cause of British economic problems has been welfare spending either before or after 1973. Successful modern states are welfare states because by securing the welfare of their citizens they enhance, rather than undermine, economic success and social stability.

Suggestions for further reading

This list follows the order of discussion in the essay.

A useful study of the past fifty years of the welfare state is Howard Glennerster, *British social policy since 1945* (Oxford: Blackwell, 1995). Rodney Lowe, *The British Welfare State since 1945* (London: Macmillan, 1993) is also helpful but says little on the period after the "oil shock" of 1973. "Whiggish" histories of the emergence of the British welfare state written between 1945 and the mid-1970s include David Roberts, *Victorian origins of the British welfare state* (New Haven: Yale University Press, 1960); Maurice Bruce, *The Coming of the welfare state* (London: Batsford, 1961); Gertrude Williams, *The Coming of the welfare state* (London: Allen & Unwin, 1967); R. C. Birch, *The Shaping of the welfare state* (Harlow, England: Longman, 1974); B. B. Gilbert, *The Evolution of National Insurance in Great Britain. The origins of the welfare state* (London: Michael Joseph, 1966). More recent surveys which take a different approach include George Peden, *British economic and social policy: LLoyd George to Margaret Thatcher*, 2nd edn 1995 (Oxford: Phillip Allen, 1985); Pat Thane, *The Foundations of the welfare state*, 2nd edn 1996 (Harlow, England: Longman, 1982).

Early sympathetic criticisms of the welfare state in the 1950s included Richard Titmuss, *Essays on the welfare state* (London: Allen & Unwin, 1958); M. Young and P. Willmott, *Family and kinship in East London* (Harmondsworth: Penguin, 1957). Less sympathetic Marxist criticism came from R. Miliband, *Parliamentary Socialism* (London: Macmillan, 1961). The extent of continuing poverty in the welfare state was revealed by B. Abel-Smith and P. Townsend, *The Poor and the poorest* (London: Bell & co., 1965) and P. Townsend, *Poverty in the UK* (Harmondsworth: Penguin, 1979).

Studies of the complex motivation for new forms of state social action at the beginning of the twentieth century include: G. Searle, *The Quest for national efficiency* (Oxford: Blackwell, 1971); D. Dwork, *War is good for babies and other young children* (London: Routledge, 1987); Jose Harris, *Unemployment and politics, 1886–1914* (Oxford: Oxford University Press, 1972); Jane Lewis, *The Politics of motherhood* (London: Croom Helm, 1980) and John MacNicol, *The Movement for family allowances, 1918–45* (London: Heinemann, 1981).

For uses of "social control" see J. R. Hay "Employers' attitudes to social policy and the concept of social control, 1900-1930", pp. 107-125 and J. Brown, "Social control and the modernization of social policy, 1890-1929", pp. 126-47 both in Pat Thane (ed.), *The Origins of British social policy* (London: Croom Helm, 1978); A. J. Donajgrodski (ed.), *Social control in nineteenth century Britain* (London: Croom Helm, 1977). Criticisms of the concept include F. M. L. Thompson, "Social control in Victorian Britain" *Economic History Review* **XXXIV**(2), pp. 189-208. G. Stedman Jones, *Languages of class* (Cambridge: Cambridge University Press, 1984), xxx.

On the history of philanthropy see F. Prochaska, *Women and philanthropy in 19th century England* (Oxford: Oxford University Press, 1980); *The voluntary impulse* (London: 1988); "Philanthropy" in F. M. L. Thompson (ed.), *The Cambridge social history of Britain, 1750-1950 3* (Cambridge: Cambridge University Press, 1990), pp. 357-94. G. Finlayson, *Citizen, state and social welfare in Britain, 1830-1990* (Oxford: Oxford University Press, 1994); D. Thomson "Welfare and the historians" in L. Bonfield *et al.* (eds), *The World we have gained* (Oxford: Blackwell, 1986). M. Daunton (ed.), *Charity, self-interest and welfare in the English past* (London: UCL Press, 1996).

On the role of the family see M. Anderson, *Family Structure in 19th century Lancashire* (Cambridge: Cambridge University Press, 1971); M. Dupree, *Family structure in the Staffordshire potteries, 1840-80* (Oxford: Oxford University Press, 1995); Pat Thane, "Old People and their families in the English past" in Daunton, above, pp. 113-36. Studies of the recent past include H. Qureshi and A. Walker, "Caring for Elderly People: the Family and the State" in C. Phillipson and A. Walker (eds), *Ageing and social policy: A critical assessment* (Aldershot: Gower, 1986) pp. 109-27; M. Rein and H. Salzman, "Social integration, participation and exchange in five industrial countries" in Scott A. Bass, *Older and Active* (New Haven: Yale University Press, 1995) pp. 237-62.

On women as victims of poverty and makers of policy see: Jane Lewis, *The Politics of Motherhood* (see above); "Women, social work and social welfare in twentieth century Britain" in Daunton (see above) pp. 203-24. Prochaska, *Women and Philanthropy* (see above); Pat Thane "Women and the poor law in Victorian and Edwardian Britain" *History Workshop Journal*, pp. 29-51, autumn 1978; Ann Summers, "A home from home - women's philanthropic work in the 19th century", in S. Burman (ed.), *Fit Work for Women* (London: Croom Helm, 1979); G. Bock and P. Thane, *Maternity and gender policies. Women and the rise of the European welfare states 1880s-1950s* (London: Routledge, 1991); S. Koven and S. Michel, *Mothers of a new world. Maternalist policies and the origins of welfare states* (London and New York: Routledge, 1992). C. Pateman "The patriarchal welfare state" in Pateman, *The Disorder of Women* (Cambridge: Polity, 1989); for critiques of Pateman see G. Bock and S. James (eds), *Beyond Difference and Equality* (London: Routledge, 1992).

For a positive assessment of the Old Poor Law see P. Slack, *Poverty and policy in Tudor and Stuart England* (Harlow, England: Longman, 1988) and *The English Poor Law, 1531-1782* (Cambridge: Cambridge University Press, 1990) and see his guides to further reading. And of the New Poor Law compared with modern social security: D. Thomson "The decline of social security: falling state support for the elderly since early Victorian times", *Ageing and Society*, 4, pp. 451–82, 1984. See the criticism by E. H. Hunt, "Paupers and pensioners: past and present", *Ageing and Society*, 9, pp. xxx, 1989. For a negative view of the Old Poor Law in the North of England see S. King, "Reconstructing lives: poverty, poor relief and welfare in rural industrial communities", *Historical Journal* (forthcoming).

On the relationship between household structure and poor relief: P. Laslett and R. Wall, *Household and family in past time* (Cambridge: Cambridge University Press, 1972); Laslett "Family and collectivity", *Sociology and Social Research*, pp. 432–42, 1979.

On Beveridge and the postwar welfare state see Glennerster and Lowe (above); Jose Harris, *William Beveridge*, 2nd edn 1998 (Oxford: Oxford University Press, 1977); P. Baldwin, *The Politics of social solidarity: Class bases of the European welfare states, 1875-1975* (Cambridge: Cambridge University Press, 1990). For criticisms of Barnett and accounts of the postwar British economy see Jose Harris, "Enterprise and the welfare state: a comparative perspective" in T. Gourvish and A. O'Day (eds), *Britain since 1945* (London: Macmillan, 1991); D. Edgerton, *Science, Technology and British Industrial Decline* (Cambridge: Cambridge University Press, 1996); A. Cairncross, *The British Economy since 1945* (Oxford: Oxford University Press, 1992).

Chapter Six

᭜

Placing "race" in
South African history

Saul Dubow

Introduction

For many people the epic struggle to end apartheid in South Africa, which
reached a climax with the country's first fully democratic election in 1994,
stands as one of the great moral and political achievements of the twentieth
century. In order to understand this process it is necessary to go back
at least a century, and probably more. The modern apartheid state was
created in the years after the National Party came to power in 1948. As
a system, apartheid distilled the practices and assumptions arising out of
some 300 years of racially exclusive rule extending back to the beginnings
of European settlement at the Cape in the mid-seventeenth century. For
almost half a century, apartheid subjected the majority black population
to a degree of institutionalized racism that is probably unprecedented in
world history. During the apartheid years every aspect of black life was
scrutinized and regulated. Blacks were deprived of their most basic citizenship rights, exploited for their labour, permitted to work and live in the
cities and towns only under strict conditions, subjected to a grossly inferior
educational system, and denied access to most public amenities and facil-
ities. The methodical and comprehensive manner in which the apartheid
bureaucracy routinely humiliated the majority of South Africans involved an
assumption – implicit or otherwise – that blacks and whites constituted
different forms or branches of humanity.

The complexities and contradictions of this process, in a society where
blacks and whites interacted as individuals on a daily basis, can perhaps
best be understood through the outpouring of personal testimonies, novels,
drama and films that marked the apartheid era. It is not the purpose of this
essay to discuss the *experience* of apartheid racism; rather, it seeks a) to
explain some of the intellectual justifications and rationalizations of racial

difference which helped to sustain the belief of whites in their own superiority and b) to locate these ideas in a long-running historical debate about the origins and function of racial oppression in a society that was also divided along lines of social class.

Race and class

For the group of liberal-minded historians writing in the 1930s, racism was fundamentally an irrational ideology. It was, argued C. W. de Kiewiet, a premodern phenomenon associated closely with the intolerant slave-owning mentality of backward Afrikaner frontiersmen. According to this conception, the Dutch or Afrikaner *boers* (farmers) who "trekked" north from the Cape Colony in the 1830s and 1840s did so to escape the socially progressive influence of British rule. Key examples of enlightened British humanitarianism were said to include the removal of discriminatory legislation towards the indigenous Khoisan (Bushman and Hottentot) population in 1828, the manumission of slaves in the 1830s, and the work of evangelical missionaries who laboured to convert blacks to the virtues and values of Christianity and civilization.

In the 1950s and 1960s a new generation of liberal scholars came to prominence. They were not so concerned to defend the positive record of British imperialism – whose aggression towards Afrikaners during the South African War of 1899–1902 they roundly deplored. But they likewise tended to blame Afrikaners for the deteriorating racial situation in the country. They viewed the victory of the apartheid-supporting Afrikaner government of 1948 as a stubborn and tragic reaction against the nineteenth-century "imperial factor". And they argued that apartheid represented an inappropriate transposition into the twentieth century of an earlier frontier mentality characterized by prejudice and fear. Implicit in some liberal writing of this time was the notion that a modern and expanding industrial economy would tend to erode racial privilege, since prejudice amounted to an inefficient use of human and economic resources.

In the 1970s a new group of radical marxist-influenced scholars began to subject their liberal colleagues to sustained critique. Noting the fact that the apartheid economy had, by the 1960s, provided whites with some of the highest living standards of the world, they re-evaluated the notion that economic progress was incompatible with racial discrimination. Instead, they maintained that apartheid was not only a form of colour prejudice, but that it was fundamentally a system of economic exploitation underpinned by the systematic use of cheap black labour. The combination of institutions such as pass laws governing access to urban areas, prison-like closed labour compounds, and government labour bureaux established to satisfy competing sectors of the white-dominated economy, lay at the heart of a system that some now characterized as racial capitalism.

The research conducted by radical scholars like Martin Legassick, Harold Wolpe and F. R. Johnstone questioned whether contemporary racist attitudes were indeed the product of age-old prejudices. Observing that the late-nineteenth century mineral revolution had catapulted an agrarian-based society into the age of modern industrialism, they sought to explain segregation and apartheid in terms of the development of capitalism. They pointed out that the system of segregation (the precursor of apartheid) developed from the beginning of the twentieth century and that it was largely conceptualized by English-speakers closely associated with imperialism. Segregation might have built on older prejudices, they conceded, but it was a thoroughly modern response to the needs of a newly industrialising society. It represented a systematic effort to manage the emergence of a potentially uncontrollable African proletariat in the cities, to exclude Africans from political citizenship, and to maintain the migrant labour system by keeping African families in proclaimed rural reserves where officially-recognized male tribal elders held sway. With men temporarily engaged in labour contracts in the urban areas, African women were responsible for raising children and scratching a living based on subsistence agriculture. In effect, this involved an economic subsidy from the rural black to the white urban sector: capitalists were able to pay male migrant labourers mere "bachelor wages" because the costs of producing and reproducing the black labour force would principally be met by African women in the agricultural reserves. This (admittedly oversimplified) sketch of the so-called liberal-radical debate of the 1970s and 1980s bore important political overtones. If apartheid and capitalism were intrinsically interconnected, as radicals claimed, the eradication of the former depended on the destruction of the latter. On the other hand, if apartheid and capitalism were unconnected, or even inimical to each other (as liberals insisted), apartheid could be defeated politically; indeed, the progress of the race-blind free market might actually assist this outcome.

To summarize: the race/class debate, as it came to be known, centred on a disagreement between liberal and radical critics over the *function* of race. Whereas liberals argued that racism was inimical to the interests of a modern industrial society, radicals maintained that racism served the underlying interests of capitalism in South Africa. It did so by creating a super-exploitable labour force and by obscuring class differences between exploiter and exploited, thereby frustrating an attack by a unified working class on the capitalist system as a whole. In theoretical terms the race/class debate turned on the issue of whether "ideology" was an independent explanatory factor in accounting for apartheid, or whether, as some Marxists claimed, it was merely an expression of underlying economic and class imperatives. If Marxists sought to reduce racial explanations of apartheid to class terms, some liberal political economists were equally reductionist by insisting that capitalism would inevitably erode the irrational foundations of group prejudice upon which the apartheid system was founded. Although they disagreed strongly about the function of race *vis a vis* capitalism and apartheid, liberal and marxist theorists alike tended to ignore the content and nature of racial ideas. How were racial stereotypes formed and sustained? How did justifications of innate racial superiority and inferiority change over time? What was the relationship between intellectual and scientific rationalizations or essential racial difference and their manifestation in popular forms?

The ideology of race in colonial times

A body of new work is beginning to address such issues. One important finding suggests that theoretical racism – understood as the systematic expression and rationalization of the idea of superiority and innate biological difference among distinct groups of human beings – was not a strong feature of the early Cape. This is not to suggest that the settlers, travellers and commentators who wrote about southern Africa from the beginnings of European settlement were blind to human difference or that they described the many different peoples of South Africa in non-stereotyped ways; rather, it is to make the point that racial categories remained fluid and imprecise until at least the early nineteenth century.

The Christian baptism and marriage of Krotoa (also known as Eva), an indigenous Khoikhoi (Hottentot) woman fluent in Portuguese and Dutch, to the upwardly mobile young Dutch surgeon Pieter van Meerhof in 1664, is often cited as an example of the potential that briefly existed for individual Khoikhoi to be absorbed within settler society. At one stage, Krotoa mixed in the elevated social world of the governor. But the fact that she became an alcoholic and a prostitute soon after being widowed has also been held up as evidence that the Khoikhoi could never successfully adapt to European culture. In any case, the wars that soon erupted between Dutch and Khoikhoi ruled out any prospect of the emergence of a common society.

In the accounts of travellers, explorers and artists, whose descriptions of the Cape interior did much to shape European perceptions of African peoples, racialized stereotyping was commonplace. Some eighteenth and early-nineteenth century ethnographic accounts portrayed the Bushmen and Hottentots in sympathetic terms as "noble savages". But most descriptions were luridly ethnocentric and routinely denigrating of Khoisan appearance, habits, language and character. Within the classificatory schemes of eighteenth-century science (the "Great Chain of Being" in particular) Hottentots were apt to be cast as amongst the lowest orders of mankind or as a missing link between humans and primates. The Oxford English Dictionary reveals that "Hottentot" referred to "a person of inferior intellect or culture" in early eighteenth-century usage. When Saartjie Baartman, the so-called "Hottentot Venus", was displayed to the French and British public between 1810 and 1815, she was presented as an outlandish specimen of female humanity. Attention was especially on her protruding buttocks; her genitals were dissected by the leading French scientist, Baron Cuvier, and put on show in the Museé de l'Homme in Paris.

The institution of slavery which, by the end of the seventeenth century, was the dominant social institution of the Cape, ensured that hierarchies of status, colour, and descent were of central importance. Most slaves were procured from the Indian Ocean basin (especially Indonesia, and Madagascar) as well as from the East African coast. Their presence further complicated an already diverse array of humanity: white settlers (themselves divided in terms of origin and status), imported slaves, indigenous Khoisan, manumitted slaves ("free blacks") and creoles were all constituents of an increasingly heterogeneous and divided society. By the early eighteenth century Cape society was highly stratified and there was a close correspondence between wealth and colour. However, "race" was not necessarily the single most important defining criterion of an individual's position in the social order. And, although racially discriminatory measures and categories were in place on the statute book by the end of the eighteenth century, the legal system cannot be said to have been thoroughly racialized at this time. Custom and convention reinforced division and prejudices, although the extent to which these can be said to have been firmly entrenched is open to debate. Certainly, genealogical origin and descent was an important key to status. Another very significant indicator of social inclusion and exclusion was religion: those baptized as Christians were in a position to claim superior social status, whereas those of "heathen descent" invariably occupied subordinate positions in society.

In 1806 the British regained the Cape from the Dutch as a consequence of resumed hostilities during the Napoleonic wars. From the first decades of the nineteenth century more systematic efforts were made to define the legal status of the Khoisan and this, in turn, encouraged the growth of a more racially stratified society. In 1809 the Governor of the Cape, Earl Caledon, proclaimed that the Khoisan should be treated as free people and he sought to control their abuse as farm servants by introducing new regulations about contractual rights. In practice, however, the Caledon Code worked against the interests of Khoisan labourers by investing new powers in the hands of local legal authorities who were often prejudiced in favour of employers.

The abolition of the slave trade in 1807 and the ending of slavery as an institution in 1833 had a particularly marked effect on the developing discourse of race. The evangelical work of missionaries like John Philip of the London Missionary society was directed to the conversion of the Khoisan to Christianity as well as the protection of their interests. The promulgation of Ordinance 50 of 1828 established the legal equality of all inhabitants of the Cape colony (with the exception of slaves); this measure is often seen as one of the great achievements of missionary pressure. Liberal historians proclaimed it as a humanitarian triumph for aboriginal rights, whereas settler spokesmen decried it as a prime instance of missionary meddling in colonial affairs. More recent analysis of Ordinance 50 suggests that, in removing the requirement of the Khoisan to carry passes, the act was largely a response to the growing commercialization of the Cape and efforts to create a free labour market. Undoubtedly, measures like Ordinance 50 and the emancipation of slaves did not significantly alter the structure of Cape society. Nor did it retard the growing correlation of colour with social class. The humanitarian influence on the British colonial office and on the governance of the Cape began to wane by the 1840s. In 1841 a new Masters and Servants Ordinance repealed Ordinance 50 of 1828 and, although cast in colourblind terms, greatly increased the effective powers of employers over employees in a racially polarized labour market. By the 1840s liberal beliefs in the underlying equality of all men and the universality of progress and Christian civilisation, were beginning to corrode. Even as influential an advocate of native rights as John Fairbairn was now re-evaluating his position in a manner rather more sympathetic to colonial interests. True, many liberal figures – including Fairbairn – stood by the principle of the (qualified) non-racial franchise when the Cape was granted representative government by the British government in 1853. The Cape non-racial franchise remained an important emblem for successive generations of liberals. But its force was continually eroded as ever-higher voting qualifications were introduced. And, although Cape liberalism remained a significant political tradition through the second half of the nineteenth century, it was placed more and more on the defensive and confronted with its own contradictions.

It was on the eastern Cape frontier settled by British immigrants in the 1820s that the articulation of a new racialized discourse can be seen most clearly. Contact between colonists and Bantu-speaking Africans (as distinct from Khoisan indigenes) became more frequent during the eighteenth century. From the 1770s onwards competition for land on the shifting frontier between the two groups led to a state of endemic conflict. With the arrival of the 1820 English settlers the frontier was opened up for commercial trade and agricultural development. Conflict with Xhosa-speaking Africans now became much more acute and a series of wars in the 1830s and 1840s resulted in a strong colonial military presence and a determination to secure the frontier and pacify Africans once and for all. The increasingly vocal body of settler opinion was much less amenable to the humanitarian idea that non-whites could, or should, be assimilated into colonial society.

Settler spokesmen like J. M. Bowker took the lead in articulating an aggressively anti-black racial discourse in which Africans were cast as irredeemably lazy savages posing a dire threat to the prosperity and security of white colonists. Symptomatic of the racialized discourse through which relations between whites and black were increasingly conceived was the use made by anti-liberals of the science of phrenology (which was based on the idea that human character and faculties could be correlated with the shape and form of the skull). Thus, the application of phrenology by enthusiasts like Andrew Smith and H. E. Macartney was used from the 1830s to attack liberal philanthropists and to demonstrate that the minds of blacks and whites were inherently different.

Although the adherents of phrenology were passionate in their claims, their influence was limited. Literary and artistic images of the black increasingly confirmed the idea that Africans were racially "other". But systematic biologically-based theories of racial difference had not yet coalesced. Such ideas became far more evident from the 1870s and 1880s – a period characterized by heightened nationalism in Europe and the concomitant scramble for Africa. In the case of South Africa this period also coincided with the discovery of gold and diamonds that initiated South Africa into the modern industrial age. It was the combination of mineral revolution and rapid imperial expansion that transformed South Africa from a largely agrarian patchwork of competing polities – Afrikaner, British and African – into a modern political and economic whole.

Imperialism and scientific racism

The "new" imperialism of the 1880s and 1890s was frequently justified and dignified by reference to the composite ideology of Social Darwinism. As the term suggests, Social Darwinism likened the workings of human society to evolutionary processes in the natural world. When applied to the colonial arena, it purported to demonstrate the ultimate biological superiority of white northern European males and, therefore, to explain imperialism as a necessary working out in political and national terms of the law of the survival of the fittest. The study of eugenics (or racial "hygiene") pioneered from the 1870s by the Victorian statistician, psychologist and explorer Francis Galton, linked Social Darwinism to the newly developing science of genetics. Its adherents sought to promote human racial improvement and "social efficiency" through the adoption of methods of selective breeding. In Europe and America eugenic ideas proved highly influential from the turn of the century until the early 1930s and they attracted considerable intellectual support from across the political spectrum. For social reformers and many socialist thinkers as well, "positive" eugenics offered a rational and scientific means by which the physiological and mental capacities of social groups could be enhanced – in association with environmental improvements such as better housing, nutrition and sanitation, as well as the adoption of techniques of birth control. On the other hand, hardline "negative" eugenists adopted a much stronger form of biological determinism. They subscribed to the dictum of the survival of the fittest, and considered that social welfare measures would only frustrate this process. Thus, "superior" races could only be defended through a programme of "weeding out" inferior genetic material, even if this meant the adoption of extreme measures like forced sterilization of the "unfit".

Eugenics combined an arrogant assumption of the natural superiority of the white races with fears that this superiority was threatened by physical and moral "degeneration"; indeed, for many eugenists, Western civilization itself was faced with imminent decline. For example, British military reverses during the Anglo-South African War of 1899–1902 heightened domestic public anxieties about racial deterioration amongst working-class British recruits. The victory of British imperialism in South Africa was therefore viewed as a crucial test and vindication of national prestige and prowess.

In the immediate aftermath of the war, the British administration led by a triumphant Lord Milner (who famously declared himself to be a "British race patriot") set about reconstructing a new South Africa. Milner envisaged a modern and dynamic country, underpinned by a strong mining and industrial sector, in which British values and loyalty to the empire were safeguarded. In order to secure these objectives it was crucial to establish a stable political and economic order. Milner himself was unable to carry the process through. But his successors worked assiduously to overcome Anglo-Afrikaner divisions and to create a unified white nation. This in turn necessitated finding a comprehensive solution to what was by now increasingly referred to as the "native question".

Racial segregation

The 1905 report of the South African Native Affairs Commission, appointed by Milner in 1903, set out the organizational and ideological basis for a systematic policy of racial segregation. In essence, this involved a denial of African claims to citizenship and franchise rights; guaranteeing but also restricting African settlement to designated areas in the countryside; reviving and reshaping the "tribal" system in the reserves as a fundamental element of administration; and controlling the flow of African labour from the countryside to the white urban sector. The concept of segregation involved a radical departure from the miscellany of laws and practices governing blacks in nineteenth-century South Africa. Its scope was so ambitious that it could only be achieved incrementally and through a protracted process of political bargaining. Only with the passage of the Hertzog Bills in 1936 was a unified segregationist policy finally put in place.

At an ideological level segregation drew heavily on racial thought. The assumption of white supremacy that underlay segregationist thinking rested on claims that blacks were less capable than whites and unassimilable within colonial society. The removal of Africans' franchise rights was often justified on the basis that the development of blacks' mental faculties were "arrested" after puberty. The suggestion that Africans should remain, for the most part, in rural areas and under the jurisdiction of officially-sanctioned chiefs, was reinforced by a belief that Africans were ill-suited to urban life and that "detribalization" posed a threat to social order.

Widespread psycho-sexual fears of "miscegenation" were heightened by a conviction that the "purity" of races should be preserved and that racial "contamination" or "hybridisation" was harmful to all. The prospect of "half-castes" displaying moral confusion and lacking social restraint was regarded with particular horror. An obsession with black sexual rapacity, combined with the concerns of male colonists to protect and to maintain their authority over their wives and daughters, engendered frequent outbreaks of "black peril" hysteria.

Such anxieties were by no means all the product of eugenic notions. In many instances eugenic ideas merely gave credence to old popular prejudices or helped to frame these in modern scientific discourse. Whether intellectual ideas caused racism or else served to codify and rationalize existing racial prejudice is to set up a false dichotomy: in practice, influences worked in both directions. The relationship between the theoretical racism as articulated in the academy, and popular racism as expressed in ordinary attitudes and behaviour, was dynamic and mutually reinforcing.

The highpoint of scientific or theoretical racism in South Africa, as elsewhere, was during the interwar years – a period marked by intense public debate about the form that racial segregation should take. In the newly developing field of applied psychology, the tenets of scientific racism were reflected in concerted efforts to show that blacks were inherently less intelligent than whites, or that "native mentality" was fundamentally distinct. In the field of medicine a small but vocal group of doctors discussed the eugenic implications of white poverty; others attempted to explain away the high incidence of tuberculosis experienced by black mineworkers in terms of hereditary susceptibility. Penologists and criminologists like J. T. Dunston and W. A. Willemse sought to demonstrate, in different ways, that "feeble mindedness" was the cause of criminality, prostitution and other forms of deviant behaviour. As in Britain and elsewhere, efforts to promote birth control, especially amongst working-class white women, were strongly conditioned by eugenic fears about race deterioration.

The field of physical anthropology and comparative anatomy was another area deeply affected by scientific racism. South African physical anthropology gained international prominence in the mid-1920s with the discovery in the northern Cape of fossilised remains suggesting that Africa – rather than Asia or Europe – might be the source of the crucial "missing link" in the evolution of mankind. This international pursuit for the origins of humanity attracted great popular interest and became a contest in which national pride and prestige was at stake. Yet, it was a strongly racialized pursuit, bound up as it was with the search for the origins of pure racial "types". Moreover, it was often assumed that the indigenous Khoisan peoples of southern Africa were quixotic survivals of ancestral human "types" and that, as "living fossils", they were doomed to extinction.

There is no space here to discuss the full extent of scientific racism or its purchase on the imagination of ordinary people. It is important to note, however, that eugenic and Social Darwinist ideas in South Africa were not only applied to blacks. Just as in Britain (where eugenic concerns were most often focused on issues of class and gender) and in the United States (where it became especially prominent in the context of immigration policy) the health and supremacy of the dominant white race was a matter of prime concern.

In the case of South Africa the politics of race, class and ethnicity were both closely intertwined and highly contested. By the early 1930s the existence of "poor whites", both in rural and urban areas, was a cause of major political concern. The majority of poor whites were Afrikaners, and the identification of poor whiteism as a distinct social problem demanding urgent attention had much to do with the mobilization of Afrikaner nationalism at that time. Eugenists were inclined to seek biological, organic, or climatological reasons for the existence of poor whiteism. Great concern was expressed that the "degeneration" of poor whites would lead to a weakening of the white race as a whole. But any suggestion that Afrikaner poor whites were somehow inferior to Anglo-Saxons was fiercely resisted by Afrikaner nationalists; this is one important reason why eugenic ideas were treated with some suspicion by politicians, or at least used selectively in public discourse.

Thus, in the politics of segregation and, especially apartheid, the imperative to maintain white supremacy was greatly complicated by ethnic division between English and Afrikaners and these divisions were in turn further complicated by differences in social class. Racial segregation was only achieved after a long process of compromise between competing white political and economic interests. Its appeal to whites was indeed its flexibility and its capacity to speak with different voices to different constituencies.

Notably, the most articulate proponents of segregation in the 1910s and 1920s were often English-speaking moderates, some of whom considered themselves to be of a liberal disposition. In presenting segregation as a commonsense measure deserving of widespread support, ideologists like C. T. Loram and Edgar Brookes proclaimed segregation as an historic compromise between the "assimilationist" or humanitarian traditions of the nineteenth-century Cape and the harshly exclusionist racial attitudes of the Boer republics. In terms of race theory, the equivalent of these policy alternatives was a choice between saying that differences between blacks and whites were of no consequence (because all humans were fundamentally alike), or that white political supremacy was justified by natural law (because of the intrinsic racial superiority of whites).

It was the anthropological concept of "culture" that, from the 1920s and 1930s, came to serve as a convenient device for reconciling these alternatives. The attraction of the anthropological notion of culture lay in its soft-edged relativism, its ability to incorporate – and transcend – the evolutionist assumptions of liberal "assimilationists" (who believed in the capacity of blacks to ascend the scale of civilization) and "repressionists" (who insisted that blacks were inherently inferior).

An excellent example of this mode of thought is evident in the celebrated 1929 Oxford lectures delivered by General Smuts (prime minister of South Africa from 1919–24 and 1939–48). Arguing in favour of segregation, Smuts rejected the opinion that viewed the "African as essentially inferior or sub-human, as having no soul, and as being only fit to be a slave". But he also rejected the egalitarian belief whereby the "African now became a man and a brother". Policies based on both of these assumptions, Smuts maintained, had been harmful. The solution was to be found in a policy of differential development or segregation: "The new policy is to foster an indigenous native culture or system of cultures, and to cease to force the African into alien European moulds." In this formulation "culture" therefore became a means of reconciling opposites, of insisting on difference without specifying whether such difference is biologically determined or not.

This discursive strategy was important for those who regarded scientific racism as too extreme, too theoretical, and too double-edged to serve as the sole intellectual justification of segregation. Conversely, the salience of inherent racial difference was considered so self-evident as to be undeniable. It had the added advantage of likening segregationist policies in South Africa to the paternalistic British colonial doctrine of "indirect rule", wherein central power was exercised by devolving authority at the local level to selected African "tribal chiefs".

Segregation became the hegemonic political ideology in South Africa during the 1920s and 1930s. Its flexibility and apparent lack of doctrinal rigour facilitated its adaptation to new political circumstances. During the war years, for example, when South Africa experienced a surge of industrial development, segregationist policies were relaxed in order to satisfy employer demands for black labour in the urban areas. However, countervailing political forces were in evidence. Afrikaner nationalists were becoming increasingly militant in their demands that South Africa should have no part in defending the British empire and that, indeed, an Afrikaner *volk* republic should be established. Afrikaner intellectuals and churchmen also paid increasing attention to the "native question", arguing that segregation was incoherent and contradictory and that stronger measures were required in order to protect vulnerable whites from being overwhelmed by the tide of

African urbanization. In this highly emotional and politicized environment, racist demands to defend the purity of whites (and Afrikaner women in particular) from "contamination" were a central rallying call.

Apartheid

When, in 1948, the National Party under the leadership of D. F. Malan defeated the Smuts government, the election result was a surprise to most observers. The new government came to power on the slogan of "apartheid" but it was unclear at the time precisely what this meant. Over the next decade it became apparent that apartheid was a far more rigorous and totalizing ideology than segregation had been and that it implied radical forms of social engineering designed to enforce separation between blacks and whites at every point. Some influential theorists, the so-called apartheid "visionaries", believed that complete separation between blacks and whites was desirable and, indeed, ordained by God. They considered that apartheid was a morally just solution to racial conflict; the apartheid promise of "separate but equal" was held to be a more honest and equitable solution than the segregationist system which allowed whites to make use of black labour but without according them political rights. Ultimately, it was the apartheid "pragmatists" who prevailed, realizing that the economy could not do without black labour and that total separation was not feasible, at least in the short term.

The doctrinal foundations of apartheid are often referred to as "Christian-Nationalism". Although it was often accompanied by crude racist rhetoric, Christian-Nationalist ideology sought, for the most part, to distance itself from biological theories of inherent difference. In part, this can be ascribed to a deep reluctance on the part of Afrikaner theologians to rely on biological and evolutionist models of human difference; for to do so would be to question scriptural accounts of creation as well as the central place of God in the universe. (In any case, interpretations of the tower of Babel story or the place of the sons of Ham provided ample material to explain the need to preserve racial boundaries.) Christian-Nationalism also laid great emphasis on a romantic conception of the Afrikaner *volk* as a collective organism with a distinctive soul. The *volk* was therefore defined in cultural and spiritual terms rather than as a merely physical or biological entity. Sustained efforts to "save" the Afrikaner *volk* by incorporating by uplifting and incorporating its "weaker" elements, the poor whites, was another important reason why Christian-Nationalists steered clear from an emphasis on biologically-based theories of race degeneration.

Finally, although Afrikaner nationalists professed great certainty in the God-given mission of the *volk*, they remained acutely conscious of domestic and foreign criticism. During the era of segregation white South Africa was considered a valuable member of the British Commonwealth and its racial policies were not seen as being fundamentally at odds with practices elsewhere in the colonial world. Apartheid, by contrast, was highly conspicuous because it was entrenched in the aftermath of the Nazi holocaust and, therefore, at a time when the West was rapidly reconsidering notions of race supremacy.

The UNESCO-sponsored statements of the early 1950s, wherein leading scientists publicly disavowed notions of race superiority, were landmark moments in what has been termed the international "retreat from race". South Africa, by contrast, was moving in an opposite direction. From the 1960s, especially, apartheid came to figure as an obvious target for the worldwide anti-racist movement. Afrikaner politicians and ideologists were well aware that to allow unbridled racist rhetoric to flourish would be highly dangerous for the country's reputation. Thus, they consciously portrayed apartheid as a system designed to allow "self-determination" for different "cultural groups" and rejected accusations that it was founded on the assumption of race superiority.

When it suited their objectives, apartheid's theorists were happy to quote the findings of racial science in support of white superiority, but only rarely did this constitute the basis of their arguments. The elevated pronouncements of Afrikaner intellectuals coexisted with visceral populist appeals against the dangers of miscegenation and racial contamination. However, for both pragmatic and doctrinal reasons, the language of cultural essentialism – as expressed through appeals to "national character", "*volk*" and "soul" – was preferred to the crude scientific racism drawn from the vocabulary of Social Darwinism. In the 1970s and 1980s, defenders of apartheid increasingly had recourse to the concept of "ethnicity". Rather like "culture" before it, the concept of "ethnicity" was deployed as a convenient synonym for race, though without the negative connotations of biological determinism.

Conclusion

The history of the idea of "race" in South Africa echoes, in a striking manner, its broader history in European social thought. The preoccupation with human difference, the impulse to create categories and typologies, and the fascination with the racial or cultural other, can be traced back at least as far as the eighteenth-century Enlightenment. In South Africa distinct social hierarchies were salient from the moment of European settlement. These were always racialized in one form or another, and they coincided strongly with wealth, social status and power.

A systematic *science of race* was not, however, evident until the latter part of the nineteenth century. The methodical racializing of the South

African state was likewise a feature of late-nineteenth and early-twentieth century industrial modernity rather than an anachronistic carry-over from pre-industrial times. Thus, the creation of a rigid racially-exclusivist society involved a complex (and ultimately inseparable) dynamic between race and class. Neither can be reduced to the other.

Scientific racism was widely pervasive in late-nineteenth and twentieth century South Africa, just as it was elsewhere in the world. Such ideas were often derived from Europe and America, but this does not mean that metropolitan conceptions were simply replicated in the colonial context. They reinforced existing prejudices while helping at the same time to shape new ones. Thus, the complex repertoire of racial ideas was selectively absorbed and differentially applied according to circumstance.

It is perhaps ironical that, in a society where institutionalized racial discrimination and prejudice was so apparent, scientific racism was never a central part of national ideology – as was the case, for example, in Nazi Germany. In part, this may be attributable to the fact that consciousness of racial difference was so deeply imprinted in the fabric of white social consciousness that it was easily taken for granted and did not always require formal articulation. The language of deference and paternalism, shaped over a relatively long colonial history of conquest and slavery, was a powerful force in its own right. Intra-white social and ethnic divisions, in particular the presence of largely Afrikaner poor whites, was another important restraining influence. However attractive scientific racism was in underwriting white supremacist attitudes by naturalizing social hierarchies in biological terms, it could never gain the wholehearted approval of those in power. But it was a vital adjunct to white authority and, as such, performed a key ideological role in the underpinning of racial segregation and apartheid.

Suggestions for further reading

Useful general histories of South Africa include W. Beinart, *Twentieth-century South Africa* (Oxford: Oxford University Press, 1995); L. Thompson, *A history of South Africa* (New Haven and London: Yale University Press, 1990); N. Worden, *The making of modern South Africa* (Oxford: Basil Blackwell, 1994). Key debates over segregation and apartheid are outlined and explained in W. Beinart and S. Dubow (eds), *Segregation and Apartheid in twentieth-century South Africa* (London: Routledge, 1995). Important interpretations of eighteenth- and nineteenth-century South African history, focusing on the relationship between race and class, are to be found in R. Ross, *Beyond the pale. Essays on the history of colonial South Africa* (Johannesburg: Witwatersrand University Press, 1993) and T. Keegan, *Colonial South Africa and the origins of the racial order* (Cape Town: David Philip, 1996). The literature on the science of race in South Africa includes: L. Thompson, *The political mythology of apartheid* (New Haven: Yale University Press, 1985); A. Bank, "Of 'native skulls' and 'noble caucasians': Phrenology in colonial South Africa", *Journal of Southern African Studies*, **22**(3), pp. 387–403, 1996; P. Rich, "Race, science, and the legitimisation of white supremacy in South Africa, 1902–1940", *The International Journal of African Historical Studies*, **23**(4), pp. 665–86, 1990; S. Klausen, "'For the sake of the race': Eugenic discourses of feeblemindedness and motherhood in the *South African Medical Record*, 1903–1926", *Journal of Southern African Studies* **23**(1), pp. 27–50, 1997; S. Dubow, *Racial segregation and the origins of apartheid in South Africa, 1919-36* (London: Macmillan, 1989) and, most recently, *Scientific racism in modern South Africa* (Cambridge: Cambridge University Press, 1995).

Chapter Seven

Agrarian histories and agricultural revolutions

Alun Howkins

It is the essence of many views of the rural world that it is unchanging and timeless. Thomas Hardy's poem, *In time of "the Breaking of Nations"* speaks clearly to this view with its famous lines

> Only a man harrowing clods
> In a slow silent walk
> With an old horse that stumble and nods
> Half asleep as they stalk.

> Only thin smoke without flame
> From the heaps of couch-grass;
> Yet this will go onward the same
> Though Dynasties pass

This is a view which spreads through the whole of English culture with its emphasis on heritage, on the English landscape, and even into advertising, where the countryside is used to show purity and permanence. Yet such a view cannot be sustained for long. Even in the years since the Second World War the rural areas have changed almost beyond measure. The physical appearance of the countryside has been transformed, along with the techniques of agricultural production leading to Britain being virtually self-sufficient in temperate foodstuffs. Nor is this change new. As W. G. Hoskins wrote many years ago, even in the apparently "timeless" villages of the English Midlands strata upon strata of change is there for all to see. In all this historians have sought for change, above all they have sought sudden change – revolutions. So agricultural revolutions have a long history. In the same way that the late J. H. Hexter noted the middle classes were rising at every period of English history, so historians have been able to identify an agricultural revolution in almost every epoch. V. Gordon Childe saw the very origins of agriculture in the Neolithic period as the most fundamental of all human revolutions; while in the 1980s the so-called "Green Revolution", that is, increases in productivity based on new crop varieties especially in the South (the Third World), is the most recent use of the idea. In the 14 millennia separating these dates other historians have claimed ancient Egypt and Rome, thirteenth-century England, Britain in the 1860s and again in the 1950s as dates at which agrarian revolutions had taken place. However, in the "popular" account the term "agricultural revolution" is closely linked with the hundred years after 1750. The origins of this account are diverse. Karl Marx in Volume 1 of *Capital* uses the term "agricultural revolution", but to refer, as some later historians have, to the sixteenth century. Overton in his recent study of the agricultural revolution suggests that its first application to the "classic" period occurs, like the term "industrial revolution" in Toynbee's *Lectures on the Industrial Revolution* published in 1884 and in an article by R. E. Prothero (later Lord Ernle) in the *Quarterly Review* for 1885. Prothero was to go on, in his *Pioneers and Progress in English Farming* of 1888 and especially *English Farming Past and Present* of 1912 to lay the foundations of many subsequent accounts of the agricultural revolution. Prothero's view was essentially an heroic one. In this a few "great men", most notably Jethro Tull, Lord Townshend, Arthur Young, Bakewell, and Coke of Holkham turned a conservative and backward peasant economy into a progressive and successful industry. Their main ally was innovation – turnips and clover in crops, the selective breeding of animals and limited use of machinery, for example, the seed drill. Coupled with this were wider "social" changes, particularly the continued enclosure of common field and waste, and the bringing together of small farms into larger ones, whose farming was often governed by leases which included instructions as to how a particular farm should be worked – husbandry convenants. The basis of this heroic view was clear enough and lay in England's, and to a lesser extent Britain's, ability to break out of the Malthusian trap. Malthus had argued in the early years of the nineteenth century that land was a fixed resource. This meant that ceilings were set on the amount of food land could produce and hence on the size of population. For the period from about 1250–1700 Malthus was broadly correct. In this period, population was unable to exceed 5.5 million and, although grain yields rose under population pressure, it never managed to break through a ceiling of about 18 bushels per acre of wheat. After 1700, and especially after 1750, population increased dramatically. By 1800 the English population had reached 6.42 million and by 1900, 30.51 million. Thus, when Prothero and his contemporaries looked back from the 1900s, English agriculture was a story of phenomenal success.

This view of the agricultural revolution was given its modern form by the extremely influential book by J. D.Chambers and G. E. Mingay, *The Agricultural Revolution 1750-1880* published in 1966. Although Chambers and

Mingay modified Prothero's view, they remained firmly committed to the period 1750–1850 as the key one of transition. As they wrote in their Introduction, "the changes which (the authors) describe were on such a scale and of such a character as to be justly called a revolution." However, by the time Chambers and Mingay had published their text the "classic" view of the agricultural revolution had begun to be challenged. In a narrow sense detailed work had dethroned many of the great men. "Turnip" Townshend was a boy when turnips were first grown on his estate, Tull was at best a crank and certainly not the first person to make a seed drill, and even Coke of Holkham was revealed as an able publicist, especially for his own work, rather than a great innovator.

More substantially in 1967 Eric Kerridge published his *Agricultural Revolution* which argued "that the agricultural revolution took place in England in the sixteenth and seventeenth centuries and not in the eighteenth and nineteenth". The core of Kerridge's argument was that most of the changes relevant to an increase in production and seen as new after 1750 were already in place by 1700, including many of the new crops. Kerridge's arguments were largely technical and centre especially on "convertible husbandry", at its most simple, the notion that productivity could be increased by rotating the grass "leys" around a farm giving the soil a "rest" and renewing it by grazing animals on it. He also stressed other technical changes, especially fen drainage and water meadows, and the use of fertilisers like marl and animal dung. The outcome of this was the ability of domestic agriculture to deal with the rise in population between 1550–1750 from about 2.9 million to 5.7 million.

Also in the 1960s the work of E. L. Jones and A. H. John produced another contender in the period 1650–1750. Jones and John, with differing emphasis, stressed the extent to which the techniques noted as important after 1750 were widely used by 1650, but used to feed a growing export market rather than a home population. As Overton notes, by the 1970s and 1980s it was this period which was the most popular. Basing themselves on the work of John and Jones, a number of studies stressed the innovative character of agriculture in this period, including the introduction of turnips and clover and their associated rotations, the use of fodder crops which enabled cattle to be overwintered and to produce dung to fertilize fields, thus increasing output and lowering production costs, and, finally, widespread landlord support for improvement.

The view that the period before 1750 was the most important was given further support in the 1990s by the publication of Robert Allen's very important study of the South Midlands, in which he argued that the real gains in productivity were not a product of the eighteenth century revolution but were made "by small farmers in the open fields during the seventeenth century". At its most extreme a combination of these views could lead another 1990s writer, G.Clarke in 1993, to deny the very existence of an agricultural revolution at all. However, radical changes in the factors of production do not make a revolution – we also need to consider the social relations of production. "These issues", Overton writes, "are concerned with the establishment of private property rights to land, the replacement of feudal tenures and estates with leaseholds for a period of years, changes in the size of farms, and changes in the ways in which people were employed by others on the land."

The debates on these changes have followed a similar path to those on the more technical and agricultural changes already briefly mentioned. Writings in the early part of this century tended to locate these major institutional changes within the period 1750–1850. A key text here was J. L. and Barbara Hammond's, *The Village Labourer* published in 1911. The Hammonds, taking an essentially "classic" view of the agricultural revolution, stressed the social, political and institutional changes in the countryside after 1750, and especially between 1780 and 1830. To them the key events centred around the enclosure of common fields and wastes, and the subsequent immiseration of the rural poor. Driven from the land the rural poor were forced to move to the cities of the industrial revolution as a new urban proletariat, or to remain in the countryside increasingly impoverished and demoralized, relying on the Poor Law to maintain a subsistence-level existence. Although the Hammonds' account was held on to by those on the political left , it was challenged from the 1920s by the new discipline of Economic History and, especially after 1950, by a number of local studies of enclosure. These were brought together in Chambers' and Mingay's account, and the Hammonds found wanting. Enclosure, far from destroying the peasant farmer, often fixed his title – there were more small farmers in 1815 than in the 1750s – and may even have led to the numbers of small farmers actually increasing. For the labourer and cottager who had common rights these were probably of little value, and their loss was more than compensated for by increased employment on the new larger farms. Immiseration, which certainly existed, was the result not of enclosure but of population increase. Set against this, enclosure made the advances in techniques of agricultural production, developed in the eighteenth century, viable on a large scale. "Enclosure", Chambers and Mingay wrote, "meant more food for the growing population, more land under cultivation and, on balance, more employment in the countryside; and enclosed farms provided the framework for the new advances of the nineteenth century."

The studies carried out in the 1950s and 1960s may well have left the Hammonds bereft of empirical clothing but their arguments did not go away. E. P. Thompson's *The Making of the English Working Class* paid scant attention to the countryside, and since it was published in 1963 predates some of the work on which Chambers and Mingay based their summary. However, in the 1968 edition he turned to Chambers and Mingay, albeit briefly. His central point, and one which continues to be central to debates on enclosure, is not whether those who had legal right were compensated for loss of that right, but whether those whose livelihood was supplemented by "illegal" use of common and waste suffered by enclosure. His answer is simple. Although the great mass of the rural poor – labourers and cottagers – may have had no legal right, they relied on the commons. They were not compensated for that loss since the "law" did not recognise their rights. But suffer they did.

Thompson's main contribution, however, took a different route. Improved agriculture, he argued most notably his last book *Customs in Common*, involved a change in property relations. Simply, private property in land meant the extinction of customary tenure and rights of all kinds. This was not only a legal change but represented a complete alteration in how men and women worked the land and related to it. Improved agriculture, then, was not only a matter of increased yield, or even immiseration it was "a rupture of the traditional integument of village custom and right".

By the end of the 1980s common threads emerged from all this discussion. The dating may have been imprecise, but probably between 1650 and 1750 English (and to an extent British) agriculture went through a fundamental technological and social change. On larger farms, held on leases and encouraged by improving landlords, and using new techniques and cropping, tenant farmers increased output to such an extent that the Malthusian trap was broken. This involved costs. Enclosure, the establishment of private property in land and the coeval extinction of custom may have caused short-term social dislocation, but this was far outweighed by the increases in food production necessary to support industrialization. However, questioning of this model continued. As early as 1968, F. M. L. Thompson made an argument for a "second agricultural revolution" based on the import of feedstuffs like oil-cake and fertilisers like guano which, like the eighteenth century accounts, emphasized the breaking of an old system by introducing new inputs. H. C. Darby had also argued from the 1960s that the spread of clay tile under draining of clay lands had enabled the gains made on the light soils of East Anglia to become genuinely national during the mid years of the nineteenth century. Without wishing to play down the importance of this work, I believe that it remains essentially a modification of the classic period model rather than a fundamental change. More recently still, a number of historians have stressed the importance of late twentieth-century developments in scientific agriculture, but again this has little to say about earlier periods. More fundamental has been recent work on eighteenth-century agriculture by Mark Overton and on the effects of enclosure by Robert Allen, Jeanette Neeson and Jane Humphries. Taken together, this work goes back to the classic period as the key period of transition and to an account of social change which owes much to the Hammonds. A good deal of the argument about agrarian transformation is technical, and often subtle and complex, but the general thrust is clear. Overton states his conclusions clearly. Although regional gains in productivity were made before 1750, they were short-term and based upon changing uses of existing resources plus a modest increase in labour productivity. "It was not", he writes, "until the century after 1750 that the dramatic and unprecedented improvements in output, land productivity and labour productivity, associated with equally dramatic and unprecedented changes in husbandry, were under way on a broad front." In support of this view Overton stresses three areas. First, an increase in land productivity, secondly, an increase in labour productivity and, thirdly, a transformation of the institutional and ideological frameworks of agriculture – the transformation to agrarian capitalism.

The question of land productivity first. Land productivity can be increased extensively, by increasing the area under cultivation, or intensively, by raising the yield per acre. The latter is obviously best since it offers the possibility of continuing increases. This is especially so since by the sixteenth century at least three-quarters of the land being farmed today was already cultivated. Nevertheless, there clearly was expansion of the area under cultivation in the sixteenth and seventeenth centuries, and further increases in the arable area at the expense of waste. Nevertheless, something of the order of 20% of England and Wales was wasteland in 1700 which suggests considerable room for increasing production extensively on the sixteenth-century model. However, there are problems since it is not always easy to disentangle intensive and extensive improvement. Moor and fenland was farmed before improvement, so the change is one from low to high intensity rather than simply extensive. Further, much change relied upon technical and cropping innovation rather than simply bringing new land into use.

Innovation in cropping is especially important here. The use of new crops to improve the vitality of the soil, rather than relying on a fallow period, could shorten enormously the period in which land lay idle and thus increase output. Although both clover, for nitrogen fixation and feed, and turnips for winter fodder were available in the seventeenth century they were little used. Detailed work, however, suggests that both were becoming widespread in the years after 1750. For example, even in the advanced counties of Norfolk and Suffolk less than 3% of the cropped area was under clover in the three decades before 1730, yet by 1830 the proportion had risen to 20%. A similar rise has been charted for turnip cultivation.

Alongside the introduction of new crops comes evidence of changing crop proportions as farming became more specialized after the middle of the eighteenth century with regional economies emerging to replace the "mixed" farms of the earlier period. This led to distinctive regional differences. In East Anglia the area under pasture dwindled as wheat become King, but in the Midlands and the West the process was reversed. Here the area under pasture increased in response to improvements in animal husbandry. What was to become, by 1850, a familiar division between an arable South and East and a pastoral North and West, was beginning to emerge in place of the more complex regional farming geography of the early modern period.

In the arable areas the "scientific" revolution in ideas about farming that Appleby notes in the last decades of the seventeenth century seems to have spread down the social scale to "ordinary" farmers. As well as the new crops, especially the nitrogen fixing clovers, there is also good evidence of increased use of existing manures and the beginnings of the use of new manures – for example, seaweed and human waste. Another element in increased cropping was the overwintering of animals in sheds, fed on turnips or other root crops whose dung was then spread on the fields. As with some other techniques, this was an "old" system but one which only began to have a wide impact, especially in East Anglia, in the years after 1750. These factors combined to make for real increases in yield both per acre and in total. As a result of all this, most reliable estimates point to English agricultural output rising by 2.5 to 3 times between 1700 and 1850, but more than doubling in the century after 1750.

Labour productivity is more difficult to deal with. Again, Overton, looking at a wide range of materials, argues that labour productivity doubled in the years after 1750. New tools, more "scientific" use of labour on large farms and the increased use of horse power were the major elements in this change. However, this may underestimate the contribution of labour to the productivity gains of the hundred years after 1750. Most of the new techniques of the agricultural revolution were, as Tom Williamson has argued, highly labour-intensive. Turnips, for instance, required extremely careful cultivation; marling, the most common form of manuring, required digging, carting and spreading; brush draining, widely used in many areas in the eighteenth and early nineteenth century, took many hours of cold, backbreaking winter work. Importantly, this was casual labour. The de-industrialisation of the rural South and East, where old-established outwork industries collapsed in the face of northern competition, created a labour surplus, forced to work on a day or piecework basis. This pool of cheap labour was a key element in the years after 1750.

The role of institutional and social change has also been rethought over recent years. When James Caird toured agricultural England for *The Times* in 1851, he saw a country divided into what he called "the three great interests connected with agriculture – the landlord, the tenant and the labourer . . ." The landlord owned the land, the tenant rented in from him for a fixed rent on a lease for a number of years, and the usually landless labourer worked the land. All this was in large part a product of the period 1750–1850 and was closely associated with the variety of processes lumped together under the word "enclosure".

Enclosure could, and did, mean many different things, but at core it involves a change in property rights. At its most extreme it involved the division of common field and waste ("common") into individual fields held in the concentrated form of individual farms. Here the rights to common animals, to cut wood or turf or to dig marl or stone on the waste were lost, replaced by charity lands for the many and exclusive ownership for the few. At the other extreme it simply represented a legal recognition of a system of private ownership which already existed, and may well have been carried out over many years.

That enclosure was a phenomenon of the classic period of the industrial revolution is beyond doubt; what remains at issue is the extent to which enclosure had taken place before the eighteenth century. The best answer is probably to say that regional differences were centrally important here, as elsewhere. In 1700 great swathes of the Midlands, East Anglia, Lincolnshire, Yorkshire and Durham were farmed in open fields with common and waste. By 1850 a major part of the land in all of these areas, with the exception of some moorland grazing, was farmed in individual farms. In some areas much of that change took place after 1750. For example, in the South Midlands 55% of the enclosed acreage was enclosed between 1750 and 1849, while in Co Durham it was 59%.

The social and institutional effects of enclosure were similarly varied. In many areas enclosure by Act of Parliament, the most common form practised after 1750, simply recognized an effective *status quo*. However, in other regions the effect could be traumatic and it is here the element of class has to be introduced. In 1963 E. P. Thompson wrote of enclosure as "a plain enough case of class robbery, played according to the fair rules of property laid down by a parliament of property-owners and lawyers." Many of those who found themselves denied to poor pickings of common rights felt the same. A ballad of the period runs.

> When the Romans ruled this land, the commons they did give,
> Unto the poor in Charity to help them for to live.
> But the poor are quite done o'er, we know this to be true,
> 'Twas not the way, when Bess did reign and this old hat was new.
>
> For the Commons are taken in, the cottages pulled down,
> Poor Moll has got no wool to spin her Lindsey-Woolsey Gown.
> 'Tis cold and clothing's scarce, and blankets are but few,
> But were clothed, both back and side, when this old hat was new.

Against this view historians have, until very recently, tended to take the side of the enclosers, stressing the positive gains of enclosure. For the small, landowning farmer it guaranteed his rights of ownership, enabling him to consolidate in security; for the labourer it increased the opportunities for work, and for the landowners it gave regular rents untrammelled by outdated feudal dues. In this, the most controversial areas have been the survival or otherwise of the small farmer, and the effect of enclosure on the labourers.

The small farmer first. Marx argued that enclosure destroyed the small farmer – the middle peasantry, and turned them into the landless proletariat necessary for the new factories of the industrial revolution. This view was widely supported by radical writers and critics until the 1950s, when agrarian historians, especially J. D. Chambers, began to argue that enclosure protected the rights of small farmers, by pointing to the fact that at enclosure the award – the document which said how the land should be divided up – usually recognized small tenures. However, recently J. M. Neeson has shown that, although many small owners had rights recognised, they frequently sold their land on after a short time, often to great landowners. So, although rights were recognised, these farms often did not survive as separate holdings and the children of their original owners often became landless workers. For example, at the enclosure of Wells-next-the-Sea in Norfolk during the Napoleonic Wars a number of small allotments were made, but the vast bulk of the land went to the Earl of Leicester (Coke of Norfolk). Between 1816 and his death in 1842, Coke bought nearly all of these allotments, often at above market price, a practice he carried out elsewhere on his estate. More serious were the losses to the labourers and those who had no significant land holdings, but did have common rights over common land and waste – the small peasants. Although these were compensated for by the award of small areas of land, which was usually then rented to a larger farmers and the rent used for charity, this could not compensate for their real losses.

With their holdings consolidated, landlords were able to rent them as farms to tenant farmers, increasingly men of capital, who often acted as managers, delegating the "muddy-boots" to a foreman. This left the labourer, without even limited rights on the common, with nothing to sell but his labour power. The classic tripartite division which still marks the country side today had come into being.

The great justification for enclosure was that, coupled with the changes of the agricultural revolution, it fed Britain's growing industrial population and thus broke out of the Malthusian trap. This question is much more difficult to address. Overton, in the most recent general study, is absolutely clear. Without an agricultural revolution in the eighteenth century, Britain would not have been able to feed a population of more than 5.5 million. The fact that this was done with proportionally fewer workers, especially than in, say, France, released population for the workforce of the industrial revolution. Yet we do need to pause, because this account is of more than historic interest. As Robert Allen and others have pointed out, the "English road" to industrialization became a model for how this process could be carried through. In this, the creation of large-scale agriculture was axiomatic. In order to produce a food surplus, and indeed in some cases a surplus of capital, it was necessary to destroy customary tenures, replace the peasant with the large farmer and utilize economies of scale to enable maximum output and specialization of production to be achieved. Unusually this view was shared by both left and right, who may have disagreed about costs, but agreed about the desirability and inevitability of the process. The small farmer and the peasant was dismissed as inefficient and outdated. The practical ramifications of this shared view have become apparent in the twentieth century. Whether in countries in the orbit of the former Soviet Union, the CAP or, more importantly, the World Bank and the IMF, agricultural economies have been forced down a version of the English road with often disastrous results. The collectivization of the peasantry in the Soviet Union in the 1920s derived directly from a reading of Marx's *Capital* with its insistence on the destruction of the peasantry as a precursor to industrial growth. The growing of specialist crops like mange tout or baby sweet corn for export to the North in the South in the 1990s proceeds from the essentially identical views of the IMF, as does the CAP's use of subsidies to destroy small-scale farming in Europe.

If this is the case, as I believe it certainly is, we need to pause and look again at our revolution in the longer term. The first thing to say is that it was by no means as simple as it seems. A revolution which took place over a hundred years is very different from an aid programme which seeks to bring about the same changes in five. This is especially true if we do not know if at any point in the process increased output might have been possible with different, and less violent, social and economic change. Let me explain. Even in the 1880s something in the region of 80% of all English farm units were below 50 acres. Although these farms account for only about 14% of the land area they are clearly a major part of the successful agricultural transition. We must at least know more about them before we impose our "model" on the South. Further, we are only now beginning to see the terrible environmental costs of the agricultural revolution. Scientific farming, the demand for cheap food and high profits are as much a part of the agricultural revolution as turnips, clover and new breeds of sheep. It is possible that they sowed a terrible wind in the 1750s and that we may now be beginning to reap the whirlwind of environmental disaster.

Suggestions for further reading

The most recent account of the debates around the agricultural revolution of the eighteenth century is Mark Overton's very useful, *Agricultural revolution in England. The transformation of the agrarian economy 1500–1850* (Cambridge: Cambridge University Press, 1996). It challenges but still needs putting alongside the much older book by J. D. Chambers and G. E. Mingay, *The agricultural revolution, 1750–1880* (London: Batsford, 1966). For arguments that it all happened earlier see V. G. Childe, *Man makes himself* (London: Watts, 1936); Eric Kerridge, *The agricultural revolution*

(London: Allen and Unwin, 1967); E. L. Jones, *Agriculture and the Industrial Revolution* (Oxford: Basil Blackwell, 1974); H. C. Darby (ed.), *A new historical geography of England after 1600* (Cambridge: Cambridge University Press, 1973); A. H. John, "The course of agricultural change, 1660-1750" in W. E. Minchinton (ed.), *Essays in agrarian history* (Newton Abbot: David and Charles, 1968); F. M. L. Thompson, "The second agricultural revolution" in *Economic History Review*, **21**, 1968. For a wider view, and one not touched here except by implication see T. H. Aston and C. H. E. Philpin (eds), *The Brenner debate: agrarian class structure and economic development in pre-industrial Europe* (Cambridge: Cambridge University Press, 1985). It is also useful to look at the relevant volumes of *The Agrarian History of England and Wales* (Cambridge: Cambridge University Press, various dates). On specific issues the potential list is huge and readers are referred to the bibliography in Overton. However some important titles would include R. E. Prothero, *English farming past and present* (London: Longman Green, 1912) and later editions, old but still the starting point for debates. J. L. and Barbara Hammond, *The village labourer* (London: Longman Green, 1911 and later) a key text for a grim view of change. Joyce Oldham Appleby, *Economic thought and ideology in seventeenth-century England* (Princeton: Princeton University Press, 1978) is good on changes in ideas as is Keith Tribe, *Land labour and economic discourse* (London: Routledge, 1978). On property relations see E. P. Thompson, *Customs in common* (London: Merlin, 1991). Two recent very important studies of enclosure are Robert C. Allen, *Enclosure and the yeoman: the agricultural development of the South Midlands 1450-1850* (Oxford: Oxford University Press, 1992) and J. M. Neeson, *Commoners: common right, enclosure and social change in England, 1700-1820* (Cambridge: Cambridge University Press, 1993). For the relationship between scientific agriculture, land and enclosure see Marion Shoard, *This land is our land, the struggle for Britain's countryside* (London: Paladin, 1987).

Part Two
Historians

Chapter Eight

ക്ക

The Weber thesis: "unproven yet unrefuted"

Richard Whatmore

> I protest against Popery as much as ever Luther and Calvin did, or Queen Elizabeth herself, but I believe from my Heart, that the Reformation has scarce been more Instrumental in rendr'ing the Kingdoms and States that have embraced it, flourishing beyond other Nations, than the silly and capricious Invention of Hoop'd and Quilted Petticoats.

Mandeville, *The Fable of the Bees* (1729).

The Augustan satirist Bernard Mandeville, reflecting upon the commercial prosperity of Holland and England, did not believe that the Protestantism of these states could explain their economic prominence in Europe. Rather, he was sure that the love of gain characteristic of such commercial societies could be traced to the exercise of natural human passions, since "all Human Creatures have a restless Desire of mending their condition". In making these claims Mandeville's intention was to disparage the views of eminent contemporaries, such as Sir William Petty, Sir William Temple, Joseph Addison, and Daniel Defoe, for whom Dutch wealth was in various ways related to Protestant religious practices efficacious to trade, by contrast with the Catholicism which in part explained the declining riches of Spain and Portugal.

Accounting for the successes of the British and Dutch economies became a French obsession in the eighteenth century and, with North America making a Protestant triumvirate, a German obsession in the nineteenth. Different writers gave prominence to different factors. For Voltaire, the leading *philosophe* of his day, the toleration of dissenting minorities favoured by the Anglican church was one of the secrets of Britain's strength. Still more important was the English aristocracy's support for commerce. In one of the most telling passages of his *Letters on England*, first published in 1733, Voltaire professed astonishment at discovering that "when the Lord

95

Townshend was Minister of State, a Brother of his was content to be a City Merchant; and at the Time that the Earl of Oxford govern'd Great-Britain, his younger Brother was no more than a Factor in Aleppo". As this example illustrates, Voltaire was certain that the distinct noble cultures of France and Britain, rather than their respective established faiths, explained relative French decline since the end of the seventeenth century. Writing fifteen years after the publication of Voltaire's *Letters*, Montesquieu adopted a broader perspective; in his eyes the wealth and power of states ought to be ascribed to a multitude of factors, ranging from the influence of climate to social structure and size. But he too stressed the particular importance of one factor above all others, the form of government of a state. Britain's rise had more to do with the fact that it was "one nation in the world whose constitution has political liberty for its direct purpose" than with the peculiarities of its elite culture. A mixed government, he concluded, balancing the popular, monarchical, and aristocratic elements of society, was singularly suited to increasing commerce. Montesquieu was not indifferent to the influence of religion, and was struck by the piety of the ordinary Englishman, but he could discover no necessary connection between riches and faith. A century on, and likewise reflecting upon the historical commercialization of Britain, which he called "the transition from feudal to capitalist society", Karl Marx believed he had discovered the first "scientific" rationale for the rise and fall of states with the formulation of a "materialist theory of history". All individuals, he argued in *The German Ideology* of 1845, "begin to distinguish themselves from animals as soon as they begin to *produce* their means of subsistence, a step which is conditioned by their physical organisation". In short, the first thought of every individual, and the overriding objective of every society, is self-preservation, and this can only be secured by the perpetual satisfaction of subsistence needs by increasing what Marx called "the forces of production". These forces, loosely defined as tools and labour power, determined the "social relations of production" by reference to which different historical societies could be distinguished. For example, the forces of production in Republican and Imperial Rome were primarily organized by the social relationship of citizens, who needed leisure time to defend the state and participate in politics, and the slaves who tilled the soil. In medieval Europe, the relationship between feudal lords, who owned the great estates, and the landless serfs who worked upon them, gave a unique character to that society. Most important of all, the capitalist society which had established itself in England, in the wake of the political revolutions of the seventeenth century, was organized by the social relationship of owners of capital, whom Marx labelled the bourgeoisie, and the notionally free proletarians then flocking from the land to the commercial and industrial towns. One of Marx's most sensational claims about societies was that the leading kinds of art, philosophy, politics, and culture, including religious practices, which developed within them, necessarily sustained the dominant social relations of production. Thus the forms of Protestantism of early-modern England became widespread because they facilitated the political hegemony of the bourgeoisie. Religion was a veil behind which the material interests of antagonistic classes fought to promote further the forces of production.

As the first society in history to become capitalist, Britain fascinated Marx and he believed that other nations had no choice but to develop the social structures which he perceived to be at work in nineteenth-century Britain. For example, he paired the French Revolution with the English Revolution as examples of the bourgeois ascent to political leadership. The German Empire, forged by Bismark in 1870–71 after decisive military victories over Austria–Hungary and France, was yet another case of a society whose development would be determined by the logic of bourgeois interests. His only fear was that the feudal Junkers' opposition to the bourgeoisie would be the "harbinger of still deadlier international feuds" and as a consequence underlined the need for the working men of Britain, France, and Germany to unite against "the lords of the sword, of the soil, and of capital" (*Second Address of the General Council on the Franco-Prussian War*, 1871).

The 1870s and 1880s saw the fulfilment of Bismarck's vision of an authoritarian *Kaiserreich* with a *Kulturmission* to promote pan-German nationalism, combining aristocratic and military values with a Lutheran religious establishment, and exemplified by Heinrich von Treitschke's attacks on "weak and effete" British and French culture. Based on an alliance of the land-owning Junker class with the wealthy entrepreneurs of the industrial technologies, popularly called the union of "steel and rye", the new empire was challenged by a large and cosmopolitan socialist movement and a Catholic minority, both vociferously questioning the prevailing notion of German identity. Yet this identity, Bismarck's supporters and successors argued, was being affirmed by the march of history. Germany had after all been united only after defeating Catholic France. In 1898, the ease with which the North American states achieved military victory over Catholic Spain appeared to underline the unsuitability of the old religion for the new world of international *Realpolitik*. Socialist cosmopolitanism, synonymous with atheism in Treitschke's eyes, had less appeal than virulent nationalism and was derided as utopian. Despite these perceived facts, intellectual controversy concerning the nature of Germany, and what it was to be German, marked the first decades of the new state, as Marx's concerns show. In his inaugural lecture as Professor of Political Economy at the University of Freiburg in 1895, "The nation state and economic policy", Max Weber agreed with Marx that the first consideration of any intellectual was to address these questions.

Max Weber was eminently capable of appreciating the historical problems which faced the German Empire. Although his primary subject at Heidelberg in the early 1880s was law, Weber attended additional courses in political economy, history, philosophy and theology. After national service and a doctoral dissertation on medieval trading organizations, in 1891 Weber published a study to secure the higher degree necessary for university teaching entitled "Roman agrarian history and its importance for constitutional and civil law". It is certain that the link between ancient and medieval history and contemporary political questions was evident to Weber, and evinced by his membership of the Evangelical-Social Congress during these years. In the early 1890s he began to focus directly on current issues, publishing the results of an inquiry into "The Conditions of the Agricultural Worker in the East Elbian regions of Germany", which addressed the effects upon German workers of the infiltration of cheap Polish labour. By the turn of the century Weber was arguing that the social antagonisms evident in the new Germany might be addressed by means of comparative studies of capitalism across Europe; in 1904, with Edgar Jaffé and Werner Sombart, he was instrumental in creating the Archive for Social Science and Social Policy, a journal seeking to explore "the cultural significance of capitalist development".

These remarks are intended to support the view that Weber's *The Protestant Ethic and the Spirit of Capitalism*, first published in volumes 20–21 (1904–5) of the Archive, is best understood as a response to the issue of German identity in the context of a longstanding debate about the influence of religion on the relative riches of modern states. Weber acknowledged this in the first chapter, "Religious affiliation and social stratification", which aimed to reveal inconsistencies in traditional explanations of Catholic economic backwardness. Weber confessed to being surprised by the small number of Catholic individuals among the business leaders and owners of capital in Germany, despite the fact that minority religious groups, such as Huguenots, Nonconformists, Quakers, and Jews, had historically been "driven with peculiar force into economic activity". He provided statistical support for his contention that Catholics preferred work in traditional crafts rather than industrial factories, to be educated in humanist schools rather than progressive technical colleges, and generally opposed any "emancipation from economic traditionalism". At the same time Weber rejected the conventional view that the greater otherworldliness of the Catholic religion explained these facts because Protestantism was, if anything, more ascetic still. As he put it, "the English, Dutch, and American Puritans were characterised by the exact opposite of the joy of living". It was an ironic possibility that "the supposed conflict between other-worldliness, asceticism, and ecclesiastical piety on the one side, and participation in capitalistic acquisition on the other, might actually turn out to be an intimate relationship".

The challenge to tradition presented by the modern world threw up numerous ironies, which Weber charted in his second chapter, "The Spirit of Capitalism". His first point was that the capitalist "philosophy of avarice" was not an inherently rational pursuit for historical individuals. The writings of the eighteenth-century North American polymath and patriot, Benjamin Franklin, revealed that the earning of more and more money was "so purely an end in itself that from the point of view of the happiness or utility of an individual it appears irrational and transcendental". Franklin appeared to exemplify the perception of the virtues of thrift, industry, honesty, and punctuality as an example of what Weber called an "ethic", a way of living which was an end in itself. This was signified by Franklin's justification of money-making, not by reasoned argument, but by reference to a Biblical injunction: "When asked why should money be made out of men, Franklin, although a colourless deist . . . replied, "Seeth thou a man diligent in business? He shall stand before Kings' (Proverbs, xxii, 29)". Such a philosophy was clearly irrational "from a naïve point of view" and yet had somehow become an ethic, a force which determined the character of national cultures.

Weber was fascinated by the irrationality of Franklin's moral code because he believed it underscored the force of cultural traditions. He used it to highlight different modes of behaviour in modern states and their uneven effect upon economic development. An excellent example was the more advanced capitalism of the northern American states, despite the fact that the Southern states "were founded by capitalists for business motives, while the New England colonies were founded by preachers and seminary graduates with the help of small bourgeois, craftsmen and yeomen, for religious reasons". The causal relation was the reverse of that suggested by the materialist standpoint. Weber wanted to explain why "the lack of commitment of the labourers, for instance Italy as compared with Germany, has been, and to a certain extent still is, one of the principal obstacles to their capitalistic development". In certain circumstances workers on piece rates did not respond to incentives to work harder; for example, "The present-day Silesian mows, when he exerts himself to the full, little more than two-thirds as much land as the better-paid and nourished Pomeranian or Mecklenburger, and the Pole, the further East he comes from, accomplishes progressively less than the German". Finally, it was well known that "German girls . . . especially unmarried ones . . . make bad workers" and "cannot adapt themselves to new methods, learn to concentrate their intelligence, or even to use it at all". The exceptions were girls from Pietistic backgrounds whose activities were characterized, Weber believed, by a sense of obligation and a capacity for sustained concentration. He concluded that "such a religious upbringing is a key to overcoming economic traditionalism".

These distinctions and ironies made a mockery of the neat and rational world portrayed in Marxist and *Realpolitik* justifications of capitalism. Any study of national character and its relation to economic behaviour revealed the difficulty of distinguishing between rational and irrational action, between worldly and otherworldly activity, and between self-conscious and unintended actions. The latter was the most important factor identified by

Weber in his comparative sketches and occupied the centre ground of his critique of materialism. As he said in the introduction to the 1920 revision of *The Protestant Ethic*, "The magical and religious forces, and the ethical ideas of duty based upon them, have in the past always been among the most important formative influences on conduct". It was of fundamental importance that in the history of Europe "rational economic conduct" had met with serious resistance from "spiritual obstacles". Although Weber recognised "the fundamental importance of the economic factor", the different modes of behaviour found between or within national cultures could only be explained by the study of particular historical ethics, presenting a history of cultural change to shore up materialist explanations of the rise of capitalism.

The case study Weber undertook focused on the economic effects of Catholic and Lutheran culture by contrast with the results of Calvinism, Pietism, various Baptist Sects, and Methodism. His basic assumption was that economic development in general, and capitalism in particular, necessitated rapid social change and inevitably led to conflict between traditional modes of living and the ethics of production. This was especially the case where the Catholic religion was entrenched, because the doctrine and organization of the Catholic church was uniquely suited to traditional economic behaviour. In his view, Catholicism gave a premium to leisure rather than labour, condemned usury, and described acquisition as a "sin tolerated only because of the necessities of worldly life". Above all, the believer was assured that salvation would be guaranteed to any individual who fulfilled the demands of the sacraments, obeyed the church on earth, and merited ascent to paradise by living a life at one with the Catholic moral code. The psyche of the believer, to Weber, was assured by Catholic theology and he was given confidence that a life lived for and through the church was the best possible on earth. Such self-confidence was challenged by the Reformation. Martin Luther was sceptical of any worldly guarantee of salvation and preached a doctrine of uncertainty and fear, in which the few who had true faith in God would alone be saved from damnation. Grace was a gift for the faithful who followed God's law absolutely, which, according to Weber's interpretation of Luther, entailed the fulfilment of a "calling" or pursuit of a certain mode of living. By contrast with the monkish asceticism of the Catholic Church, Luther's idea of the calling valued "the fulfilment of a duty in worldly affairs as the highest form which the moral activity of the individual could assume". In sum, "the fulfilment of worldly duties is the only way to live acceptably to God". This radical departure from traditional theology had revolutionary cultural consequences. Weber believed that this was evident from Milton's Michael in *Paradise Lost*, for whom life was a task in this world rather than the next, by contrast with the medieval Catholic view portrayed in Dante's *Divine Comedy*, at the close of which "the poet in Paradise stands speechless in his passive contemplation of the

100

secrets of God". However, Weber claimed that the impact of Lutheranism on traditional behaviour was limited after the German peasant rebellions of the 1520s, which caused a frightened Luther to stress the importance of Providence and, as a result, defend conventional ways of living:

> The stronger and stronger emphasis on the providential element, even in particular events of life, led more and more to a traditionalistic interpretation based on the idea of Providence. The individual should remain once and for all in the station and calling in which God had placed him, and should restrain his worldly activity within the limits imposed by his established station in life.

Worldly duties were no longer subordinated to ascetic ones, and the new Church preached obedience to authority and the acceptance of things as they were. Yet the unintended consequence of the Lutheran search for means to ensure the salvation of the soul was the creation of a doctrine which, in Calvin's and other radical reformers" hands, justified the transformation of accepted economic practices.

The Protestant ethic most interesting to Weber was a product of an acute fear of damnation and a belief that worldly activity was one of the only weapons available for the individual to live the godly life which was a possible sign of grace. But it derived from different dogmatic foundations. Although Weber argued that the idea of a mystical union with God impeded the Pietist adoption of capitialistic behaviour, for the majority unstinting toil was perceived to be an example of "the methodical development of one's own state of grace to a higher and higher degree of certainty and perfection". Wesleyan Methodism similarly promoted the aspiration to a higher and more godly life, called "the second blessedness", which was associated with the vigorous pursuit of labour. Equally, for the Quakers and other Baptist sects "the radical elimination of magic from the world allowed no other psychological course than the practice of worldly asceticism". Each of these forms of Protestantism promoted forms of behaviour which Weber believed to be at odds with traditional economic beliefs, by making the religious individual more concerned about his own salvation and, as a result, more devoted to worldly activity. But the most important theology which promoted worldly asceticism, because it was more widespread than any other type of Protestantism, was Calvinism.

To Weber, the doctrine of predestination was the essential tenet of the Calvinist creed; as a result,

> the Father in Heaven of the New Testament who rejoices over the repentance of a sinner is gone and taken by a transcendental being, beyond the reach of human understanding, who has decided the fate of every individual and regulated the tiniest details of the cosmos from eternity.

The psychological effects of this view of the deity were devastating. It produced generations of individuals who experienced an "unprecedented inner loneliness" because they could no longer rely for salvation on the words of a priest, the practice of a sacrament, or even the sure knowledge of a God "because even Christ died only for elect". One unanticipated consequence was a "disillusioned and pessimistically inclined individualism" which Weber believed could still be identified in Calvinistic cultures, evinced by Anglo-American distrust of friendship, and a view of life "not for self-humiliation before God but as a restless and systematic struggle". To a German Lutheran, American and British people appeared to be victims of "narrowness, unfreeness, and inner constraint".

In one of the most important passages of *The Protestant Ethic*, Weber sought to explain how a doctrine which "tore the individual away from the closed ties with which he is bound to this world" justified "labour in a calling which serves the mundane life of the community". Because the world existed to serve the glorification of God alone, the elected Christian lived only to fulfil His commandments to the best of his ability, requiring specific kinds of social achievement. As Weber put it,

> Brotherly love, since it may only be practised for the glory of God and not in the service of the flesh, is expressed in the first place in the fulfilment of the daily tasks given by the *lex naturæ*; and in the process this fulfilment assumes a peculiarly objective and impersonal character, that of service in the interests of the rational organisation of our social environment.

Questions about the meaning of the world and of life were overcome by faith in the sanctity of labour, and the necessity of the calling as a sign of grace and election. The idea that "God helps those who help themselves" was, Weber claimed, singularly suited to the rejection of traditional forms of economic behaviour.

Weber gleaned evidence for the relationship between Calvinism and capitalism from predominantly English theological sources, such as Richard Baxter's *The Saints' Everlasting Rest* (1650) and *A Christian Directory* (1673). For Baxter, he argued, industriousness "is God's command for divine glory". Wealth was evil "only as a temptation to idleness", but "as a performance of duty in calling it is not only morally permissible but actually enjoined"; wealth "has the highest ethical appreciation of the sober, middle-class, self-made man". The greater the wealth of an individual, the greater the duty to labour for God through the community. Once direct consumption was replaced by injunctions to invest for the future "the inevitable practical result is obvious: accumulation of capital through ascetic compulsion to save". Weber concluded that Calvinism's unexpected cultural effects "favoured the development of a rational bourgeois economic life"; "it stood at the cradle of modern economic man".

The Protestant Ethic and the Spirit of Capitalism, in the form of the first edition of 1904–5, was intended as a subtle critique of German nationalists, for whom Lutheran culture was superior to any other, and the Marxists who neglected to give cultural factors an independent role in their studies of modernity. Weber wanted to point out the limits of rationality, self-awareness, and self-control, by showing the potential richness of an analysis which took irrational and accidental forces seriously as historical agents, and was thereby able to provide explanations for the distinct cultures of modern European nations. He also intended to associate the economic effects of Lutheranism and Catholicism, by contrast with Calvinism and other forms of Protestantism, in order to give reasons for the relative backwardness of Germany as opposed to Britain or America. Although he was not an uncritical viewer of the Anglo-American world, he believed Germany had a great deal to learn from the more tolerant culture and less hierarchical social structures which he associated with Calvinist origins. This was stated explicitly in the notes to the edition of 1920 where Weber contrasted "the relative immunity of formerly Puritan peoples to Cæsarism, and, in general, the subjectively free attitude of the English to their general statesmen" with "many things which we have experienced since 1878 in Germany positively and negatively". His work ultimately sought to shed light on the differential growth paths of modern Occidental states and to provide counter-arguments for those who feared the anti-democratic rhetoric of uncritical Germanophiles. When these aims were carried out in the rigorous and imaginative manner of Weber's writing, controversy was bound to be fuelled. Although Weber put the shelf life of an intelligent work at fifty years, the thesis remains a vibrant source of disputation almost a century on. There are now libraries of material devoted to different aspects of Weber's *Protestant Ethic* and it is beyond the capacity of any scholar to do justice to the range of questions and issues which have been raised. All that is intended here is a review of certain common themes and several misunderstandings, and a brief examination of some of Weber's responses to the debate as it raged during his lifetime.

One of the most common attacks on Weber's thesis is the claim that capitalism did not develop in union with Calvinism, but has in fact existed throughout the history of human societies, and is therefore compatible with a multitude of cultures, including Catholicism. An early exponent of this view was the political economist Lujo Brentano, for whom the "acquisitive ethic" had certainly reached its apotheosis in the Catholic courts of the Renaissance, as well as in the republics of Venice and Florence. Similar claims were made by Weber's colleagues, Simmel and Sombart, for whom "economic rationalism was developed to its farthest conclusions as early as Cato", and have continued to be made against Weber, most recently by Alan Macfarlane in *The Culture of Capitalism*. A corresponding attack came from those in whose eyes Weber had neglected economic explanations of the rise of capitalism in Europe, including the role of the discovery of South America, the influx of silver and gold moneys in the sixteenth century, and the increasing ability of states to make use of their natural resources in production. This view, as William Lamont shows in his chapter, stemmed from the otherwise adulatory pen of R. H. Tawney in his own study of *Religion and the Rise of Capitalism*, but has been associated with the Marxist tradition of European historiography above all others. A number of historians have become convinced that Weber was mistaken in his association of Calvinism and capitalism because of the existence of counter-cases, such as Scotland, whose economic backwardness in comparison with that of England was noted from long before the Act of Union. Hugh Trevor-Roper, following Sombart, concluded from such evidence that capitalism developed where the emigration of religious groups into different states, and the pressing need for survival in foreign cultures, stimulated economic activity. Sombart had made a powerful case for associating the nomadic Sephardic Jews with economic development, on the grounds that the Old Testament's view of rationality was singularly capitalistic. Weber's thesis became an example of the use of Old Testament ideas by Calvin rather than the description of the birth of a new kind of culture.

It must be said that all of these views misinterpreted Weber's argument and intentions in writing *The Protestant Ethic*. Against Brentano he pointed out that the spirit of capitalism was not synonymous with the lust for gain of the Cortez figure who could be found in every society "among waiters, physicians . . . artists, prostitutes, . . . soldiers, nobles, crusaders, gamblers, and beggars". Nor was it necessarily linked to the luxury consumption aspired to by every Renaissance courtier, the finance capitalism associated with the history of banking and moneylending, or the pariah capitalism of autonomous communities and above all the Jews. For Weber, "the impulse to acquisition, pursuit of gain, of money, of the greatest possible amount of money, has in itself nothing to do with capitalism". What he meant by the spirit of capitalism was a culture which justified "the pursuit of profit, and forever *renewed* profit, by means of continuous, rational, capitalistic enterprise". Examples of capitalistic *activity* could be found "in all civilized countries of earth – China, India, Babylon, Egypt, Mediterranean antiquity, and the Middle Ages". But the constant industriousness the capitalist *spirit* demanded, and the sobriety, thrift, and prudence it strictly enjoined, characterized a culture unique to the early-modern Occident and facilitated "developed capitalism both to a quantitative extent and in types, forms, and directions, which have never existed elsewhere". It was part of the story of Western uniqueness, of generating forms of life and thought "having *universal* significance and value", which Weber spent his life trying to define through comparative studies of the great civilizations of India, China, Babylonia, and Egypt. As he said at the end of the work, he had only touched upon the significance of ascetic rationalism, and ought to have studied "its relations to humanistic rationalism . . . to philosophical and scientific empiricism, to technical development and . . . its historical development from the medieval beginnings of worldly asceticism to its dissolution into pure utilitarianism". The book was a brief and compressed study of a very important causal relationship between carefully defined phenomena.

Weber did not intend to be exhaustive. In particular, he made it absolutely clear that he did not believe Calvinism was a sufficient condition for capitalism; economic factors were equally essential to any causal analysis. He did not seek "to substitute for a one-sided materialist an equally one-sided spiritualistic causal interpretation of culture and of history". For example, he argued that economic development "required the separation of the business from the household" as well as "rational book-keeping". Capitalism would develop only where economic and other factors facilitated it; these were singularly lacking in certain Calvinistic cultures, such as Scotland, Geneva, and Bohemia. Ultimately, Calvinism was not even a necessary condition for the unique capitalism of the modern West; in time "the monastic struggle" always gave way to "the temptations of wealth". Baxter's "care" for external goods, which in his words "should lie on the shoulders of the saint like a light cloak", became an iron cage, constraining all cultures which entertained it, and undermining the very religious beliefs which had fostered its growth. In the United States, Weber claimed, the pursuit of wealth had become "stripped of its religious and ethical meaning . . . associated with purely mundane passions, which often give it the character of sport".

Sombart's association of Jewish communities with capitalist practices was a more powerful attack on Weber's claims, especially because its analysis of the Old Testament promised to make Calvinism one example of a more general ideology. In addition, Weber never denied the challenge to traditionalism presented by a cultural diaspora, and likened the Babylonian exile of the Jews to that of the Jains in India, and the Protestants in America, admitting "a great deal of American development is due to this factor". But he saw the Jews as "representatives of financial and political capitalism" rather than "the rational organisation of labour", which was in any case precluded by the "pariah" nature of Jewish communities and the resulting differential economic treatment of believers by contrast with non-believers. Weber turned Sombart's criticism back on its author with the argument that Jewish communities were particular cases, and had only indirectly influenced the development of the Occidental spirit of capitalism. Other scholars have chosen to attack Weber for his misunderstandings of Calvinist theology in general, and in particular the use of English Puritans such as Baxter as paradigms of the capitalist spirit. There can be no doubt that Weber's use of "ideal types" in his analysis greatly simplified it, and the end product was an exaggerated view of the unity of Calvinist doctrine and the divisions between Catholicism, Lutheranism, and Calvinism. Modern historians have recognised the difficulties of identifying the doctrinal, liturgical, or organizational traits which defined particular churches, and convincingly challenged the rigid distinction between Protestant and Counter-Reformation Europe. Perhaps the greatest problems arise in disentangling Puritanism from Anglicanism, and explaining the former's special role in the rise of capitalism in England. Few writers would now be as emphatic as Weber in his association of Calvinism with the peculiarities of capitalistic development in England or North America. Another problem arises with the case of France, economically supreme in Europe between the seventeenth and eighteenth centuries, and, many economic historians would argue, not far behind the commercial and industrial development of Britain. Given the enforced flight of the Huguenots after the Edict of Nantes in 1685, and the power of the Catholic church until the Revolution, it would be very difficult to explain French capitalism in religious terms. Weber recognised this, and drew parallels between the Calvinist and Jansenist conceptions of predestination, although he considered the latter too mystical to have fostered rational attacks on traditional doctrine; this said, it is probably the case that the relative decline of France by the end of the nineteenth century led him to underestimate the cardinal role of the French state in early-modern Europe.

If Weber's thesis becomes more narrow than he conceived and less important than he believed in explaining the rise of capitalism, it remains very difficult to give no credence at all to Weber's views. His description of the psychological trauma generated by Protestant theology, and the wealth of evidence acknowledging a relationship between Protestant states and economic success, means that Weber's thesis remains *one* plausible interpretation of the movement of early-modern ideas, in its way as impressive as those of more contemporary intellectual historians, such as John Pocock's magisterial study of the early-modern debate about the relationship between commerce and virtue. It must also be remembered that Weber's critique of materialism succeeded by means of a breathtaking comparative study of the major civilizations of Eastern and the Western history; studies of the influx of silver coin into India under the later Roman Emperors, the inventiveness of Chinese technology and the populousness of the Chinese state, were used to great effect in challenging parochial explanations of Western capitalism founded on economic forces alone. Part of the greatness of Weber is his focus on cultural factors and emphasis on unintended consequences. In many respects he was returning to the cautious, modest, and critical approaches to modern European history which flourished during the Scottish Enlightenment and in the work of Adam Smith, in particular. Weber saw himself as a member of the great German "historical school of political economy", and the contemporary interest in Adam Smith appears to have influenced Weber; in his use of irony, his focus on the role of the unexpected and the accidental, and his eschewal of all-encompassing theory, Weber is distinctly Smithian. In the context of the twentieth-century search for a social scientific theory which is as unified and coherent as those of the natural sciences, Weber is a problematic figure and the intellectual role he defended in his life and his writings is a far cry from the popular ideal of the academic as technician. Any study which gives the irrational such prominence is by nature very difficult to justify comprehensively and also to refute convincingly. One consequence is that students and scholars will continue to return to Weber's great exercise of the historical imagination for insight and stimulation.

Suggestions for further reading

For Weber's thesis itself Talcott Parsons' 1930 translation of *The Protestant Ethic* remains both excellent and in print; in addition the essay "The Protestant Sects and the Spirit of Capitalism" in H. H. Gerth & C. Wright Mills, *From Max Weber: essays in sociology* (London: Routledge, 1991) is useful, as are the sections of *Economy and Society* dealing with "Magic and religion" **II**, pp. 422–39, "Asceticism, mysticism and salvation" **II**, pp. 541–56 and "The Great Religions and the World" **II**, pp. 611–34, and the "Anticritical last word on the Spirit of Capitalism", *American Journal of Sociology*, 83(112), 1978.

The best contemporary work on Weber's thesis is undoubtedly *Weber's Protestant ethic: origins, evidence, contexts*, H. Lehmann & G. Roth (eds) (Cambridge: Cambridge University Press, 1993), and especially the essays by Roth, Graf, Münch, Lehmann, Mackinnon, Von Greyerz, and Benedict. Other good recent studies include Gianfranco Poggi, *Calvinism and the capitalist spirit. Max Weber's protestant ethic* (London: Macmillan, 1983) and Gordon Marshall, *In search of the spirit of capitalism. An essay on Max Weber's Protestant ethic* (London: Hutchinson, 1982); Marshall's bibliography gives a broad synopsis of recent literature and should be used in conjunction with that of Lehmann & Roth.

Relating Weber's ideas to the themes of modern intellectual history is best achieved by contrast with the interpretations of early-modern Calvinism to be found in J. G. A. Pocock's *The Machiavellian moment* (New Jersey: Princeton University Press, 1975), Q. Skinner, *The foundations of modern political thought* (Cambridge: Cambridge University Press, 1978), and W. Lamont, *Puritanism and historical controversy* (London: UCL Press, 1996).

The next step is to put Weber's work in the context of his broader writings and also in the intellectual context of his time. This is a difficult task, but students continue to be aided by Reinhard Bendix, *Max Weber: An intellectual portrait* (Berkeley: California University Press, 1977), Marianne Weber, *Max Weber. A biography* (New York: Wiley, 1975), and W. J. Mommsen's studies, *Max Weber and German Politics 1890-1920*

(Chicago: University of Chicago Press, 1984) and *The Age of bureaucracy* (Oxford: 1974).

For more current discussion see W. Hennis, *Max Weber. Essays in reconstruction* (London: Allen & Unwin, 1988), L. A. Scaff, *Fleeing the iron cage. Culture, politics and modernity in the thought of Max Weber* (Berkeley: University of California Press, 1989), and Derek Sayer, *Capitalism and modernity. An excursus on Marx and Weber* (London: Routledge, 1991). Of course, there is no better source than Weber's writings themselves; students might begin with the essays in Keith Tribe's *Reading Weber* (London: Routledge, 1989) and P. Lassman and R. Speirs' *Weber's political writings* (Cambridge: Cambridge University Press, 1994), before moving on to the more difficult, voluminous, but rewarding, *Economy and society*. To understand fully the latter work it is essential to be aware of the writings of Weber's colleagues and opponents, and especially Werner Sombart's *The Jews and modern capitalism* (Glencoe: Free Press, 1951) and *Luxury and capitalism* (Michigan: University of Michigan Press, 1967), Georg Simmel's *The Philosophy of Money* (London: Routledge, 1990), and Ernest Troeltsch's *The Social teaching of the Christian churches* (London: Allen & Unwin, 1931).

Chapter Nine

.ᴥꜱ

R. H. Tawney: "Who did not write a single work which can be trusted"?

William Lamont

R. H. Tawney died in 1962, but he remains a deeply controversial figure. He was the spectre haunting G. R. Elton, when he gave his inaugural lecture as Cambridge Professor of English Constitutional History six years later, under the title "The future of the past". "With great regret", he would say on that occasion (and how the words must have been squeezed out of him!), he was "coming to think increasingly that there is not a single work which Tawney wrote which can be trusted". More than 20 years on, Elton was back on the attack, in an essay on "Europe and the Reformation": Europe had no future *because* of what Tawney had done to its past.

A different view of Tawney, and of Elton, however, was given in 1995 by Elton's successor as Regius Professor at Cambridge, Patrick Collinson. His lecture was called "*Tudor England revisited*." Its tone was sombre, but the jokes were light. Collinson was respectful of his predecessor's achievements, but not of his legacy. The legacy of Elton's "Tudor England", in Collinson's view, was: political history which was skewed towards the governing class; parliaments minus ideas; economy and the society relegated to noises-off. As a sixteenth-century historian, Collinson regretted that the seventeenth century was now having all the best tunes: would future undergraduates *want* to study Tudor England? Collinson's title was a pun: he was revisiting Tudor England in two senses – referring both to the field of study, and to the book of that title. For he chose the sixth annual Bindoff lecture at Queen Mary and Westfield College, University of London, to commemorate S. T. Bindoff's *Tudor England*, first published as a Pelican History in 1950. And he did so by honouring the insights which Bindoff had derived primarily, in his view, from Tawney.

This made me feel good. For years I've told my students to begin their studies in early modern English history, not with Elton's *England under the Tudors*, but with Bindoff's *Tudor England*. I wondered how far that was prompted by filial piety: I had studied history as an undergraduate under Bindoff. My students' response to Bindoff was generally favourable. Perhaps only the first chapter of a very different book, Sir Keith Thomas's *Religion and the decline of magic*, can match it for conveying, to the newcomer to Tudor studies, the feeling of what it would be like to live in those times.

When *History Workshop* – subtitled then "a journal of socialist historians" – asked me to write Bindoff's obituary in 1980 it seemed an odd thing to do. Bindoff was a man of conservative principles. *Past and Present* – a companion scholarly journal which rapidly shook off its Marxist origins – was still too radical for Bindoff: it was banned in my undergraduate days from the Queen Mary College History Department library! He seemed to be, in many ways, an old-fashioned political historian. His London mentors were Pollard and Neale: the same stable from which Elton came. He would end his days compiling entries on the House of Commons, 1509–58, for the History of Parliament Trust. If Bindoff hadn't written *Tudor England*, few *History Workshop* readers would have heard of him. But those who had heard of him did so *because* of that book: for so many, with no background in academic history, *Tudor England* was their passport to higher education. Was it fortuitous? The Pelican Histories in paperback were cheap, accessible and short. That didn't save many of the companion volumes in the series from (merited) extinction. Its format was deceptively old-fashioned and chronological, signalled by chapter headings such as "Henry Tudor and Son" and "Succession and Supremacy". The style was at times sub-Arthur Bryant: "Henry VII's subjects were still warmed by the golden rays of the medieval sunset". But the *vision* was anything but Bryant's. The epigrams rattle across the pages with enviable gusto, but the tone of the book is overwhelmingly dark. Nobody could read this book and fall for "Merrie England" claptrap. Politics were not left out, but their role was now seen as essentially trivial: "scarcely more than a sport which great men indulged in while the country as a whole clung doggedly to the more important business of feeding, warming and clothing itself". That great insight (expressed in the book's prologue) governs the work. We see the Earl of Essex's tawdriness as an indictment of the society, as much as of the man; we see the villein's disabilities as the precondition of the nobleman's privileges; we feel (in an extraordinarily prescient passage) the injustices that were perpetrated on women in Tudor society. These were the insights which Tawney quickened to. When he reviewed the book in *The Manchester Guardian* in 1950, he was rapturous: "it deserves to become a classic". What Collinson recognises in his lecture is how much Bindoff himself draws upon Tawney's own early masterpiece of 1912, *The agrarian problem in the sixteenth century*, and the three volumes of *Tudor economic documents* which Tawney co-edited with Eileen Power in 1924 (the latter would be the documentary basis of Bindoff's own Special Subject class at University College London from 1935 onwards). Tawney's conviction, that the distribution of land and its product was fundamental to an agrarian society, held good for twentieth-century China no less than for sixteenth-century England. His *Land and labour in China* (1932) remains a recommended text in Jonathan Spence's definitive *The search for modern China* (1990). William Hinton would quote directly from Tawney's work in his classic account of revolution in a Chinese village, *Fanshen* (1966): the Chinese rural population, Tawney had said, was like "a man standing permanently up to the neck in water, so that even a ripple is sufficient to drown him". In Elton's revision of the canon, one guesses that he would be seen as not drowning but waving.

Elton's quarrel with Tawney can therefore, it seems, be reduced to a contest about the proper subject matter of history. W. G. Hoskins, whose *The age of plunder* (1976) is seen by Collinson as the work of an angry old man in the Tawney tradition, had demonstrated, from his study of the 1520s tax returns, that in London and Coventry 5 per cent of the population owned anything up to 80 per cent of the total wealth. Was history primarily then to be a study of the 5 per cent or the 95 per cent, victor or victim, mandarin or peasant? But Elton's quarrel with Tawney ran deeper than that; it focused on one work of his, *Religion and the rise of capitalism*, and the implications of that quarrel will provide the theme for the rest of this essay.

Elton objected to the very use of terms like "victim", or indeed "plunder". They injected in his view, into the study of history, an unnecessary moralism, and their effect on the development of European capitalism itself had been catastrophic. These were the consequences spelled out in Elton's curious 1985 essay, "Europe and the Reformation". There are not many essays without footnotes in the Elton *oeuvre*, but this is one. The man who commended factual history, derived from the archives, became here the proponent of Arnold Toynbee-like breadth and generalizations. He sketched out the triumph of European capitalism, and linked it to the Reformation in a way which was not wholly unlike Max Weber's. Things went wrong in the twentieth century only when men were made to feel guilty about it. Lord Dacre (by no stretch of imagination the rising hope of the stern and unbending Marxists) expressed drily in a review his failure to be convinced that the history of Europe in the twentieth century would have taken a quite different turn if Tawney and Christopher Hill had never existed. But in that essay, Elton did argue that *Religion and the rise of capitalism* had created "an entrenched hostility to the Reformation as the champion of false and materialist gods"; to be particular, "speaking indeed with the tongues of Hugh Latimer and Thomas Lever, who saw in the reform the only hope of social improvement, Tawney denied to the adherents of Latimer's and Lever's religion the right to regard themselves as capable of producing social betterment"; the next generation of "really aspirant young Protestants" in the twentieth century were, therefore, turned off Protestantism and were fatally redirected to "the religion of Marx". Thus it was that

Christopher Hill, "one of nature's Calvinists", ended up as a proponent of "the Asiatic version of historical materialism". Elton said that he was not "judging but describing" a process: what, one is tempted to wonder, would he have written if he *had* been judging?

Richard Whatmore describes in chapter 8 the misconceptions surrounding Max Weber's pioneering work, *The Protestant ethic and the spirit of capitalism* (1904-5), but we can see, from even these quotations from Elton's essay, why his target of attack would be Tawney, not Weber. Tawney's most important qualification of Weber was indeed his revised reading of the Puritan *mentalité*. Weber had once called himself self-mockingly "religiously unmusical". But there is nothing crass or simplistic about his discussion of Calvinist theology in that work. He never argued that ideal factors alone could be agents of change, but noted their importance to be recognised *alongside* the material factors. And he never said that Calvinism by itself *caused* capitalism. More importantly, he never argued that Calvinists, in their sermons and pamphlets, had meekly acquiesced in the rise of capitalism. Two of his earliest critics, Sombart and Brentano, were wrong to suggest that he had. But he argued that the crisis of proof for the seventeenth-century predestinarian Calvinist believer produced an *unintended* spiritual sanction for labour. The Protestant ethic emerges in this watered-down Weber, in John Updike's harrowing description of his grandfather:

> He was born tired. His life smells of financial failure and of the guilt and shame that attaches to such failure in the United States. It was the inspiriting genius of Calvinism to link prosperity and virtue, to take material thriving as a sign of salvation; and Presbyterians would be especially sensitive to this link.

What Updike called "the stain of unsuccess" ate away at his grandfather's whole life because of this belief that "a failure of economic fortune must be a moral failure".

Tawney had been ruminating on this connection, independent of Weber. We have fascinating evidence of this from this entry in his *Commonplace book* of 1912: "I wonder if Puritanism produced a special attitude towards economic matters". He goes on: "I believe Schulze-Gaevernitz has some remarks on this". No knowledge at that date, it would appear, of Weber: an omission which would be rectified, of course, when in 1922 he delivered the Scott Holland Memorial Lectures, which would be the basis four years later of his book, *Religion and the rise of capitalism*. An admiring, but critical, preface to the 1930 edition of Weber's work by Tawney makes clear where he parts from him. Weber had undervalued the "iron collectivism" in Protestantism which had acted as a check on its ethic; it was the abandonment of that concept of a "godly discipline" in England and Holland, in the latter part of the seventeenth century, which was to mark the true watershed. That belief determines the structure of *Religion and the rise of capitalism*. Christianity in the Middle Ages had attempted to control the acquisitive spirit – not always consistently or successfully, but it *had* tried. Catholic casuists, from Aquinas onwards, had tried to determine the "just price": "The last of the Schoolmen was Karl Marx" is one of those memorable Tawney epigrams which make the book live on, independently of the controversies which it has engendered. Luther and Calvin had not meant to collude with market forces; but that was the tragic consequence, however unwilled, of the doctrines that they taught. Whatever else can be said of Tawney, he at least was "religiously musical" (though Elton would say that he consistently struck the wrong note). In his 1914 notebook he had written: "one of the things which strikes me as I grow older is the extraordinary truth and subtlety of the religious dogmas at which, as an undergraduate, I used to laugh". "Original Sin" was one such concept; another was that " 'Grace' does what 'will' cannot . . . all the discussions worth making are as old as the hills." Hence Tawney's preoccupation with the sermons and pamphlets of Protestant divines, and with the paradoxes of how a determinist creed like Calvin's released entrepreneurial energies.

Weber had identified with the forces of industrial change before the First World War; Tawney reacted against them. Between 1911 and 1912 he observed the dockers', railwaymen's and miners' strikes, and the bankruptcy of the response of the Fabian Society (home of the progressive intellectuals), to that challenge. Tawney became a member of the Independent Labour Party, and was a failed parliamentary candidate in 1918, who was increasingly attracted to guild socialism (that is to say, militant industrial action). In his diary entry of 10 September 1913 he commented: "Marxian socialists are not revolutionary enough". Tawney was indeed no ivory-tower academic, which was clear from the start with his involvement in the Workers Educational Association (he would be its President from 1928 to 1943). In 1916 he contributed to a report on *Christianity and industrial problems*; he joined with the great Christian social evangelist, William Temple (later to be the only socialist Archbishop of Canterbury in the history of the Church of England), in founding an organization called "Life and liberty movement"; he would serve on the Sankey Commission on the Coal Industry which deepened his critique of economic privilege when he saw, at close scrutiny, the damaging effects of a privately-run industry; through his influence on his brother-in-law William Beveridge he would have a part to play in the Beveridge Report, which laid the foundations of the modern Welfare State and the National Health Service.

Did all this political partisanship get in the way of his primary function as a historian, of re-creating the experiences of the sixteenth- and seventeenth-century religious preachers about whom he wrote? That was, remember, Elton's specific charge: that "he denied to the adherents of Latimer's and Lever's religion the right to regard themselves as capable of producing social betterment". I believe that to be wholly wrong: that it is precisely because he was "religiously musical" that William Temple's old colleague could enter so sympathetically into those sevententh-century minds which dreamed up their "holy commonwealths". Elton has a better case, in this connection, to be made against Hill (whom he too readily lumps with Tawney in his attack). Hill's book (in many ways brilliant but flawed), *The English Bible and the seventeenth-century revolution* (1993), it is true, will not have it that religion is merely a "cloak" for secular motives. But this is less of a concession than it appears; it often means no more than that he thinks that men of that time were self-deceived. His interest in Puritans does not, therefore, imply a concession to "religious" explanations for the Revolution: "to say that the English Revolution was about religion is tautologous: it took place in the seventeenth century". He even argues perversely that in many senses the seventeenth century was "a less religious age than ours". If we turn to one case study, we can see why Weber, Tawney and Hill – so often bracketed together for a common view of the relationship of religion and capitalism – actually have very different perspectives.

Richard Baxter is the case study. His importance derives from the fact that he was a leading English Puritan minister, who wrote in 1673 the longest, most ambitious and influential guide, *A Christian directory*, on how Christians should behave in social matters. In Hill's book, *The world turned upside down*, Baxter is seen quite straightforwardly as the spokesman for that section of his book entitled "The Protestant ethic". He is the man against whom the Digger, Gerrard Winstanley, and his allies were fighting in the next section, "Beyond the Protestant ethic". Now it is true that Hill can produce many quotations from *A Christian directory* to buttress his position. We learn of Baxter's respect for property, his horror of levelling, and his awareness of the necessity of using one's time methodically. The quotations are not made up, although sometimes there is sleight of hand in their presentation. When Hill tells us, for instance: " 'The rich will rule in the world', sighed the well-to-do Richard Baxter philosophically, 'and few rich men will be saints' ", we may recognise that the "well-to-do" is irrelevant and that the "sighs" are a Hill invention. But who would know, from that account alone, that it was drawn from a correspondence between two millenarian activists about the time when they expected the entire world to become a "Divine College"? Weber, on the other hand, fully empathizes with Baxter's revulsion from avarice; there is no sense that he caricatures his Protestant divines in order to make his point. His mistake – and it is a serious one – is to take Baxter as a classic example of the tensions within *Calvinism*, when the thrust of Baxter's arguments from his first pamphlet in 1649 onwards is to detach English Protestantism from its predestinarian origins, in fact to make the case *against* Calvinism.

Tawney said – another of those epigrams! – that "puritanism was the schoolmaster of the English middle classes." We might add: "discuss". It

114

comes from the opening of a truly brilliant section of Tawney's fourth chapter entitled "A Godly discipline versus the religion of trade". As he points out, "it is a strange school which does not teach more than one lesson". There was in puritanism the lesson of individualism, but there was also the lesson of collectivism. The tension in Baxter's work comes not, as Weber thought, from his Calvinism (which he was rapidly shedding), but from the attempt to accommodate those conflicting impulses. The "attempt to crystallize social morality in an objective discipline" – which Tawney recognises as the great aim of Baxter's *A Christian directory* – "was possible only in a theocracy". The short-lived Barebones Parliament of 1653 was the last practical effort of English puritanism to construct just such a "theocracy". But it failed. "Expelled from the world of faith" it "survived in the world of ideas". "The most learned, the most practical and the most persuasive" of the champions of those ideas would be Richard Baxter. His *Christian Directory* was a "Puritan *summa theologica*". But it failed because it was now (in 1673, that is) anachronistic: "The rules of Christian morality elaborated by Baxter were subtle and sincere. But they were like seeds carried by birds from a distant and fertile plain, and dropped upon a glacier. They were at once embalmed and sterilized in a river of ice."

And one half of Baxter knows that truth. When he wrote *A holy commonwealth* in 1659, it had been from a conviction that, under Richard Cromwell, a godly discipline *could* be created. But in 1673 Baxter, Tawney believed, was a representative symbol of that fatal loss of confidence in the clergy, which would lead him to offer "Memorandums" to the laity where he once had given them "Directions". And his *Christian directory* can only, in the final analysis, offer sincere, *but toothless*, injunctions to the ruling class to behave itself. The whole, very careful, construction of his work – from rules for the individual, then for the family, then the Church, then the State – in four separate sections, collapses in wretched anti-climax. When he concludes: "But alas! who should first reform the Landlords?", it is his shrug of the shoulders, his confession of moral bankruptcy, his recognition that the rules of the political game had changed for good.

Tawney's Baxter is therefore far more credible than Weber's or Hill's. If in the end it fails to convince, any more than theirs do, it is because of fresh findings from manuscript sources. We know now how much of the politics of *A Christian directory* had been governed by Baxter's need to survive Restoration persecution. He had been forced already in 1670 publicly to revoke *A holy commonwealth* (although his private papers tell a different story of his personal beliefs). What is striking is how the change of national politics, the accession of a Protestant King (William III) in 1688, revived the old 1659 yearnings for a Cromwellian "holy commonwealth". His *National church* pamphlet of 1691 envisages the restoration of a godly discipline under William III, acclaimed by Baxter as "a wise and godly King". The programme of reform which he outlines is rigorously prescriptive. Baptism in the future would not be – as it is now – "an infant ceremony" but one where parents were taught to *know* what was meant by entering their child into a covenant. Adults for their part would have their own baptismal covenant. The scandalous would be kept out of the Sacraments. The universities would be purged until there were only "godly careful Tutors". Toleration of religions was not an absolute virtue, but one which was dependent upon the will of the law-giver. It was the "Rich Mans oppression of the Poor" that would destroy the fabric of a commonwealth. This conviction would inspire the last work he wrote in the same year, *The poor husbandman's advocate*. It became his posthumous testament; not to be made public until (appropriately enough) the year of the General Strike, 1926. For three hundred years nearly, it lay in manuscript form, having been repressed by his literary executors, Daniel Williams and Matthew Sylvester, because of its radical content. It was found in the Baxter archive by F. J. Powicke who published it – four years too late for Tawney, whose Scott Holland Memorial Lectures, which would later be published as *Religion and the rise of capitalism*, had been given in 1922. As a social document, Baxter's last work can be compared with Part One of George Orwell's *The road to Wigan Pier*. The tone is passionate and impenitent: if the doctrine propounded in it seems to "savour of the Levellers or Quakers", so what? Baxter asks Christians "what would you have done if you had lived when the Spirit of Love made all the Christians sell all that they had and live in common?". That devastating question, and the invective in his work against class exploitation, derive their force when seen as part of a whole, of a design in 1691, as he said, to restore "the full power of Church discipline". Elton thought, that in offering this alternative view of Baxter, I had dealt "handsomely" with Baxter, "that protean creature – once Weber's chief exponent of a protestant commercial ethic, [becomes] now a rather more credible millenarian". At the same time, had I not strengthened Elton's case that there was not a single Tawney work "which can be trusted"? While it was clear that Tawney *had* misread Baxter; that his *Christian directory*, far from being his definitive statement of a *laissez-faire* philosophy, could now be seen as a parenthesis between two "theocratic" (Baxter's own words) testaments in 1659 and in 1691; and that the public statement could be put right by recourse to the manuscript source – all these in line with Elton's definition of good practice in writing history – they could hardly become the basis for the more swingeing Elton accusation. For what we are dealing with here is the small change of historical controversy: the process we are all subject to, of having our hypotheses modified by detailed investigation. Lamont revised Tawney's Baxter, but soon – how long, O Lord, how long? – somebody else will revise Lamont's Baxter. It was a process which Tawney himself understood perfectly: as he said, "all flesh is grass, and historians, poor things, wither more quickly than most".

116

On the big things, however, Tawney saw further than his critics. Weber had been wrong to see *A Christian directory* as a model of Calvinist dialectics, and Hill had been wrong to see it as individualism run riot. Tawney, more sensitively, saw how it mirrored the civil war within Puritanism itself, between individualism and collectivism. He was only wrong to think that the war had ended, in Baxter's case, in victory for one side, and that as early as 1673. But he was not wrong to think that a momentous shift had occurred in England in the latter part of the seventeenth century in the puritan *mentalité*, and one which would have vast social and economic consequences. But how, and where, to locate it?

That historian's quest continues, but two recent contributions now may take it significantly forward. David Underdown's *Fire from Heaven* (1992) showed how the great fire which devastated Dorchester in 1613 would be turned to evangelical advantage (an Act of Providence) by the charismatic preacher, John White. Dorchester became a sort of Geneva, with a repressive holy commonwealth which made it stand out from its Dorset neighbours. Hospitals, schools, an embryonic welfare state were created. This reconstruction is based on good Eltonian principles: a local study, factual, rooted in archival research. It also has a poetic quality: the story from the archives of one particular episode is juxtaposed with Thomas Hardy's reconstruction of it from oral testament and the transformation of it into fictional form in *The Mayor of Casterbridge*. It does what Elton (wrongly) accused Tawney of not doing: it empathises with White's efforts to do a Latimer and Lever for his century. It was the Tudor "commonwealth" idea that was indeed revived in White's Dorchester, as it was in Baxter's pastoral work at Kidderminster in the 1650s. Baxter's creation of Ministerial Associations to export these ideals across the English counties was the very practical basis of his "Holy Commonwealth" programme of 1659. Underdown believed that the Dorchester godly reformation did not cease at once with the Restoration any more than Baxter's programmes of reform had, and that indeed its echoes "died away only towards the end of the century", but that, nevertheless, "after 1662 the vision of a reformed, godly community which had inspired Dorchester's leaders ever since the fire of 1613 gradually faded". And one symptom would be the slackening of the townspeople's philanthropic generosity. Another historian, Derek Hirst, argues powerfully for us to think again about the 1650s and recognise that it marked "a central place in the internal, as well as the more famous external, commercial development of the nation".

While, in that same period, Baxter was building his Kidderminster "holy commonwealth", London's coffee-houses of the 1650s were shaping a new and altogether different political culture: "offering as they did sites for exchange of all kinds, and in particular for the reading and discussion of the newsbooks, that print form perfected in the mid-century turmoils". A Jew called Jacob, we have been told elsewhere, had opened the first English

117

coffee-house at Oxford in 1650; four years later he had been driven out of business by a fellow Jew who set up shop in the High Street. It was in this milieu that James Harrington composed his famous political reform treatise, *Oceana*, in 1656. John Aubrey has unforgettably described the meetings of his clique at the Turk's Head in London. A large oval table was provided, with a passage in the middle for "Miles to deliver his coffee". There was a ballot-box set up for votes on their debates (far superior to those in the Commons, says Aubrey); there was a formal taking of minutes; the room was crammed with disputants every evening. At one time a rival clique came in, the worse for drink, and tore up their minutes. Aubrey says that "the soldiers offered to kick them downe stayres, but Mr. Harrington's moderation and persuasion hindered it".

In 1941 Tawney had launched another historical controversy, when he related the coming of the Civil War to the economic rise of the gentry in his famous lecture on "Harrington's Interpretation of his Age". For the controversy on the rise of capitalism, with which this essay has concerned itself, however, it may be the case that what Harrington himself had to say in *Oceana* is less important than the ambience in which he created it. For historians today – it is a humbling thought – are no further forward than Tawney was in his day, in identifying the date of that crucial process which Tawney characterized as "the transition from the anabaptist to the company promoter", let alone in naming its cause. We might do worse than make a start with Miles and his coffee.

Suggestions for further reading

A full bibliography of R. H. Tawney's published writings is to be found in: R. Terrill, *R. H. Tawney and his times* (London: André Deutsch, 1974). A good analytical monograph is: Anthony Wright, *R. H. Tawney* (Manchester: Manchester University Press, 1987). There are some fascinating insights to be found in *R. H. Tawney's commonplace book*, J. M. Winter and D. M. Joslin (eds), (Cambridge: Cambridge University Press, 1972). The entries are for the years 1912 to 1914, which were crucial in Tawney's evolution as an historian. G. R. Elton's attack on Tawney – which provides the title of the essay – was given in his lecture of 1968 entitled "The future of the past", reproduced in: G. R. Elton, *Return to essentials* (Cambridge: Cambridge University Press, 1991), pp. 75–98. Patrick Collinson's defence of Tawney against Elton is to be found in his *Tudor England revisited* (the sixth annual Bindoff lecture, 1995 Queen Mary and Westfield College, University of London, Department of History). W. G. Hoskins, *The age of plunder* (Harlow, England: Longman, 1976), writes (like Tawney) with "mud on his boots". Elton's attack on Tawney and Christopher Hill (for altering the course of European history!) is to be found in his essay, "Europe and the

Reformation", *History, society and the churches*, D. Beales and G. Best (eds) (Cambridge: Cambridge University Press, 1985), pp. 89-104. A striking testament to the Calvinist "stain of unsuccess" is to be found in John Updike's memoirs of his grandfather: *Self-consciousness* (London: Penguin, 1989), pp. 156-201. Christopher Hill's ideas on religion are best found in his *The English Bible and the seventeenth-century revolution* (London: Allen Lane, The Penguin Press, 1993), but, for a critique of them, read: W. Dray, "Causes, individuals and ideas in Christopher Hill's interpretation of the English Revolution", *Court, country and culture*, B. Y. Kunze and D. D. Brautigan (eds) (Rochester: Rochester University Press, 1992), pp. 21-40. On Baxter, see: F. J. Powicke (ed.), *The Reverend Richard Baxter's last treatise* (Manchester: Manchester University Press, 1926) and the seventh chapter of my *Puritanism and historical controversy* (London: UCL Press, 1996), pp. 103-128. David Underdown, *Fire from Heaven* (London: Harper Collins, 1992), describes Dorchester's Cultural Revolution, and Derek Hirst's "Locating the 1650s in England's seventeenth century", *History* (July 1996), pp. 359-383, asks old Tawney questions in a refreshingly new way.

Finally, an anecdote from a World War Two memoir provides a revealing insight into Tawney the man (William Stevenson, *A man called Intrepid* (New York: Ballantine Books, 1976), pp. 373-4):

"Professor R. H. Tawney had been sent from London as a link on the question of labour relations. Tawney was impressed by the need for discretion. He kept no diary and memorized his engagements. One was lunch with a millionaire in Washington. He arrived on the wrong day. The host, with typical American courtesy, greeted him as if he had come on the right day. During lunch, the host indicated a painting on the wall: 'Professor, I think you will find that is the finest Manet to have crossed the Atlantic.' Next day, Tawney was reminded that he was to have lunch with a prominent businessman. Tawney was driven off to the same millionaire. The host again displayed tact. Nothing was said about yesterday's lunch. The same ritual was observed with regard to the Manet painting: 'the finest to have crossed the Atlantic'. Professor Tawney paused with his fork in midair, thought carefully, and said: 'Oh no, I'm afraid you're wrong. I was shown the finest Manet in America by my host at lunch yesterday.'"

Chapter Ten

୶ଽ

Lawrence Stone and interdisciplinary history

Michael Hawkins

The editors of his *Festschrift* described Lawrence Stone as "one of the towering figures of the historical profession". This is true both literally – he is enormously tall – and metaphorically – for all his academic life he has been at the centre of innovation and controversy in British historical writing, particularly in the early modern period. My purpose is to use Stone's writings as a barometer to illustrate some of the changes over the last half century in the writing of history in this country, particularly the way it has interacted with other disciplines. Historical writing is itself a dialectical process: innovators in the field respond positively or negatively to the state of the discipline as they find it in their formative years. At the very real risks of simplification and of adopting too schematic an approach, it may still be helpful to present initially a brief outline of the earlier development in professional historical writing in this country before the beginning of Stone's academic career during the Second World War. For much of the later nineteenth and earlier twentieth centuries many leaders of the emerging historical profession were fascinated by the problems of medieval English society and by the fields of politics and law. Medieval history seemed to offer the greatest opportunities for progress: it appeared that there the gap was largest between the levels of understanding which could be derived, on the one hand, mainly from traditional chronicle sources and, on the other, from the newly available archives of central government, made more accessible by the rapid expansion of editing and publication. For the first time medieval history could be put on a serious academic footing: this was clearly a period in which disciples of Ranke or Comte could show what progress was possible from precise attention to the records of judicial, administrative and political history. At the same time adherents of various historical schools saw the Middle Ages as a key to many of the developments on which they wished to focus: whether their main concern was to emphasize the evolution of political and personal liberty through representative institutions and a principled legal system, the development of the nation state, the (often connected) growth of strong institutions of central government, or even the disappearance of old English liberties before Norman centralization, it seemed that medieval history was of central concern. Fierce debate arose, for example, over the origins of the open-field system, the effects of the Norman Conquest, the significance of Magna Carta, the early history of the jury, the evolution of Parliament and the role of the Commons. Most of these disputes had contemporary political resonance, perhaps most famously (or notoriously) in the many adaptations for different political purposes of the notion of a "Norman Yoke" still often seen, even in the nineteenth century, as dominating English class relations. Medieval history generated the greatest professional interest, the most marked progress and the most heated controversies.

Perhaps the greatest achievements of this period were the works, both titled *The constitutional history of England*, by Stubbs and Maitland (published respectively in 1874–8 and 1908), Maitland's *Domesday Book and beyond* (1897) and, of a slightly later generation, Tout's *Chapters in the administrative history of mediaeval England* (1920–33). But the study of history could not be confined to the political, legal and institutional spheres: many of the main topics of interest – for example, the origins of the open-field system and the impact of the Norman Conquest, unavoidably mixed social and economic questions with government, law and politics. Work on agricultural practices and the origins of serfdom and manorialism by Maitland, Seebohm and others already marked a switch of interest to social and economic history in the late Victorian and Edwardian periods, of which Maitland's *Domesday Book and beyond* was perhaps the most notable manifestation. In 1912 appeared R. H. Tawney's *The agrarian problem in the sixteenth century*, indicative in its polemical approach of a change of emphasis as well as of period. But it was perhaps some of the consequences of the First World War which encouraged and facilitated a switch of emphasis to economic history *per se* and to the early modern period. The Soviet Revolution and the crises of inter-war capitalism gave great *cachet* to Marxism as a blueprint of historical development, a political tool to be used in the study of history and, for even non-Marxists, a method through which to approach the masses of new documentary evidence now becoming available. For the economic and social pressures on the old English landed elites led to the much wider availability of their archives through sale or deposit in public repositories (national and, increasingly commonly, local). New empirical precision and a more secure theoretical underpinning to social and political change could, it was hoped, be provided by economic history. There was among many, though by no means all, historians less unquestioning confidence in the excellence of English political, legal and administrative structures and more willingness to investigate the social realities they saw underlying them. As so often the opening of new fields of academic study was eventually followed by the creation of new posts and periodicals: in 1923 Tawney was promoted to Reader (Professor in 1931) at the London School of Economics; and in 1927 appeared the first issue of the *Economic History Review*, the first specialist historical periodical in Britain not to be devoted to the older fields of ecclesiastical, legal or local history. Tawney was one of its first two co-editors.

At the same time the period from the late fifteenth to the mid-eighteenth century, now often called 'early modern', became the new focus of innovatory writing and fierce debate. Both Marxist and non-Marxist historians saw it as of especial significance. In the first place, to Marxists and those influenced by Marxism it was the period of the transition from feudalism to capitalism, the best-documented, most recent and most significant transformation in world history to date. The origins of capitalism were particularly worthy of study also to non-Marxist economic historians, whether they were influenced by Weberian notions of the growth of modern rationality or by economic growth in its own right. For historians of a liberal or "Whig" persuasion the sixteenth and seventeenth centuries had always rivalled the Middle Ages as a formative period in the growth of English liberties, but, prior to Tawney, without generating the heat of medieval debates. The magisterial and multi-volumed works of S. R. Gardiner seemed to combine the best document-based historical scholarship with an apparently unimpeachable assertion of the role of the House of Commons in defending liberty against the arbitrary Stuarts. It established a tradition of meticulous narrative focused particularly on the Commons, which was especially influential at the University of London from the time of A. F. Pollard to that of J. E. Neale in the 1950s and 1960s.

Especially significant was the English Revolution of the seventeenth century. For Marxists it had long been identified by Marx himself as the first successful bourgeois revolution. For a particularly succinct, indeed even brash, statement of this, see one of Christopher Hill's first published works, his essay, "The English Revolution", in a collection he edited, *The English Revolution 1640*, issued on the Revolution's tercentenary in 1940. Tawney, who like so many historians of his generation was influenced by Marx, although no Marxist himself, attempted to give the Revolution an underpinning in economic change. It appeared as the first revolt against the Crown which was neither an aristocratic nor a peasant rising, and Tawney tried to show that there had been a significant shift in the century before 1640 in the pattern of English landownership. The Crown, Church and aristocracy had lost land to the emergent, entrepreneurial class of middling landowners which Tawney tended to equate with the gentry. He thus attempted to give statistical precision to a movement in the balance of English wealth first detected, he claimed, by James Harrington in *Commonwealth of Oceana* (1656). Like Harrington he held that the English Revolution, far from being an essentially disinterested struggle for liberty, was an attempt by *nouveaux riches* to gain political influence to match their already acquired economic preponderance. His article, "The Rise of the Gentry", first published in the *Economic History Review* in 1941, became the benchmark for one of the most notorious and bitter historical debates in England during the two decades after the Second World War.

It is at this point that we may at last introduce Stone's work, since he first became well-known in the historical profession for his contribution to the gentry debate. Stone has always stressed the significance of the early modern period, seeing it, as he wrote in *The Past and the Present Revisited* (p. xi), as one in which "the social, economic, scientific, political, ideological and ethical foundations" for modern Western Europe were laid, a process first developed in England. Stone's writing has combined concern for such large issues with scepticism about received interpretations and openness to new directions of inquiry. It is characteristic of his early interest and finely-tuned antennae that most of his first articles were for the *Economic History Review*. If they have a common theme it is perhaps that they were concerned to destroy aspects of the Elizabethan myth. An early article on the Armada, written while on active service in a destroyer during the War, undermined the idea of the efficiency of the Elizabethan naval administration; "State control in sixteenth century England" analyzed the mixture of public and private influences which contributed to the making of government policy in social and economic questions, a theme pursued in his early biography of Sir Horatio Palavicino, essentially a study of "the seamier side of early international finance capitalism" and its links with government; and an analysis of the economics of "An Elizabethan coalmine" focused on the small-scale realities of Elizabethan industrial activity.

These themes can also be seen at work in Stone's first, somewhat ill-judged, contribution to the gentry debate. The minutiae and the methodological errors in this controversy have been much mulled over. Stone, for example, mistook bonds entered by aristocratic debtors as equalling their capital debt. This had the effect of doubling aristocratic indebtedness, since the bond was normally for twice the principal. This produced a vituperative attack by H. R. Trevor-Roper introducing a level of acrimony into the debate which still makes it notorious. Rather than pursue the debate, which like so many other historical controversies has rather run into the ground than been resolved, it is more profitable from our point of view to use the controversy to focus on trends in English historical writing. Stone's intervention was devoted to attempting to underpin one of Tawney's themes, the financial difficulties of the Elizabethan aristocracy. Stone has written in his autobiographical essay of Tawney's influence on him. It is significant that Tawney's own stature and the questions he raised should so influence a young scholar, particularly given the differences in personality and political creeds between them. Tawney's humility and Christian socialism were not shared by Stone, who has always laid about him with apparent self-confidence, who is not a religious believer, and whose political radicalism took rather the form of liberal individualism: he has called himself the "last of the Whigs".

Stone's early disaster gave an impetus to his research which eventually led to one of his major works, *The Crisis of the aristocracy, 1558-1641*, a massive work of nearly 900 pages and appendices published in 1965. This widened the argument: no longer was the main emphasis simply on the economic difficulties of the aristocracy or on what Stone later referred to as a "simplistic model" derived from Marxism. Instead Stone argued that the aristocracy underwent a general social, military, political, economic, ideological and moral crisis, to which the decline of power, in a variety of forms, was central. In an amendment to earlier views generally held by the "Tawney camp", he recognised that the aristocracy had revived their landed income in the generation from 1603 to 1641, but maintained that this was only at the expense of a loss of military and moral authority over their tenantry. They had come to see their estates as sources of income rather than of authority over men. This meant a loss of prestige and military authority, which in turn was compounded by the "inflation of honours", the extensive sale of titles and the easy creation and promotion of peers by the early Stuarts.

This was a move away from "narrow" economic history and indeed from early, rather straightforward Marxist assumptions towards a wider intellectual focus. It is paralleled in Stone's periodical writing and, as so often, reflects a shift in direction for the more lively English historians. As I have said, Stone's early articles were mostly for the *Economic History Review*, a measure perhaps of its status as a focus for innovation in historical writing to the generation which spanned the Second World War. But the study of economic history was perceived as becoming increasingly narrow in its subject matter and technical in its methods, a trend which has continued with the rise of econometric history (sometimes known as "cliometrics"). Stone, like most historians, has never used technical economics in his work. Instead, in the 1950s he was early associated with the journal *Past and Present*, which began publication in 1952. Stone's first article in *Past and Present* appeared in 1958, the year in which he joined its editorial board. This reflected a wider interest in social change. *Past and Present* published very few articles which could be regarded as narrowly, or even primarily, economic history. Increasingly significant was the influence of a wider range of social science disciplines, particularly sociology (he himself has referred to the influence of Weber on him at this time) and, a little later, social anthropology. Also of relevance here is Stone's contemporary attempt to reform the Oxford History syllabus, the failure of which helped to precipitate his move from there to Princeton in 1963.

Marxist influence was present, but never exclusive, both on the editorial board and in the content of many early articles in *Past and Present*: the first fifteen issues (1952–8) were subtitled "A Journal of Scientific History", a term which then had strongly Marxist overtones. From the beginning of *Past and Present* this influence was seen as compatible with other social sciences, and, for example, a fruitful Marxist sociology emerged. But the change of subtitle in 1959 to "A Journal of Historical Studies" may be seen as significant in widening *Past and Present*'s appeal to a broader band of historians interested in new approaches to their discipline.

It is here perhaps that Stone's work has been methodologically most significant. He has applied models derived from the social sciences to history without (in my view despite some contrary opinion) losing touch with empirical evidence. There is a sharp division between his approach, with its conscious use of models, and Elton's rejection of them in his account of historical method in *The Practice of History* (1967): indeed it was largely against historians such as Stone that Elton was reacting. I shall discuss below a specific criticism of Stone in this book but, on the central issue of the use of models, I believe Stone has the stronger case. Elton argues (*The Practice of History*, p. 83 in the 1969 Fontana edition) that the historian, having made an initial choice of area of study (he does not say how this is decided), should then "ask no specific questions until he has absorbed what [the evidence] says". This concept, of the historian approaching the evidence without presuppositions or apparently even an hypothesis to be tested, is unrealistic: it is difficult to envisage how an historian with such an approach would ever get started on research or proceed to choose between or ascribe significance to the mass of potential evidence available to them. The hypothesis used normally has an implicit or explicit model of explanation underpinning it: the model used by the historian is that which seems fittest to his or her understanding of human social behaviour over time. Elton's own initial seminal work, *The Tudor revolution in government* (1953), can be read as an excellent example of the application of the Weberian model of growing rationality in administration, and was clearly undertaken to revise historians' current judgements on Thomas Cromwell.

Be that as it may, examples of Stone's application of a wider range of social sciences have dominated much of the rest of his career. It is nevertheless possible to distinguish several stages. One arose from his continuing attempt to explain the English Revolution. Here Stone was much influenced by the interest among sociologists and political scientists in the 1960s in comparative theories of revolutions and in related discussions of modernization theory. In a study called *The causes of English revolution, 1529–1642* (1972), he made effective use of the work of Chalmers Johnson, Harry Eckstein, Crane Brinton, Louis Gottschalk and others. Holding to his view that the English Revolution had long-term causes and resulted from deep-rooted tensions in society and political structure, he produced a hierarchy of causes, methodically arranged as presuppositions, preconditions, precipitants and triggers. Presuppositions he saw as the structural tensions in English government and society, preconditions as long-term developments going back to the Reformation, precipitants as policies producing a rise of tension in the 1630s, and the immediate triggers of revolution as those events leading to an irremediable breach in the first two years of the Long Parliament. Stone saw pre-revolutionary England as marked by the presence of many of the main dysfunctional features which sociologists saw as usual in a society ripe for revolution: an intransigent governing elite unable and unwilling to adapt to new pressures; an alienated intellectual class providing an alternative ideology to the currently dominant one; an obsessive revolutionary mentality; and relative economic deprivation marking the end in the 1620s of the long sixteenth-century boom.

But Stone had also become more interested in social change for its own sake, not simply as a precursor of civil war. Here we should note the growing influence of a wider, more diversified, cultural history and, in particular, of the discipline of social anthropology with its stress on the implicit meanings and significance of cultural phenomena. Perhaps the most famous work of this stage of English historical writing is Sir Keith Thomas's *Religion and the decline of magic: studies in popular belief in 16th and 17th century England* (1971). We should also be aware here of Stone's ambiguous attitude to the *Annales* School. He acknowledges its work in broadening historians' intellectual horizons while retaining rigour, but criticizes it for an overemphasis on the material base of society and on quantification. For example, he specifically refers to Braudel's underestimating of the role of religion in his great work on *The Mediterranean in the reign of Philip II*. Stone perhaps exaggerates the rejection by the *Annales* School, given their interest in *mentalités*, of the cultural, political and religious superstructure as epiphenomenal. An alternative criticism of other members of the *Annales* School besides Braudel might indeed be rather differently focused. One could see their explanatory pattern as admitting *too eclectic* a range of phenomena, although still denying the influence of *les événements* on the substructure of society. I shall return briefly to these issues when discussing Stone's 1979 article on "The Revival of Narrative", but for most of the 1960s and 1970s Stone's work encompassed this new thinking.

Four fields – education, social mobility, crime and the history of the family – attracted his interest. Of these he first focused on education and social mobility. They clearly interacted with each other and developments in them had indeed been seen by Stone as relevant to his account of the causes of the Revolution in England. In 1964 he produced an article in *Past and Present* on what he saw as an educational revolution in the period 1560–1640. Those years were marked by a peak of numbers and a significant growth of provision in what we would call secondary and tertiary education, in the grammar schools and the two universities. Such an expansion had helped to generate both new ideas and a greater demand, which could by no means always be satisfied, for professional employment and advancement. It was both a cause and consequence of greater pressure in the sixteenth century for upward social mobility. This mobility Stone discussed more widely in another *Past and Present* article in 1966: "Social Mobility in England, 1500–1700". Here he used more complex models to replace what he saw as a simplistic established view of a simple pyramidal structure to English society. Early sixteenth-century England he saw as conforming to a "United Nations" model, a high skyscraper perched on a wide base with an elevator conveying up or down the successes and failures of agricultural society (the latter more numerous), while around it several ramps offered opportunities to rise in the fields of the church, law, commerce and government office, although those who took them were always likely to prefer the security of land – that is, life inside the skyscraper. By 1700 England had begun to change to a "San Gimignano" model in which five towers offered opportunities for rising in the four ways above with land added. Land no longer had the special status of being the focus of all aspirations, but was merely one way of progressing (or declining). Stone also wanted to stress the general decline of social mobility and the "closing" of English society after the Restoration, especially in education, in reaction against what were perceived as the radical excesses of the Revolution. Elton argues (p. 46 ff. of *The Practice of History*) that Stone fell in this article into what Elton perceived as one of the traps of using models, forcing the evidence to fit the model. In my view, there are some strains in the uses of Stone's models, but I do not see Stone as liable to the criticism Elton made. In fact, contrary to Elton's view, Stone is so little dominated by his models in his article that he refers to them only once, after initially setting them out. This relative neglect does perhaps suggest that Stone was not altogether at ease with the models he portrayed. To me it is not clear how the models incorporate some of the crucial elements of Stone's thesis – for example, the greater equality among the upper ranks of English society before 1640 with the relative decline of the aristocracy and rise of the gentry, or the blurring of distinctions between the gentry and other upward aspirants after 1660, marked by a rise of "pseudo-" (essentially non-landed) gentry and the greater diffusion of the title, "Mr". In general the models do not seem to build on a developmental principle: there is nothing in them intrinsically or logically necessary so that one should naturally lead to the other. Be that as it may, we may also note here that developmental argument and several other strands of his earlier work in the field of social mobility were united in a later book, *An open elite? England 1540–1880*, written with his wife and published in 1984. Here Stone's earlier concern with the aristocracy, his increasing interest in a broader sweep of English history and his iconoclasm came together in a thesis denying easy access by the upwardly mobile to an open English elite, particularly in the eighteenth century: this fitted well with his view of a relative "closing down" of English society, leading to the establishment of a "broad-based but relatively closed oligarchy".

This broad sweep was even more marked in a survey of the history of crime in England. In a *Past and Present* article in 1983 Stone focused on interpersonal violence in England from 1300 to 1980. But perhaps the most fruitful outcome of Stone's increasing breadth of approach to English history is his work on the history of the family, marriage and divorce. Family history, particularly in its relation to demography, has been a growing field of historical research at least since the foundation of the Cambridge Group for the History of Population and Social Structure in 1964, but Stone has preferred to focus on the *mentalités* of English society as revealed by its attitude to such fundamental issues as the nature of marriage (and latterly its breakdown), relations between genders, attitudes to children and, more generally, the complex relationship between public and private morality, law and religion. He regards the emphasis of the Cambridge Group on demography or household and family structure as important but ultimately less productive of historical understanding.

Again it may be said that this work derived its initial impetus from Stone's work on the aristocracy, perhaps in particular *Family and fortune*, a volume of case studies of aristocratic family history and finances. This was, however, widened into an attempt at a full history of the English family in *Family, sex and marriage, 1500–1800*, published in 1977. In this Stone, while denying a wholly linear evolution, accepts a stadial approach to the history of the family and gender and sexual relations in England. He discerns three stages: the first, lasting from *c.* 1450 to *c.* 1630 and characterized by an "open lineage family"; the second from *c.* 1550 to *c.* 1700 by a "restricted patriarchal nuclear family"; and the third from *c.* 1640 to *c.* 1800 by a "closed domesticated nuclear family". There is also a brief discussion of developments in the last two centuries. The book has been criticized for relying too much on the nobility and gentry for material. Indeed it may be said that Stone himself has been somewhat ambiguous about how far he intended to continue in these later works his earlier focus on the English elite. He is prepared, properly and strongly (see *The First modern society* . . . pp. 585–6), to defend this emphasis against those historians who seem to want a social or even a political history of England without its governing class, but that is not a claim that the social behaviour of that small section of English society can be taken as representative of the whole. A more fundamental criticism of *Family, sex and marriage* has been made by Alan MacFarlane, who in his book, *Marriage and love in England: modes of reproduction 1300–1840* (1986) denies the existence of these stages at all.

It can perhaps be argued that, despite the apparent schematic approach outlined above, Stone has been less concerned in his later career with applying overarching models to historical situations. Indeed he has said he used model-building too enthusiastically and indiscriminately earlier in his career. He is, however, certainly still prepared to use models as a way of explaining particular historical developments. For example, his discussion (in a later work, *Road to divorce: England 1530-1987* (1990), pp. 18-20) of the processes by which the law is changed has elements reminiscent of Kuhn's paradigmatic shift in scientific change: an accumulation of incongruities and incompatibilities which quite suddenly makes the current law seem "intolerable". But the work on the family presents a scheme of development which does not imply the universality of the model used to understand the causes of the English Revolution. Instead more emphasis has been placed on the role of the past in framing the present. In fact, he chose to begin *Road to divorce* with a quotation from Bernard Bailyn arguing that the "greatest challenge" facing the historian was to show how the present had emerged "from a very different past". There is an element of Whiggery here picked up by Edward Thompson in his *New Society* review of *Family, sex and marriage*.

This concern with the relationship of the present to the past has certainly been the inspiration of Stone's most recent major works: a trilogy on divorce, research for which dominated his later years before retirement. This comprises *Road to divorce: England 1530-1987*; and two volumes of case studies, *Uncertain unions: marriage in England, 1660-1753* (1992) and *Broken lives: separation and divorce in England, 1660-1857* (1993) (the relationship of the latter two volumes to the first mirrors that of *Family and fortune* to *The crisis of the aristocracy*). The history of divorce and marital breakdown presented Stone with the difficult problem of explaining the sharp distinction between the past situation, which until very recently made divorce or even separation impossible or very difficult ("a scandalous rarity"), and the current one in which it is merely an "administrative procedure", easily available and commonly used (*Road to divorce*, p. 2). Unlike the development of the family as Stone saw it, the history of divorce does not lend itself so appropriately to a stadial approach. Inevitably there is some tension between focusing on the evolutionary influences which enabled change to occur and on a sharp contrast between the past and the present in the history of divorce. The shift away from overarching models is consistent with the argument Stone put forward in an article on "The revival of narrative" in historical writing in *Past and Present* in 1979. Stone detected, and was prepared to give a qualified welcome to, the revival of a special sort of narrative, not the older political or biographical narrative of much standard and unadventurous historical writing, but a deep analysis of the significance of events or situations in their "total" cultural context. This development marks a further stage in the growing influence of the study of *mentalités* and the discipline of social anthropology on historians. Stone saw several strands contributing to it: a revived belief in human free-will; an acceptance of a two-way interaction between the realm of ideas and the economic and social substructure; a recognition of the significance of power as an independent variable in society; and, negatively, disillusion with the lack of the hoped-for results in the work of the three main innovative groups of historians of the previous generation – the Marxist economists; the *Annales* School with its structural analysis and rejection of *l'histoire événementielle*; and the "cliometricians", whom Stone dismisses as "statistical junkies". Stone's reservations about what may perhaps be more appropriately called "new" rather than "revived" narrative concern the issues of representativeness and significance, which older quantifying historians had tried to address. The new emphasis on the dramatic or sensational event, and on the records of crime and of the poor and obscure imply, to Stone, an abandonment of any attempt to comprehend society as a whole, let alone elucidate the general mechanics of social change. One could say that Stone's own use of narrative in his more recent works – for example, on the family – is an attempt to avoid these difficulties, Whiggish though some of the applications may be. But he has also been concerned, increasingly so later in his career, with attempting to assess the impact of contingent events.

History has always been important to Stone. The contributions to his *Festschrift, The first modern society*, reveal the breadth of interest of his research students. This is paralleled by the lively work of the Shelby Cullum Davis Center for Historical Studies at Princeton, which he played a leading part in founding and of which he was the Director from 1968 until retirement. As one reviewer wrote, as a preface to some damning criticism, Stone "asks important questions". Stone has always demonstrated a ready willingness to admit errors, which may (or may not) be thought consistent with his reputation for not suffering fools gladly. As has been pointed out above, he has always been enthusiastic about, and sensitive to, new trends which promise to enlarge the historian's understanding of the past. But he has also, despite openness to others' influences, always remained his own man. This concern for the significance of history and independence of judgement has meant little sympathy for modern "revisionists", those who purport to deny the significance or the deep-rooted causes of the English Revolution. He has always focused on politics in the widest sense. Stone does not make the vulgar error of separating social history from political and denies what some social historians are prone to assume, that the history of the upper classes – the holders of power – can somehow be ignored, or that the study of them is somehow "politically incorrect", even though he may occasionally have been too much influenced by his earlier preoccupation with them. Generally he has never worried about political correctness, as may be seen in his comments on the significance (or rather insignificance) of early feminist writing in *Road to divorce*. Finally, let me turn to something rather different to try to show that not all can be explained in terms of the pattern-making which has dominated this essay. Stone's first major work was a book on medieval sculpture in Britain. Undergraduates discussing historiography are often taken with E. H. Carr's dictum – study the historian before studying what they write – which coheres well with their frequent reductionism. An historian of English historiography might make something out of Stone's box brownie camera and peculiar circumstances, which Stone has recounted, in which he was given the commission to write this volume. But those circumstances reveal more about the workings of academic patronage than Stone's own intellectual preoccupations. The concerns which interested Carr – Stone the historian's social and political assumptions – would, I suggest, not be useful in understanding this.

Suggestions for further reading

Stone's first article, "The Armada campaign of 1588", appeared in *History* (1944). "State control on sixteenth century England"; "Elizabethan Overseas Trade"; and "An Elizabethan coalmine" were published in the *Economic History Review* in 1947, 1949–50 and 1950–1 respectively. The early books were *Sculpture in Britain: The Middle Ages* (London: Penguin, 1955) and *An Elizabethan: Sir Horatio Palavicino* (Oxford: Clarendon Press, 1956). General contributions to the gentry debate, as opposed to studies of specific topics, may be found in the *Economic History Review* in 1948 and 1951–2, *Explorations in Entrepreneurial History* (1957), *Past and Present* (1958) and *Comparative Studies in Society and History* (1961). His books on this subject were *The Crisis of the Aristocracy, 1558–1641* (Oxford: Clarendon Press, 1965), *Social Change and Revolution in England, 1540–1640* (Harlow, England: Longman, 1965) and *Family and Fortune: Studies in Aristocratic Finance in the 16th and 17th Centuries* (Oxford: Clarendon Press, 1973). Also relevant to this stage of Stone's career is *The Causes of the English Revolution, 1529–1641* (London: Routledge & Kegan Paul, 1972). His article on the educational revolution in *Past and Present* (1964) was followed by a further article in the same journal in 1969 extending coverage until 1900 and by his edition of a two-volume collection of essays on the history of European universities, *The University and Society* (Princeton and Oxford: Princeton University Press, 1975) and *Schooling and Society: Studies in the History of Education* (Baltimore: John Hopkins University Press, 1976).

The related topics of social mobility and the history of the family and divorce were dealt with in *Past and Present* (1966), *The Family, Sex and Marriage, 1500–1800* (London and New York: Weidenfeld, 1977), *An Open Elite? England 1540–1880* (with J. C. F. Stone, Oxford: Clarendon Press, 1984), *Road to Divorce: England 1530–1987* (Oxford: Oxford University Press, 1990), *Uncertain Unions: Marriage in England, 1660–1753* (Oxford: Oxford University Press, 1992) and *Broken Lives: Separation and Divorce in England, 1660–1857* (Oxford: Oxford University Press, 1993).

A volume of his collected essays was published as *The Past and the Present* (London and Boston: Routledge, 1981), reissued in an extended form as *The Past and the Present Revisited* (London and New York: Routledge, 1987).

Stone's work was celebrated by his research students in a volume edited by A. L. Beier, D. Cannadine and J. M. Rosenheim, *The First Modern Society: Essays in English History in honour of Lawrence Stone* (Cambridge: Cambridge University Press, 1989): most of the quotations above are taken from this volume, particularly the preface, prologue and the epilogue (the last an account by Stone of his own intellectual development). This book also contains a full bibliography up to 1988. See also for a discussion of Stone's work, P. Scott, "Putting Flesh on the Bare Bones of History", *Times Higher Education Supplement*, 23 September 1983; the profile of Stone in J. Cannon *et al.* (eds), *The Blackwell Dictionary of Historians* (Oxford and New York: Blackwell, 1988), 392-3; and a videotape interview of Stone by Keith Wrightson, issued by the Institute of Historical Research in 1988.

Chapter Eleven

৬১

Jacob Burckhardt: romanticism and cultural history

Malcolm Kitch

In 1860 a retiring and then little-known Swiss historian Jacob Burckhardt published what was to become one of the most famous and enduring historical works written in the nineteenth century, *The civilisation of the Renaissance in Italy*. Initially, like many famous books, it made little impact, but later editions established the reputation of its author. Burckhardt had been born in 1818 into a minor, clerical branch of a distinguished Basel family. After his student days and a brief and unhappy spell as editor of the *Basler Zeitung* (an occupation that "devours the poet in one") and lecturing at the university of Basel, he took up an appointment at the new Federal Polytechnic in Zurich. Then in 1858 the forty-year-old Burckhardt was appointed Professor of History at the small provincial university (only 200 students) in his native town. He also taught at the Basel Pedagogium and gave popular public lectures. In 1874 he added the professorship in the History of Art to his chair of History. He resigned the latter in 1885 but remained professor of the History of Art until 1893. He died four years later. The great appeal of Basel was that it allowed him intellectual freedom ("I can say what I like"). He turned down offers of more prestigious positions elsewhere, including perhaps the most distinguished history post in the German-speaking world as successor to his former teacher Leopold von Ranke (1795–1886) at the University of Berlin.

He later wrote "Berlin in my time was . . . the best place in which to learn history and the history of art". His main reason for studying there between 1839 and 1843 was to attend Ranke's lectures and seminars. Other professors who impressed him were the classical scholars Johann Droysen (1808–84) and August Böckh (1785–1867) and Franz Kugler (1808–58). Kugler was one of the founding fathers of art history and an influential writer on it. He became friendly with the young Burckhardt and encouraged him to develop his interest in the subject. Burckhardt later revised some of

Kugler's books and several of his ideas are echoed in Burckhardt's work, including his stress on the national element in the development of Italian art and the idea, derived from the Romantic movement, of the individual artist as a liberated spirit.

The greatest influence was Leopold von Ranke, the professor of history and the central figure in the development of modern methods in the study of history. Though Burckhardt admired Ranke as an historian he despised him as an individual and he was contemptuous of his cultivation of the great and the powerful. Even so he acknowledged that he learnt much from him, although he applied what he had learnt to writing a different sort of history. He wrote in August 1840 after attending Ranke's lectures, "I now begin to suspect what historical method means" and many years later he commented that he knew parts of Ranke's earlier books by heart. Ranke's methods were new but his subject matter was for the most part traditional – narrative political and diplomatic history, though he had included a section on Italian art in his first book and as a young man wrote a *History of Italian art*. He famously stressed the fundamental importance of facts and the need to derive them from contemporary sources, from the "purest, most immediate documents". Both the facts and the sources had to be critically evaluated. He was by no means the first historian to work in archives and study documents. His method owed much to the German School that had developed at the University of Berlin after 1810, but he was the first to use documents so systematically and thoroughly. His history seminar at the University of Berlin provided a novel and widely copied training ground for many distinguished historians of the next generation. Less commonly emphasized than Ranke's methodology was his belief, shared by Burckhardt, that history should be written in an attractive style; an idea that owed much to Romantic writers. Early nineteenth-century Germany witnessed two important developments in the evolution of modern historical writing: the rise of historicism and the development of history as an academic subject. Ranke contributed much to both. Historicism has more than one meaning. Here it means the development of a crucial modern historical consciousness, a recognition that each age was different and had its own character and standards. Historians must try to understand, not judge the past and they should not look at it from the standpoint of their own time. As Ranke wrote in a famous passage in his first published work, *The history of the Latin and Teutonic peoples* (1824):

> History has had assigned to it the task of judging the past, of instructing the present for the benefit of the ages to come. To such lofty functions this work does not aspire. Its aim is merely to show how things actually were.

In a similar vein Burckhardt wrote in 1882 "we have no business sitting in judgement on any past age . . . It is questionable whether we possess specifically superior historical insight [though] if we turn to knowledge of the past, our time is certainly better equipped than any previous one". He was familiar with the developments in history as an academic discipline in his life-time, but he was not in sympathy with the minute scholarly monographs that by the end of the century had become the hallmark of the academic historian in Germany, although as a young historian he had written them as a member of Ranke's seminar.

Several factors contributed to the development of historicism, including the influence of Romanticism. Romanticism, which developed in the late eighteenth century and flowered in the first decades of the following century, is a familiar term, though it eludes any universally accepted definition. It was not just a movement in literature. It fostered new ways of looking at life and the world that had a significant impact on European culture in the early nineteenth century and beyond. Romantic writers rejected what they saw as the excessive cult of reason and rationalism of the previous era, the age of the Enlightenment. They turned instead to feelings and the imagination and they manifested a love of nature and a fascination with the picturesque and the middle ages. They affirmed the importance of individual freedom and often expressed a sense of personal anxiety and melancholy that was occasioned both by the human condition and the impossibility of achieving the personal goals the artist must set himself. As a young man Burckhardt too had pictured himself as the frustrated young artist, plunged in melancholy by his inability to express, either as a poet or as a artist, what lay deep within him.

Though few Romantic writers were serious historians, Romanticism had a considerable impact on the writing of history. From the mid-1840s, after his student days and the decline of his enthusiasm for German mediaeval culture, Burckhardt would perhaps not have been conscious of his continuing debt to the Romantic movement, but the influences survived. In the 1850s he lectured on Byron's *Childe Harold*, one of the key texts of European Romantic literature, and he followed Romantic writers in arguing that it was wrong to view history as the inevitable march of progress, in contrast to the optimism of many nineteenth-century thinkers. Different periods were different, not morally or intellectually inferior – though he did not regard all periods or all civilizations as equally worthy of admiration.

Romanticism exerted other influences on him too. It is perhaps the source of his highly personal method of writing history, the unusual connections he made between history and poetry and above all his emphasis on individualism. However, he rejected the sentimentalism often associated with Romantic historical writing and art criticism as well as the misuse of the unfettered Romantic "imagination" in writing history. Ranke had taught him to eschew imagination and *a priori* ideas and to start with facts. "I cling", Burckhardt wrote, "by nature to the concrete, to visible nature and to history". Imagination was a necessary attribute for poets and painters but

137

not for historians. In place of imagination and *a priori* ideas he substituted what he called "contemplation" – a term previously used by the great German writer Goethe (1749–1832). Burckhardt "contemplated" sources: that is, if they were written sources he read them; if they were works of art he looked at them and allowed impressions to surface. "I include in contemplation", he wrote, "spiritual contemplation . . . historical contemplation issues from the impression we receive from sources". He goes on "What I build up historically is not the result of criticism and Speculation, but on the contrary of imagination, which fills up the gaps in contemplation". There was a place then for imagination, but its function was limited to filling in gaps, although it could be argued that what he called contemplation was in fact an historically conditioned imagination.

As a student in Berlin he realised that he was not to be, as he like many young Romantics had hoped, a lyric poet and saw that his talents lay in the writing of history. However, he made unusual connections between history and poetry. "History for me is always poetry for the greater part" he wrote, "a series of the most beautiful artistic compositions". Many Romantic poets held high claims for poetry – for example, Shelley's celebrated aphorism that "poets are the unacknowledged legislators of mankind" – but no other major historian could have made this connection between history and poetry. History he declared:

> is poetry on the grandest scale; don't misunderstand me, I do not regard it romantically or fantastically, all of which is quite worthless, but as a wonderful process of chrysalis like transformations of ever-new disclosures and revelations of the spirit. I stretch my hands towards the fountain for all things and that is why history to me is sheer poetry, to be mastered by contemplation.

Poets, he believed, gave expression to the spirit of the age in which they lived. Consequently, "history finds in poetry not only one of its most important, but also one of its purest and finest sources. Firstly, it is indebted to poetry for insight into the nature of mankind as a whole; further for profound light on times and peoples. Poetry, for the historical observer, is the image of the eternal in its temporal and national expression" – a strongly Hegelian observation.

The influence of the German idealist philosopher Hegel (1770–1831) was still dominant in Germany and Burckhardt's relationship with his ideas is a contentious subject. He always claimed to reject Hegel's philosophy but he shared with Hegel (and many other German scholars since the late eighteenth century) a strong belief in the *Zeitgeist*, the spirit of an age, and the *Volksgeist*, the spirit of a people.

His goal as an historian was to interpret an historical period and reveal the spirit that connected all aspects of the age. He never questioned the existence of this *Zeitgeist*, a basic assumption of Romantic writers. Although he always claimed to eschew philosophy and affirmed he that he no head for it, in his lectures on history at Basel he articulated theories of history that drew a good deal from the Hegelian philosophy he had rejected as a student. He claimed that "As the result of drawing ceaseless analogies between facts I have succeeded in abstracting much that is universal". These theories (discussed below) along with his perceptive if pessimistic observations on his century and his prophetic vision of the twentieth century have helped to create his modern reputation as an important historical thinker. They were induced from experience and study, not deduced from *a priori* abstractions. He respected philosophers in their attempts to penetrate the secrets of the universe but he could not follow them. Philosophers saw eternal truths but he saw only "mystery and poetry"; a quintessentially Romantic attitude.

His years in Berlin were crucial to his intellectual development, but he soon lost the deep admiration for Germany and the German middle ages of his student days. In April 1841 he had written:

> I often want to kneel down before the sacred soil of Germany and thank God that my mother-tongue is German! I have Germany to thank for *everything!* My best teachers have been German, and I was nourished at the breast of German culture and learning; . . . What a people! What wonderful youth! What a land – a paradise!"

But in the 1860s he witnessed with alarm the rise of Bismarck's Germany and the cult of state power that fascinated German historians for the next two generations, seducing even Ranke in his later years. He also distrusted the power the state and organized religion could exercise. He saw them as enemies of culture if they were too powerful, as he believed religion had been in the middle ages, when it restricted artistic creativity. He disliked too the new nationalistic element in much German historical writing. He even extended his increasing distaste for Germany to the German tourists he encountered in his beloved Italy, the country to which he had transferred his affections, "the Italy I still love so deeply", he wrote in 1891. Italy was not only the home of great art and great buildings, both Renaissance and classical, but also in his view it was less corrupted by the values of the nineteenth century, at least when he first came to know it after 1837. He had visited Italy six times before writing *The Civilisation of the Renaissance in Italy* in 1860. Before then, in 1855, he had published, though with no great commercial success, his often-reprinted *Cicerone,* subtitled *An instruction how to enjoy the works of art in Italy*. The word "enjoy" is characteristic of his passionate attitude towards art and culture.

The first sign of his intellectual independence had come before he went to Berlin. By 1838 while studying theology in Basel he had decided that Christianity was a myth. Though he duly completed his degree in theology he did not follow his father as a Protestant minister. To reject Christianity was still a bold step and one that he knew would upset his father. However, he retained belief in a personal God and Divine Providence and later felt that some form of spiritual revival was a possible solution to the problems of his day.

Burckhardt's history was scholarly but also personal and subjective and he never aspired to Ranke's goal of objectivity, though he too (usually) eschewed moral judgements. He broke with mainstream traditional history with its concern with political narrative history to write cultural history. In 1842 he wrote that he intended to devote himself to cultural history (*Kulturgeschichte*), a subject close to his other great interest, the history of art, though until the 1860s he argued that they were distinct and unrelated disciplines. He wrote several works on the history of art and his *Cicerone* remained a popular work of reference until well into this century. A full discussion of his work and ideas should devote attention to his contribution to the history of art, but lack of space means that this topic is neglected here, as it tends to be in most general studies of Burckhardt.

The word culture is used in very different ways, including the familiar terms "popular culture", or "elite culture". As Burckhardt himself observed of cultural history in 1882, "Definitions of the concept vary" and cultural history still has no agreed definition. For Burckhardt its prime concern was to demonstrate the interconnectedness of all aspects of life in a civilization. "The history of civilisation [that is to say, culture] overlaps with church history, the history of law, literary history, the history of communications, the history of morals, etc., according to its requirements". Like many German scholars, his approach to cultural history was posited on the idea of the homogeneity of a culture, derived from the prevailing *Zeitgeist*, what the art historian E. H. Gombrich has described as "an independent supra-individual collective spirit". In order to discover the spirit of a culture/civilization, to establish the "constant, recurrent and typical" he sank what he called "cross-sections through history". Cultural history required different sources from those used to write narrative political history and they had to be used in a very different way. The cultural historian, more than most historians, selects evidence not according to any fixed rules, apart from relevance, but to demonstrate a hypothesis. Modern cultural historians would agree with Burckhardt that a wide range of sources was necessary to study cultural history, not just the official documents that Ranke had used. For Burckhardt "Everything is a source . . . including literature". "Sources are of interest to the history of civilisation as the monuments and pictures of a certain period and nation . . . the historian of civilisation reads with different eyes than does the historian . . . the history of civilisation can only be learnt from sources instead of handbooks". His objective was not to write an historical narrative or produce a comprehensive history of an age. He dealt with the civilization of the Italian renaissance not chronologically but by topics in a series of parallel discussions. His approach to cultural history was close to that of the anthropologist: to look at the totality of a culture, including everyday life, as well as political and social institutions and the arts and ideas in order to establish its common and distinctive features.

The belief that ages possessed different and distinctive spirits and that these differences could be seen in art and literature was not peculiar to Burckhardt. Ranke as well as Hegel and many German writers and historians believed that every nation was distinct and distinctive. But few non-German historians have given the idea of the *Zeitgeist* such a central place. Though cultures are never completely homogeneous, many cultural historians still assume that a culture has an internal unity, though this can be attributed to factors other than the *Zeitgeist*. Gombrich has argued that cultural movements do not mysteriously emerge as the manifestation of an abstract spirit; they are created by individuals. Other historians have cited the importance of material factors such as the dominant mode of production (Karl Marx) or, more loosely, social factors as the key to understanding a culture. Much cultural history is now concerned with investigating themes rather than the examination of a culture as a whole, and the subject has been extended to embrace new concepts, such as the cultural significance of forms, symbols and words. Burckhardt's approach and writings marked an important development in the development of cultural history and he is often described as the father of the subject. Though his works are still read, his form of cultural history has been criticized for its presuppositions, methodology and limited subject matter.

Cultural history is usually held to have been created by Voltaire (1697–1778), although its roots can be traced to many writers. In the early nineteenth century it was a minor field of study, distinct from mainstream narrative political history but complementary to it. It had two forms: one was close to what later became known as social history. Its concern was to describe the daily life of a whole society at a particular time and it often related to studies of folklore and national character. The other, more Hegelian form, sought to define and explain the stages and development of human progress. By the late nineteenth century national political history had became dominant and cultural history languished, enmeshed with Romantic nationalism and Hegelian philosophy. Burckhardt spent much time defending his subject and his conception of it. However, unlike his predecessors and many subsequent cultural historians he focused not on society as a whole (or like later writers on particular aspects of a culture) but on the elite and on the European high culture that was his consuming passion.

In Berlin he had believed that Europe, led by Germany, was on the verge of a new, great cultural age, but by the mid-1840s he came to feel that not only Germany but the whole century was fundamentally philistine and threatened his cherished cultural values. The creative individual was menaced on all sides. The production of great works of art had become impossible because culture was corrupted by materialism, what he contemptuously called "money-making". Equally dangerous for high artistic achievement was the ignorant populism engendered by democracy and the dangerously half-educated masses of the nineteenth century. Democracy, he wrote, was "the product of mediocre minds" and it only used mediocre men. Unlike the elitist and undemocratic city-states of classical Greece or Renaissance Italy, nineteenth-century democracy stifled the creative genius of artists and writers. Socialism was even more dangerous. It meant not only democracy and materialism but also revolution and the physical destruction of culture on the grounds that it was "the secret ally of capital". Not that he liked capitalism either. He believed that the dominant commercial spirit of his century tempted creative artists to sell out and not to listen to their inner voices.

Italy, and the study of history, provided an escape from an uncongenial present. He was aware of the escapist element in his attachment to Italy. In a letter written in 1846, in which he foresaw the turmoil that was to hit Europe two years later, he wrote "[I] am escaping to the beautiful, lazy south [i.e. Italy], where history is dead". There he would avoid radicals and industrialists; there he would, as he put it, "strike up new relations with life and poetry". There he would also find the things he found most dear, "art and antiquity".

Although he admired Greek antiquity and the Renaissance that had revived knowledge of the culture of the classical world and its values and had handed them down to his day, he pessimistically, if accurately, observed that "the spirit of antiquity is no longer our spirit". As he became increasingly disenchanted with the modern world, even the Renaissance that had witnessed the birth of the modern world began to lose some of its attraction. His interests shifted to classical Greek antiquity, the foundation of all that was finest in European culture. However, he continued to lecture on a range of historical periods and subjects and in 1867 he published his final though incomplete work on the Italian Renaissance. This was *The History of the Italian Renaissance*, a study of Renaissance architecture. From then on his main interest was Greek culture, although, surprisingly, he never visited Greece. He refused to publish the manuscript of his lectures on *History of Greek culture* because he knew that it would be savagely "plucked apart" (as it indeed was) by the *viri eruditissimi*, the classical scholars who regarded him as an amateur in this field, largely because of what they saw as his neglect of philology and his preference for reading sources, especially Greek literature, rather than keeping up with the latest scholarly literature.

For Burckhardt history was not, as it was for Ranke and the scientific historians of the nineteenth century, an objective science. He observed that "History is actually the most unscientific of all the sciences." It was essentially a subjective study, the investigation of "what one age finds remarkable in another". At the beginning of the *Civilisation of the Renaissance in*

Italy he stressed that his long book was an essay, a personal interpretation. He wrote "To each eye, perhaps, the outlines of a given civilisation present a different picture". "What changes most of all is the picture created for us by the art and poetry of the past". For him as a cultural historian, art and poetry provide evidence that allowed him to create a personal "picture" of a past age. "We need", he wrote, to take "personal possession" of the past. His perception of the inner spirit of a civilization derived from his contemplation of sources, including his deep knowledge of art and literature.

He had clearly taken "personal possession" of the Italian Renaissance when he wrote his most famous book, *The Civilisation of the Renaissance in Italy*. Though it omitted art and architecture, because he planned a separate volume on them (which he never wrote), many of the ideas contained in the book derived from his interpretation of Italian art. The spirit of the Italian Renaissance was characterized by a cluster of attitudes that he called "individualism". He challenged the prevailing idea that the Renaissance was brought about by the revival of classical antiquity alone. His explanation of the Renaissance combined individualism with the *Zeitgeist* and *Volksgeist*. In the late eighteenth century the influential German writer Johann Gottfried Herder (1744–1803), whom Burckhardt greatly admired, did much to popularize the concept of "nations" as distinct entities. Nations were not just political entities. Every nation had its distinct customs, institutions and culture. Romantic writers followed Herder in believing that each nation produced a distinctive culture, which expressed the special character of that nation. Böckh in his lectures in Berlin that Burckhardt had attended had also affirmed the central role of the *Zeitgeist*. Burckhardt stressed the distinctive spirit of the Italian people at the time of the Renaissance and related it to the unique and volatile political situation of Italy. Elizabethan England had been simultaneously shocked and fascinated by contemporary Renaissance Italy and Romantic writers too, like the French novelist Stendhal (1783–1842), had seen Renaissance Italy as a uniquely violent and what Ferguson calls "pleasantly shocking" society. Burckhardt took over and embellished this attitude. He also followed the Romantics in contrasting the spirituality of the art of the middle ages and the sensuality of Renaissance art. Individualism was at the core of the Romantic attitude to life. It was perhaps in this belief in the importance of individualism that he was most indebted to Romanticism. Romantic writers greatly valued originality and imagination. All human beings were unique. It was imperative to assert one's individualism, reject convention and express one's ideas and feelings, though this might lead to a self-conscious cult of singularity for its own sake (something Burckhardt rejected) or the destructive individualism that he regretted was also an aspect of Renaissance Italy. In his *History of Greek Culture* he argued that, when the culture of ancient Greece was at its apogee, "self-expression and the concept of individual genius" flourished and thinkers could be "free, spontaneous, original and aware", although his

143

often harsh depiction of Greek life was strongly anti-Romantic. The Renaissance, too, had been an age that fostered creative individualism and permitted great men of all kinds to emerge and artistic talent to flourish. Its decentralised, small-scale, competitive political structure allowed, indeed encouraged, the flowering of individual genius. Thus, men became aware of themselves and their potential and they became conscious of themselves in a way that people in the middle ages never were. Thus, the unique political state of Italy encouraged great men to flourish as rulers, artists or villains. Romantic writers had often tended to hero-worship great men, especially those creative geniuses who represented the spirit of their people. In lectures given in 1870 Burckhardt sought to define what constituted the great man – there were no great women. Unlike some German writers he did not argue that it was the role of great men to act as agents of the World Spirit or of Divine Providence. Like Constantine the Great and Napoleon the great man must be irreplaceable – his contribution must be uniquely personal. The great poets, painters and scholars had remained uncorrupted by materialism and popular ideas and had listened to their "inner voice". Their "inner voice" was the expression not only of themselves but also of the spirit of the age in which they lived – they gave, he wrote, "ideal form to the inner content of time". Their individualism, however, was not the misguided, self-centred subjectivity of his day. There have been great scientists and mathematicians, even a few great statesmen (though he distrusted great political leaders) but no great historians. Even though he found no philosophical system satisfactory, he argued that philosophers were the greatest of all great men because they sought to answer the big questions. After them came poets who, like artists, represented inward things in outward forms. "They alone can interpret and give form to the mystery of beauty". Beauty was what Burckhardt, like many Romantics, deeply prized – "Beauty is truth, truth beauty" wrote Keats. For Burckhardt in his later years beauty was essentially classical beauty. "Devotion to the true and the good in their temporal form . . . is splendid in the absolute sense. The beautiful may be exalted above time." Great artists not only expressed the spirit of their own age, but they also spoke for all time. They needed imagination and vision as well as technical skill to create works of beauty. Their message was eternal. He had nothing to say for the "masters" of his age – when culture was commercialized and third-rate and nothing of beauty was produced. He had witnessed a great "levelling down" that made the emergence of great men less likely. "Art and poetry themselves are in our day in the most wretched plight, for they have no spiritual home in our ugly, restless world, and any creative spontaneity is seriously menaced."

As a student at Berlin he had moved in liberal circles but even then he had confessed conservative views. Any tendencies he may have had towards liberalism (except in its elitist, non-radical form) disappeared soon after he returned to a Switzerland that did not escape the political turmoil of the mid- and late-1840s. From this time he became increasingly pessimistic. He believed that the French Revolution marked a turning point in history, although the ideas that it promoted derived from the eighteenth century. It ushered in the era of the all-powerful, centralized, secular, militaristic state. By the 1870s he feared that "times of terror and the profoundest misery may come". Chaos would result, in the form of war or revolution or both, but he believed that educated men such as himself who had managed to stand outside events would be able to salvage something from the chaos. In "the crisis of the declining nineteenth century" he wrote "things can only be changed by ascetics, men who are independent of the enormously expensive life of the great cities" – that is by men like Burckhardt himself, the cosmopolitan Swiss patrician. Although he was pessimistic and cynical about the world in which he lived and was always conscious of the role of unhappiness in human history (even in Greek civilization), he was never a fatalist. He never fell into despair. Civilization was fragile but nevertheless much of classical civilization had managed to survive the Fall of the Roman Empire, to be recovered in the Renaissance, and much could be retrieved from a future disaster. His first book, *The Age of Constantine* (1852) was about an earlier age of disintegration as the Roman Empire and its civilization began to break up. In the Italian Renaissance what remained of this great classical civilization, preserved though not properly understood in the middle ages, was recovered and the modern world began.

Others shared his pessimism about a century in which states were becoming threateningly more powerful and militaristic, in which industrialization, mass culture and excessive freedom were undermining culture: de Tocqueville (1805–59), liberals like J. S. Mill (1806–73), conservatives (especially in Germany) and even some radicals. Characteristically his concerns about his time centred not on the conditions industrialization created for the masses but on its cultural consequences. Thus, in 1870 he was tormented for several days by the erroneous rumour that the Louvre had burnt down in the Siege of Paris.

His fears about the future and his pessimistic view of the world in which he lived did not, however, impinge on his writing of history, though they may have influenced his choice of subject. Whatever his subject, he emulated Ranke and the Romantics in striving for a readable, attractive style. He aimed, as he affirmed in his introduction to *The Age of Constantine*, to "address himself primarily not to scholars but to thoughtful readers of all classes", that is to the general educated public, not like most historians by his books but more by his well-attended and popular public lectures. He did not seek to train narrow scholars but to encourage his pupils, like him, to take personal possession of the past and to learn from it.

I never dreamt of training scholars and disciples in the narrower sense, but only wanted to make every member of my audience feel and know

that everyone may and must appropriate those aspects of the past
which appeal to him personally, and that there might be happiness in
so doing. I know perfectly well that such an aim may be criticised as
fostering amateurism but that does not trouble me overmuch.

The purpose of studying history was not to acquire knowledge of the facts
but to understand eternal values and to be able to differentiate between
what was lasting and what was transitory.

We could not, as Ranke believed, use the past to explain the present.
History provided human beings not with lessons to be applied but a perspective that allowed us to grasp the eternal truths that explain the human
condition. In a significant passage that sums up his humanistic beliefs he
wrote "We . . . shall start out from the one point accessible to us, the one
eternal centre of all things – man suffering, striving and doing, as he is and
was and ever shall be". Much of his history writing was a reflection on the
themes of human freedom and the creativity that produced what he valued
most. His book on the Italian Renaissance is still in print, although its
arguments, particularly about the modernity of the Renaissance and individualism as its defining characteristic, have often been criticized. His high
reputation today rests more on his prophecies of twentieth-century developments and his perception of the major political developments of his day
as well as on his theories on history based on the historical forces – "state",
"religion" and "culture". Culture was used by Burckhardt in this context
to denote that part of human existence that was free from the restrictions
of religion and the state.

For Burckhardt the achievements of the great poets and artists of the past
allowed "the man of culture to sit down to the banquet of the art and
poetry of past times". One should enjoy the arts while they lasted – a new
age of barbarism was dawning. He himself was essentially such a "man of
culture". He lamented that there would be no more great art culture and
was saddened by the philistinism of his day. Modern painting, he believed,
had abandoned beauty. He wrote in 1881 that most European art from
Delacroix was "a personal insult to one's sense of beauty". He felt deeply
about what he called the "culture of old Europe", the high culture that had
begun in classical Greece and which, after its revival in the Renaissance,
had lasted to the beginning of his own century – he had no interest in non-
western culture.

He had the acute aesthetic sense of the Romantic. He responded strongly
to the beauties of art and the Swiss and Italian landscapes. His sensitive
nature made him regard keeping birds in cages as barbarism. He was hor-
rified by the way Italians treated animals and could break off a lecture on
Raphael with his voice choked by tears. However, this sensitivity was combined with detachment. Although he had many correspondents and friends,
none were very close. He was a reserved and solitary man, at times proving

difficult in his relationships with friends. As early as the age of 25 he observed that he avoided going into society, although with his love of beauty he was not immune to female charms - he was attracted to an English "beauty" who attended his lectures in Basel, but she proved cold. He was for a short time engaged, but he seemed surprisingly unconcerned when his fiancée terminated the engagement. He felt that as a man of "strong passions" he would not have made her a good husband. However, although he admired beautiful women, these passions seems to have been directed less towards them than towards what moved him most - pure beauty. He was never to marry and for 26 years lived simply in Basel surrounded by his books, his ever growing collection of photographs of works of art and his piano. Though a reclusive and modest man, who characteristically told Basel university that he did not want his retirement marked by any celebration, he was never an ascetic. His letters show a strong sense of humour and until his health declined he continued to enjoy travel, especially to Italy which he visited annually for many years. He appreciated the pleasures of life: good food, red wine (although not the "so-called half bottle of Bordeaux" that was served to him in London), cigars, concerts, playing the piano, evenings spent talking in cafés (although not to his academic colleagues - he preferred "to live *par distance* with clever people") and walking. For all his pessimism about the world in which he lived he enjoyed life and retained close and warm connections with his family.

For him the past was ultimately a mystery, the present uncongenial and the future threatening. The fame that came late in life meant little to him. Ultimately what really mattered was beauty and the culture that past ages had bequeathed to those who could appreciate it, although even beauty was not for ever. He wrote of Leonardo da Vinci's fading *Last Supper* "The most beautiful art on earth must perish, and death delights in devouring that which is most glorious in the world of man".

Two years before he died he summed up his beliefs in a letter to a young theological student: "Be true to art in all its branches, to music, to poetry and to painting and persevere in believing that it is not for nothing that it is given to one to have one's life exalted by these glorious things". For all his pessimism he was part of a long humanist tradition. He prized the "glorious things" that human beings were capable of and the joy they bestowed. It was enough that as a teacher and cultural historian he had done his best to preserve and hand down eternal values in an age of decline.

Suggestions for further reading

The main German edition of his works is *Jacob Burckhardt-Gesamtausgabe [14 vols.]* (Stuttgart/Basel: Schwabe, 1929-34). The complete edition of his letters, *Jacob Burckhardt: Briefe*, was edited by Max Burckhardt [10 vols.]

(Basel: Schwabe, 1949–86). His most important books have been translated into English, beginning with *The Cicerone* in 1873 (London: John Murray) (but only the section on Painting), followed by *The Civilisation of the Renaissance in Italy* in 1878 (London: Kegan Paul & co.). In this century there have been translations of *The Age of Constantine the Great* (London: Routledge, 1949); *The Architecture of the Italian Renaissance*, P. Murray (ed.) (London: Secker, 1985) and an abridgement of *The History of Greek culture* (London: Constable, 1964). A selection of his letters have been translated by Alexander Dru, *The Letters of Jacob Burckhardt* (London: Routledge & Kegan Paul, 1955). His *Historische Fragmente* (selections from his notes for history lectures given between 1865 and 1885) have been translated as *Judgements on history and historians* (London: George Allen & Unwin, 1959) and, more important, some of his other lecture notes between 1868 and 1871, the *Weltgeschichtliche Betrachtungen* as *Reflections on history. Jacob Burckhardt* (London: George Allen & Unwin, 1943). An enormous amount has been written about Burckhardt, mostly in German. The standard biography is Werner Kaegi's monumental *Jacob Burckhardt: eine Biographie* [6 vols.] (Basel: Schwabe, 1947–82). Writing in English on Burckhardt includes: F. Gilbert *History: politics or culture? Reflections on Ranke and Burckhardt* (Princeton, New Jersey: Princeton University Press, 1990); Francis Haskell, *History and its images* (London: Yale University Press, 1993), 331–46; H. R. Trevor-Roper's lively lecture, "Jacob Burckhardt", *Proceedings of the British Academy*, **70**, 1984 and Karl J. Wientraub, *Visions of culture* (Chicago: University of Chicago Press, 1966). G. P. Gooch, *History and historians in the nineteenth century*, 2nd edn (Boston: Beacon Press, 1952) was first published in 1913 but is still the fullest work on historical writing in the nineteenth century. W. K. Ferguson, *The Renaissance in historical thought* (Cambridge, Mass.: Riverside Press, 1948) remains the best overview of evolution of the concept of the Renaissance up to 1948 and Burckhardt's contribution to it. There is no good general account of the development of cultural history but E. H. Gombrich, *In search of cultural history* (Oxford: Clarendon Press, 1969); J. Huizinga "The task of cultural history" (1929), reprinted in his *Men and ideas* (London: Eyre & Spottiswood, 1959) and Peter Burke "Reflections on the origins of cultural history", in *Interpretation and Cultural History*, J. H. Pittock and A. Wear (eds) (London: Macmillan, 1991) are useful.

Chapter Twelve

Anthony Blunt and Lucien Goldmann: Christianity, Marxism and the ends of history

Brian Young

This essay is concerned with two twentieth-century writers, both Marxists, one of them a spy, who sought to interpret two seventeenth-century Christian figures. Study of their interpretations raises important concerns about historiography – for example, do we have to study the historian before studying the history? – and about the competing claims of Marxism and Christianity as ideological forces in the twentieth century.

To begin with Anthony Blunt, the spy: one route to him may be traced through a novel by Evelyn Waugh. Charles Ryder, the artist-narrator of *Brideshead Revisited*, Waugh's novel concerning nostalgia and its discontents, recalls early on a potent moment of aesthetic conversion:

> For me the beauty was new-found.
>
> Since the days when, as a schoolboy, I used to bicycle round the neighbouring parishes, rubbing brasses and photographing fonts, I had nursed a love of architecture, but, though in opinion I had made that easy leap, characteristic of my generation, from the puritanism of Ruskin to the puritanism of Roger Fry, my sentiments at heart were insular and medieval.
>
> This was my conversion to the Baroque. Here under that high and insolent dome, under those coffered ceilings; here, as I passed through those arches and broken pediments to the pillared shade beyond and sat, hour by hour, before the fountain, probing its shadows, tracing its lingering echoes, rejoicing in all its clustered feats of daring and invention, I felt a whole new system of nerves alive within me, as though the water that spurted and bubbled among its stones, was indeed a life-giving spring.

Set in the 1920s, Ryder's conversion is not untypical of that of other, non-fictional contemporaries. Sir Denis Mahon, whose recent bequest to the nation of a magnificent collection of Italian baroque paintings has been one of the most refreshing instances of private generosity overcoming governmental meanness in the provision of aesthetic education for the public. He discovered his taste for the work of Guercino and his contemporaries as an undergraduate at Oxford in the 1920s. At much the same time, Anthony Blunt, as an undergraduate in Cambridge, deepened his interest in the work of the artist Nicolas Poussin, writing a successful fellowship dissertation at Trinity College on the work of this then neglected French master. Just as Ryder had to unlearn the prejudices against seventeenth-century art instilled into Edwardian youths by the influence of the Victorian sage John Ruskin, whose enthusiasm for medieval culture dictated so much of his contemporaries' tastes, so Mahon and Blunt had to progress beyond such strictures. This was made easier for Blunt by the example of an older Cambridge figure, Roger Fry, whose revolutionary exhibition of Post-Impressionists had educated so many English art-lovers in the appreciation of modern art and away from the Victorianism against which other Bloomsbury figures had reacted. Fry achieved for the figurative arts what Lytton Strachey had pioneered in the undoing of Victorian reputations in his seminal collection of essays, *Eminent Victorians*. The freedom experienced by the young of the 1920s and 1930s, when the world of their parents and grandparents had been so brilliantly and sometimes rather unfairly attacked, was considerable. With the dismissal of Victorianism came a sense of the "modern" that would have considerable repercussions in the arts, as is most apparent in the novels of Virginia Woolf, the sister-in-law of another of Fry's Cambridge friends, Clive Bell.

The initial conversion to modernism in the arts made later conversions possible. As Waugh's Charles Ryder made plain, it was Fry's influence that moved him away from inherited aesthetic ideals, later allowing him to experience a stronger conversion to the Baroque. "Conversion" is an apt word to describe these experiences, whether it be to the Baroque, Roman Catholicism or Communism. Waugh had himself also famously converted to Roman Catholicism, and this was a direction followed by others of his contemporaries. In the turbulent political atmosphere of the 1930s, other philosophies attracted the allegiance of the young, and a host of other "conversions" were made at that time. For instance, modernism sometimes notoriously colluded with fascism, as illustrated in the enthusiasm for Mussolini evinced by the American poet Ezra Pound; T. S. Eliot occasionally expressed an interest in the more dubious politics of the French Right and his work is famously open to the charge of voicing anti-semitic sentiments. Younger poets, such as W. H. Auden, flirted with Communism and this proved to be an enthusiasm shared by Julian Bell, Clive Bell's son, who died fighting Franco's forces in the Spanish Civil War. Communism was particularly successful in Cambridge, and it was there that Blunt joined the Communist Party, sowing the seeds for future treason. Blunt, then, underwent a double-conversion, from the aesthetic which had dominated English art criticism since Ruskin to that inaugurated by Fry, and from the comfortable political pieties of the times to an alluring Communism.

The first part of this essay will examine the congruence between these two conversions, and their implications for intellectual and cultural historians. The second, considerably shorter, part of the essay will be concerned with the analogous study of Poussin's contemporary, the religious writer Blaise Pascal, made by the emigré Rumanian Communist, Lucien Goldmann, Blunt's contemporary. In so doing, this essay will raise the question of the relationship between Christianity, as represented in the works of Poussin and Pascal, and Communism, as evinced in the interpretations of these two men made by Blunt and Goldmann. Since we are told that ours is a time witnessing what the American theorist Francis Fukuyama has called "The End of History", it is invaluable to examine two of the dominant ideologies of recent history. Much ink has been spilled in addressing the consequences of the alleged disappearance of Christianity and Communism; this essay will seek to demonstrate that such speculation is largely misplaced.

> An entire arsenal of ruses and tricks is needed if discourse is to explore painting.

> (Louis Marin)

The section of *Brideshead Revisited* in which Ryder traces his aesthetic conversion is entitled "Et in Arcadia Ego". This deliberately wistful and nostalgic phrase, with its evocations of the immanence of death, provides the title of two of Poussin's most famously enigmatic paintings. Translatable as "I also was in Arcadia" it may also be translated as "I too am in Arcadia": "Et in Arcadia Ego" can therefore refer either to Death itself, or to the unknown inhabitant of the tomb portrayed in the paintings, and this ambiguity is central to addressing the meaning of the paintings, one of which is to be found in the Louvre, the other at Chatsworth House. There is a deeply nostalgic quality in Poussin's work, a sense of the fragility of happiness, of the grief brought about by change, and the phrase "Et in Arcadia Ego" also evokes much of the atmosphere of youth and promise which informed the ideological conversions of the 1920s and 1930s, when some were prepared to die for their beliefs (or, occasionally, to allow others to die for them). The atmosphere of the time and the influence this was later to have on those shaped by it is made manifest in a sequence of novels written by another product of the troubled world of the 1920s and 1930s, Anthony Powell.

Like Waugh's Ryder, as well as Mahon and Blunt, Powell had obviously experienced his own conversion to the aesthetic world of the seventeenth century. While Ryder and Mahon explored the baroque, it was the predominantly neoclassical work of Poussin which most appealed to Blunt and Powell. Something of a "Tory" novelist like Waugh, Powell entitled his sequence of interlocking novels *A dance to the music of time*, also one of the titles of a work by Poussin which is to be found in the Wallace Collection, and which provides something of a *leitmotif* in the novels. The painting depicts four figures dancing in a circle to the music played by Time, while two playful *putti* represent the passing of time by examining an hourglass and blowing bubbles respectively. Described by Blunt, following a friend of Poussin, as a "Wheel of Fortune", the painting acts as a magnificent summary of the major themes of Powell's novels. A profound sense of melancholia is conveyed by Poussin's Arcadian paintings, and this coldness in an otherwise sunny landscape finds a most apt analogue in the notoriously inscrutable character of Blunt and his "conversion" to Marxism in the 1930s. Blunt's initial interest in Poussin seems to have come about through his interest in Cézanne, the Post-Impressionist artist whose work had been ably promoted by Fry. Cézanne was a strong admirer of Poussin, and this affected the young art historian's interest in the older of the French masters. Blunt had been largely brought up in Paris, and his Marlborough contemporary and fellow art historian Ellis Waterhouse noted this as an important element in Blunt's maturing into a Poussin scholar. In a short memoir prefaced to Blunt's 1967 *festschrift*, Waterhouse also suggestively noted something that would only later make full sense. As Waterhouse innocently wrote:

> It was at Trinity, Cambridge, that the style of his mind was formed. The imprint of the Cambridge of that decade on her sons is something which perhaps only an Oxford man can fully savour – and that thirty years later, for, as was normal for Oxford men of that generation, it never occurred to me to visit Cambridge . . .

Exposed as a former Soviet agent in 1979, Blunt's place was made clear in what the writer Andrew Boyle has called the "climate of treason" which he delineated in the Cambridge of the 1930s. Had Waterhouse taken the trouble to travel to the Fens he might have been rather surprised to learn of the turn of his schoolfriend's mind, although this would have involved him in the improbable feat of penetrating the inner circles of the Apostles, the élite and highly secretive debating society of which Blunt had early become a member.

Waterhouse also wrote in 1967 that "It is not fashionable now to recall the thirties with approval, but there was much to be said for them". If Cambridge formed the style of Blunt's mind, the politics of the 1930s furnished it. The son of an Anglican clergyman, Blunt absorbed the new faith of Marxism in a period of fascist growth which could only have aided a burgeoning admiration for revolutionary Russia. There was nothing unusual in Blunt's conversion. What singled him out was his decision to work for the Soviets, to act as a "mole" throughout the period of the Second World War and beyond, and to aid and abet Donald Maclean and Guy Burgess, the "Cambridge Spies", whose defections to Moscow in 1956 (the year of the Suez crisis) followed by that of Kim Philby in 1963 (the year of the Profumo affair) marked a great change in the otherwise rather complacent atmosphere of post-Second World War Britain. The defection of Philby led to Blunt's reluctant confession to MI5 in 1964, when he was granted immunity from prosecution and a "Royal Pardon". When confronted by his actions in 1979, Blunt claimed that his betrayal had been a matter of conscience when the political map of Europe had been unpropitious for those who saw themselves as liberals and reformers. That this thoroughly establishment figure, a Fellow of the British Academy, longstanding Director of the Courtauld Institute and, ironically, Keeper of the Queen's Pictures, should have been of all clichéd things, a Soviet agent, was difficult to accept in the changing world of a Britain whose new Prime Minister, Margaret Thatcher, had felt ready to reveal Blunt's treachery when journalists and spy watchers had all but sniffed him out. The results were all too inevitable: he was stripped both of his knighthood and his fellowship of the British Academy, the latter leading to A. J. P. Taylor's resignation as a fellow in disgust at what he considered to be the shabby treatment of a scholar whose scholarship was untainted by his secret life as a spy. Just what was lost by these revelations, and how influential Blunt had been in his chosen field is nicely summarized by Waterhouse, who also marked the changes in the acceptance of the seriousness of art history in a country which had not always rated it as an academic subject. It is, perhaps, not too fanciful to detect a shadow of Blunt the establishment "mole" in Waterhouse's depiction, and the word "recruits" acquires particular resonance in this connection:

> Before the war the Courtauld had something of the air of a curiosity in the London scene: by the end of the war, as a result of the change in our sense of values, it had almost inevitably become a force . . . The Courtauld, under Anthony's directorship, has trained recruits for the country's Museums, Universities and Art schools, as well as for the art trade, and the various sides are now very much concerned with the same standards than could have been said before . . . But it is teaching as much by example as by precept, and the qualities of intellect and moral integrity which are the foundation of his books and lectures are conveyed to pupils willing to absorb them without pressure or any parade of doctrine.

Although many could only read such words with a sense of irony after the exposure of 1979, many of Blunt's pupils continued (and continue) to concur with Waterhouse's judgement, and A. J. P. Taylor was plainly at one with them.

Was Taylor right in his judgement of Blunt's scholarship? Was it untainted by his covert beliefs? Did Blunt's actions not inform his interpretation of Poussin's work as a painter and a thinker? In an article arising from the splendid 1994–5 quatercentenary exhibition of Poussin's paintings, Marc Fumaroli, a professor at the Collège de France, accused Blunt of attributing to Poussin a mentality which was more applicable to himself as a spy long taken to the establishment's bosom. According to Blunt, Poussin was an outsider who adhered to the philosophy of Neo-Stoicism, a man leading a double life of apparent respect to the religious and cultural status quo but who found consolation in a revival of a pagan philosophy which divided him from the views of the common herd. As Fumaroli put it:

> There is little doubt that Blunt was tempted to attribute the double life of the spy to Poussin, his favourite subject throughout his life, suggesting that he was apparently perfectly adapted to his surroundings, while in his heart betraying it for a cause known only to himself and a handful of confederates.

According to Fumaroli, Blunt was identifying his own position with that of Pousssin, and thereby crucially misunderstanding him. Poussin, Fumaroli insists, was a devout Catholic whose Christian Neoplatonism was common within a learned and open circle in Rome, where the artist lived and worked, and that his painterly ideals were very much those of a French tradition of religious thought expressed in art. Fumaroli felt that this realization of the essentially Christian nature of Poussin's art and thought was "enough to demolish Blunt's notion of him as an Enlightenment spy, carefully disguised behind a façade of Stoical caution in Papal Rome".

The image of Poussin which Fumaroli attributes to Blunt is an image which the playwright Alan Bennett used to depict Blunt himself in his play *A Question of attribution*, which, at a pivotal moment, confronts Blunt with his erstwhile employer, the Queen, who engages in gentle but revealing badinage over the question of fakes. By this time, the late 1980s, Blunt had begun to serve his turn as an image of what the "establishment" managed to cover up, and what it means to betray that "establishment". Blunt's portrayal of Poussin's thought is not quite so exposed, but it does contain something of that sense of immanent danger. This is not to say that his criticism of Poussin can *only* be understood in this way, not least since so much recent Poussin scholarship remains indebted to him as the premier historian in the field. What can be said is that Blunt's personality and experience definitely informed his appreciation of Poussin's life and work. Oscar Wilde once famously declared that "All criticism is a form of autobiography", and this considerably illuminates Blunt's discussion of Poussin.

Blunt was above all an intellectual, a position which notoriously put him at odds with the attitudes of all too many of his countrymen. His reading of Poussin was conducted largely in terms of an intellectual appreciating the mind of a fellow-intellectual. This approach to Poussin is not without its critics, and Denis Mahon, in a study inspired by the 1960 Poussin exhibition which had been largely organized by Blunt, made some formidably trenchant criticisms of Blunt's treatment of the artist's work. Mahon wanted to draw attention back to Poussin as an artist, and it was his stated intention to understand Poussin as a *painter* rather than as a scholar or an intellectual. Interestingly, Mahon's criticisms have gained much acceptance, and his delineation of Poussin's progress as a painter has won him many admirers as a connoisseur with a uniquely attentive and penetrating eye. Mahon also demonstrated his possession of other essential desiderata of an art historian: a good knowledge of the subject-matter of art in the early modern period, principally classical mythology and episodes from the Bible; a thorough grounding in the learning of the period he studied; awareness of the iconography then in use; and an immersion in the scholarship in the field of art history which developed in Germany in the nineteenth century. Mahon describes himself as having sat at the feet of Nikolaus Pevsner, famous now as the author of critical studies of the architecture of the English counties, but, in the 1930s, a recently arrived refugee from Hitler's Germany lecturing on the Italian Baroque at the Courtauld Institute. Similarly, the world-famous Warburg Institute had been transplanted to London from its German base in Hamburg as a result of the rise of Nazism. Art history was just one of the fields of scholarship which grew in Britain as a result of the work of émigré scholars fleeing fascism. Once again, one can see how Blunt's commitment to the hitherto neglected discipline of art history was significantly affected by the tense politics of the 1930s.

Art history of the type encouraged by the German-inspired teaching of the Warburg and Courtauld Institutes emphasized its connection with intellectual history. Blunt's work on Poussin has much in common with the trade of the intellectual historian, and it is from this perspective, rather than from that of the trained art historian, that the present essay is written. Art history and intellectual history are frequently closely allied as modes of historical enquiry, and this becomes a necessary union in the case of an artist such as Poussin, known to several of his contemporaries as the painter-philosopher, "le peintre-philosophe".

It was with Poussin's ideas, and those of the circle in which he moved in the Rome of the 1630s through to the 1660s, that Blunt was most concerned, although, naturally, it was how these ideas were reflected in Poussin's paintings that principally exercised him. A great deal of the work on Poussin is thus given over to an analysis of Poussin's Stoicism, his supposed commitment to the ancient philosophy which was growing in vogue in early seventeenth-century intellectual circles. Blunt stressed that this was for Poussin an ethical rather than a metaphysical system: it was how this philosophy of resignation and loyalty to friends affected his relations with the world that preoccupied Poussin, and not grander questions of the nature of reality. It is not difficult to read in Blunt's depiction of Poussin something akin to a disclosure of his own secret life of commitment to an ethical and political system, Marxism, at odds with that followed by most of his contemporaries. Friendship, central to the Stoic ethic, was also vital to the Cambridge world in which Blunt had grown up: it was, after all, E. M. Forster who famously asserted that, if asked to choose between betraying his country and betraying a friend, he hoped that he would have the courage to betray his country.

As Blunt's life developed in what must have been to him an increasingly disappointing atmosphere of the post-Second World War flurry of active, Cold War anti-Communism, one senses a hint of fellow-feeling in his distillation of Poussin's experiences in the 1640s: "Resignation in the face of misfortune is a theme to which Poussin frequently returns in his letters." Similarly, he draws back from portraying an apolitical Poussin in a language that could once again be used to describe his own position: "The fact that Poussin believed that a wise man should keep out of politics does not mean that he had no views on them. His code is on the whole a simple one, based on a love of peace and fear of any disturbance." Other instances of this kinship abound in Blunt's study of an artist he had held in high regard since childhood, as, for instance, when he wrote that "This picture of the grave, deliberate, and serious artist, living apart from the world and contemplating it with detachment and even a little scorn, was something of a rarity in the Baroque period". Poussin's attitude, again like Blunt's, may have weakened his prospects, but he gained a peace of soul from it: "He sacrificed much, but he achieved *tranquillitas animi.*"

The commitment to the Communist cause which was nurtured amongst a self-selecting band in the Cambridge of the 1920s and 1930s can also, perhaps, be discerned in Blunt's image of the commitment to Stoicism which flourished in a circle dominated by a friend of Poussin in early seventeenth-century Rome:

> Cassiano del Pozzo and his friends seem to have formed a close group of enthusiastic students living apart from the main stream of political and ecclesiastical life, and pursuing their interests in peace and quiet; and it was into this haven that Poussin was drawn . . .

If such a reading is permissible, then might Blunt be seen as lamenting the failure of his fellow-intellectuals to effect the political changes they had desired when he declares that "the world in which Cassiano del Pozzo and his friends were at home, [was] the world of allegory rather than that of physical reality"? There certainly does seem to be more than a hint of self-identification in Blunt's portrayal of the older Poussin, who had "become even more completely detached from the world than in the middle period of his life; he lived only for his art and for the company of a very restricted circle of friends who really understood him". If this claim was true in the mid-1960s, when only *very* few people were aware of Blunt's treachery, then how much more true was it of his life after the public exposure in 1979?

However one might choose to interpret the details of Blunt's deeply personal engagement with Poussin, it cannot be doubted that the specifically Cambridge elements in his understanding of art history inform this book-length study. This would have come as no surprise to Ellis Waterhouse, who noted the importance of the Cambridge classicist Andrew Gow on Blunt's development as an art historian. Furthermore, the impact of Fry's introduction of post-Impressionism was also registered by implication, this time in the conclusion to the study:

> The great tendency during the present century toward an intellectual approach to painting has inevitably brought with it a return of interest in Poussin. The doctrines of the Cubists and of a certain number of nonrepresentational schools are close to Poussin's ideas on art, and some of them claim descent from him through Cézanne.

It is possible, then, to place Blunt's reading of Poussin into a firmly historical perspective. What does this tell one about the relationship between intellectual history and art history?

Blunt's own work demonstrates the potential richness of the intellectual historian's approach to the arts; a reading of Blunt's work in terms of his own, personal history also demonstrates the importance of historicizing the assumptions of historians themselves. Historians frequently identify with their subject-matter, and the relationship between Poussin's supposed Stoicism and Blunt's Marxism may best be understood as such a fruitful collusion. Without its interpreters the past is merely inert, and without intellectual passion it is all too easily lost from the view afforded by the present. This can have a tragic as well as a liberating effect, a lesson that may well be present in Poussin's Arcadian paintings.

Blunt considered the "Et in Arcadia Ego" paintings to be a firmly Stoical lesson in the transience of innocent pleasure, enacted in the shade of mortality. Scholars have been much concerned with understanding these most complex of paintings, and one of the most rewarding, if difficult interpretations of the Louvre version was made by the French semiotician, Louis Marin. In the conclusion to his essay "Towards a theory of reading in the visual arts: Poussin's *The Arcadian Shepherds*", Marin made a claim about the past that might usefully be borne in mind when considering the nostalgia for the lost commitments of the 1930s that seems to inform Blunt's analysis of Poussin's resignedly constant Stoicism:

> *Et in Arcadia Ego* could be read as a message sent by Poussin in order to signify that from the representation of death – that is, the writing of history – to representation as death as delight, history in the history painting is our contemporary myth.

The pleasure of writing history is, then, to be considered as a distinctly aesthetic pleasure, albeit one necessarily fraught with an irreparable sense of loss.

Marin wrote about Poussin with a knowledge derived from an extensive acquaintance with the wider intellectual world of seventeenth-century France. He was especially conversant with the ideas of Port-Royal, an intellectual circle whose brightest star was Blaise Pascal. Pascal's *Pensées* were studied

157

by another Marxist scholar, Lucien Goldmann, in terms of a sense of tragedy stronger than any conveyed by Poussin. Pascal, it has to be admitted, was undoubtedly suspicious of painting: "Quelle vanité que la peinture qui attire l'admiration par la ressemblance des choses, dont on n'admire point les originaux!" ("How vain painting is, exciting admiration by its resemblance to things of which we do not admire the original!" Translation by Alban Krailsheimer).

> Mien, tien.
> Ce chien est à moi, disaient ces pauvres enfants. C'est là ma place au soleil.
> Voilà le commencement et l''image de l''usurpation de toute la terre.

> (Pascal)

> Mine, thine. "This is my dog," said these poor children. "That is my place in the sun." There is the origin and image of universal usurpation. (Translation by Alban Krailsheimer.)

Blaise Pascal was almost thirty years younger than Poussin, dying young in 1662, a few years before his older contemporary. Similarly, Lucien Goldmann was some six years younger than Anthony Blunt, dying prematurely at the age of fifty-seven in 1970. Goldmann was a Rumanian scholar who fled from the Nazis to Switzerland, becoming an eminent academic in post-Second World War Paris. A Marxist humanist, Goldmann was always an anti-Stalinist, having been so long before this was generally acceptable amongst members of the Communist Party. It would be interesting to compare his views with those of Blunt on this matter; the beliefs of the spy, however, are difficult to reconstruct, and hearsay is never a particularly valuable source in constructing reliable histories. Four years after Blunt had made his private confession to MI5, Goldmann was revelling in the *événements* of 1968 in Paris, optimistic that the way to his version of market socialism was being opened in this brief revolutionary uprising of workers and students.

That heady mood was far from apparent in 1956, when Goldmann produced his study of Pascal and the tragic vision, *Le Dieu Caché* (*The Hidden God*). Influenced both by the Marxist aesthetic and literary theory developed by Lukàcs, and the psychology of his Swiss friend Jean Piaget, Goldmann sought to develop in his work on Pascal an ideal of the "transindividual subject" in cultural and historical action. In a development of the Marxist theory of history, Goldmann attempted to develop an intellectual history of what he called the "tragic vision" and its resolution into some form of realistic hope which could be traced from Greek drama to Pascal, and thence from Kant to Hegel and Marx. Aware that this was very much an experiment in historical and philosophical method, Goldmann noted that "Both philosophers and historians are concerned with the same facts, but they approach them from different points of view and with different ends in mind".

158

The tragic vision was one which rejected rationalism and empiricism on the grounds that they were both deeply unsatisfactory means of understanding the world, being both amoral and irreligious. The tragic vision was a return to morality and religion, especially as religion involved a widening of the set of values which transcended the mere individual, whose perspective was otherwise cherished by rationalism and empiricism. For Pascal this transcendence was only to be found in God, since individualism led only to selfishness and irresponsibility (as can be appreciated from the fragment in the *Pensées* quoted at the head of this section). For Goldmann, this transcendence was to be achieved in the dialectic of history as this unfolded in the hopes of Marxist humanism. While Pascal was confident only of the ultimate consolation of religion and faith in God, Goldmann paralleled this in what one might call a nostalgic appeal to the Marxist future. Pascal famously wagered that worldly rewards could be foregone in favour of belief in the existence of a God who rewarded His followers with the pleasures of Heaven, allowing Goldmann to make an explicit comparison with the earthly *telos* of Marxism:

> Marxist faith is faith in the future which men make for themselves in and through history. Or, more accurately, in the future that we must make ourselves by what we do, so that this faith becomes a "wager" which we make that our actions will, in fact, be successful.

Such parallels were drawn from Goldmann's claim that Pascal's *Pensées* constituted the first expression of a coherently tragic vision in Western thought, a vision which fed into the dialectical theories of Hegel and Marx. For Goldmann, Pascal was the first modern man, and his image of a universal man made possible "a new ethic that is still awaiting its full realisation". Just as Goldmann and his fellow Marxists were confident that the revolutionary potential of humanity was knowable and yet tantalisingly distant, so for Pascal the realization that God "should be always absent and always present is the real centre of the tragic vision".

Pascal's famous wager on the existence of God was translatable as a profound insight which similarly informed Marxist dialectic. For Pascal, faith justified itself as a wager on the ultimate reality of God as being greater than merely worldly rewards. By choosing to believe, the Christian conquered lower passions and became honest, humble and devoted to good works. The Christian had gained something certain and infinite for which nothing had been paid. For Goldmann, a secularized version of Pascal's ultimate hope readily transformed tragedy into something essentially positive in this synthesis of otherwise disparate elements:

> Risk, possibility of failure, hope of success and the synthesis of these three in the form of a faith which is a wager are the essential constituent elements in the human condition. It is certainly not the least of Pascal's

titles to glory that he was the first man to bring them explicitly into the history of philosophical thought.

Pascal was no proto-Marxist in this interpretation, and Goldmann properly appreciated his subject's essentially conservative social and political temper. More importantly, Pascal was presented as a theorist of the human condition whose vision fed into a resolution of that plight in directions which he could not have foreseen. As Goldmann expressed it:

> One could certainly show today that the historical wager on the future existence of the human community (in socialism) also possesses all these qualities; that, like Pascal's Christianity, it is incarnation, the joining up of opposites, and the fitting of ambiguity into a pattern that makes it clear and meaningful.

As with Blunt's reading of Poussin's Stoicism in terms reminiscent of his own earlier commitment to Marxism, so for Goldmann Pascal's explicitly Christian vocabulary informed his own hope in the Marxist dialectic. It is now generally considered somewhat jejune to draw parallels between Christianity and Marxism, but they certainly exist, and this consolation in an ultimate resolution of current tragedy into future hope, known both to Christians and to some Marxists as the *"eschaton"*, is clearly to be seen in Goldmann's appeal to Pascal's thought. There can be no doubt that Goldmann's reading of Pascal is a controversial one; at times it is downright eccentric. It is important to realise, however, that it is very much the work of a philosopher rather than an historian. Indeed, much the least satisfactory aspect of this study is Goldmann's attempt to relate Jansenism – the revival of the teachings of St Augustine on the disputed and highly technical questions of grace – to the socio-political conditions of the *noblesse de robe*, from which group came many of Jansenism's most famous sympathisers, in the mid-seventeenth century. As Robin Briggs, a recent historian of Jansenism has remarked, it was primarily a religious and an intellectual movement: its "sociological" appeal to particular groups therefore requires a good deal more subtle and detailed refinement than Goldmann was prepared to elaborate.

Parallels have played a considerable part in the argument of this essay, and it is obvious that more could be made of the parallels between the lives of two seventeenth-century French Christian intellectuals than those of two twentieth-century European Communists (one signally more committed than the other), whose major works concerned appreciations of the achievements of those earlier lives. A sense of tragedy pervades all four of these men: Poussin's awareness of its essential role in human lives; Pascal's development of it as the centre of his religious understanding; Blunt's treachery and its great personal costs; Goldmann's fleeing both Nazis and Stalinists, and dying in the wake of the delusive hopes of the defeated *soixante-huitards*.

Much the strongest link between the four was described by Goldmann when developing his Lukàcs-derived notion of the tragic vision: "there is only one way of entering the world of tragedy: by conversion". All four of the subjects of this essay, like so many of their contemporaries, were converts, Poussin to Stoicism, Pascal to a profoundly Augustinian version of Christianity, Blunt and Goldmann (albeit of differing levels of intensity) to Marxism.

If, as Fukuyama and his ilk claim, we are entering the end of history (in altogether less dramatic terms than those foreseen by Pascal and Goldmann), then not the least of the probable consequences is an end to the impulse to conversion, and with it a dynamic that it would be truly tragic to lose. One of Goldmann's most appreciative critics is Alasdair MacIntyre, who described him as "the finest and most intelligent Marxist of his age". MacIntyre, a philosopher and an historian of philosophy, has himself recently converted to Roman Catholicism, and his writings on private and public philosophy reflect this change. Perhaps the dialectic of history has played a trick on Goldmann full of appropriately Pascalian irony, with Christianity gaining new converts as Communism loses its ideological grip in Europe and North America. Either way, the disappearance of Christianity and of Communism remains a somewhat distant prospect. This study of one of the interesting twentieth-century byways of the relationship between the history of Christianity and Marxist historiography is offered in confirmation of the essential vitality of both perspectives.

Suggestions for further reading

For some sense of the world of Bloomsbury in this context, and for an astute analysis of the Cambridge which produced Blunt and other spies, see Noel Annan, *Our Age: Portrait of a Generation* (London: Weidenfeld & Nicolson, 1990). For a vehemently condemnatory account, see Andrew Boyle, *The Climate of Treason* (London: Hutchinson, 1979), the second edition of which in 1980 finally revealed his part in the unmasking of Blunt in 1979. For the significance of Denis Mahon's work, see Michael Kitson, "Sir Denis Mahon: Art Historian and Collector", in Gabriele Finaldi and Michael Kitson, *Discovering the Italian Baroque: The Denis Mahon Collection* (London: National Gallery Publications, 1997), pp. 8–21. For Mahon's technical criticisms of Blunt as a Poussin scholar, see *Poussiniana: afterthoughts arising from the exhibition held May–August 1960 at the Louvre* (Paris: Gazette des beaux-arts, 1962). The seminal work by Anthony Blunt on Poussin, first published in 1967, is now available in a single-volume edition, *Nicolas Poussin* (London: Pallas Athene, 1995). For further work on Poussin which engages with Blunt's interpretation, see Elizabeth Cropper and Charles Dempsey, *Nicolas Poussin: Friendship and the Love of Painting* (Princeton: Princeton University Press, 1996), and Marc Fumaroli, "Prayers for a secret Platonist", *The Times Literary Supplement*, October 7th 1994, pp. 22–3. For some appreciation of Blunt by a fellow art historian, who was also his contemporary at Marlborough, see Ellis Waterhouse, "A Personal preface" to *Studies in Renaissance and Baroque Art presented to Anthony Blunt on his 60th birthday* (London: Phaidon, 1967), pp. ix–xi. Alan Bennett's *A Question of Attribution* has been published with the play with which it was originally paired, *An Englishman Abroad*, as *Single Spies* (London: Faber, 1991). *An Englishman Abroad* is concerned with Blunt's colourful Cambridge contemporary, Guy Burgess. For a challengingly theoretical approach to Poussin, see Louis Marin, *To Destroy Painting* (English translation of *Détruire la peinture*), (Chicago: University of Chicago Press, 1995), and the same author's "Towards a theory of reading in the visual arts: Poussin's *The Arcadian Shepherds*" in Norman Bryson (ed.), *Calligram: Essays in New Art History from France* (Cambridge: Cambridge University Press, 1988), pp. 63–90. Marin also wrote perceptively on Pascal, see especially "Réflexions sur la notion de modèle chez Pascal" in *Etudes Sémiologiques: écritures, peintures* (Paris: Klincksieck, 1971), pp. 189–208. For some understanding of the structuralism used by Marin, see Jonathan Culler, *Structuralist Poetics: structuralism, linguistics and the study of literature* (London: Routledge & Kegan Paul, 1975). The best single-volume edition of Pascals' *Pensées* is that edited by Louis Lafuma (Paris: Pléiade, 1962). The English translation of the *Pensées* made by Alban Krailsheimer, which I have used in this essay, is available as a Penguin Classics edition (Harmondsworth: Penguin, 1966); Krailsheimer also provided a good study of Pascal in the Oxford Past Masters series, *Pascal* (Oxford: Oxford University Press, 1980). The major work by Goldmann is *The Hidden God: a study of tragic vision in the Pensées of Pascal and the tragedies of Racine* (English translation of *Le Dieu Caché*), (London: Routledge & Kegan Paul, 1964). For appreciation of Goldmann on Pascal, see Alasdair MacIntyre, "Pascal and Marx: on Lucien Goldmann's *Hidden God*" in *Against the Self-Images of the Age: Essays on ideology and philosophy* (London: Duckworth, 1971), pp. 76–87, and Mitchell Cohen, *The Wager of Lucien Goldmann: Tragedy, Dialectics, and a Hidden God* (Princeton: Princeton University Press, 1994). For a recent appraisal of the religious atmosphere of Le Grand Siècle see Robin Briggs, "The catholic puritans: Jansenists and rigorists in France" and "*Idées* and *mentalités*: the case of the catholic reform movement in France" in *Communities of Belief: Cultural and social tension in early modern France* (Oxford: Clarendon Press, 1989), pp. 339–63, and pp. 364–80. For a study which analyzes the religious context in which the work of both Pascal and Poussin was undertaken, see Henry Phillips, *Church and culture in seventeenth-century France* (Cambridge: Cambridge University Press, 1997). On the "end of history thesis" see Francis Fukuyama, *The End of History and the Last Man* (London: Hamilton, 1992). I am grateful, as ever, to Mishtooni Bose for commenting on an earlier draft of this essay.

✦

Chapter Thirteen

Bernard Bailyn and the scope of American history

Colin Brooks

I want in this essay to use the example of the works of the American historian, Bernard Bailyn, to provide illustrations of some of the characteristic questions which agitate historians: how do they define the questions they ask? How do they delimit their subject? From what standpoint do they approach their material? And on what grounds do they disagree with each other? First, I discuss the focus and the lines of development in Bailyn's work. Secondly, I show how Bailyn has attempted to get a particular purchase on that most slippery of subjects, "American history", and to indicate the disputes that exist, less over the question of whether his way of encompassing early American history makes disciplinary sense than as to whether the leverage it gives is not only partial but also morally inappropriate for the needs of contemporary America. Thirdly, I outline the strengths and the limitations of his approach, in particular with respect to the questions of "American exceptionalism", and of the aptness of a celebratory tone in writing about early America. Finally, I suggest that Bailyn's work leads naturally into consideration of a further central question posed by the American experience: how do, and why should, independent citizens submit themselves to government? How can authority be established in America?

Bailyn was born in Connecticut in 1922. An undergraduate at Williams College in Massachusetts, he served in the United States Army at the end of the Second World War. He then went to Graduate School at Harvard University, was appointed to the History department there in 1949: he served continuously on the faculty until his retirement in 1987. He is a New Englander through and through, but he comes from a family whose origin in the United States was actually very recent and he married into a family who were emigrants from Germany during the Second World War. So, he has very much a sense of place within the United States, but also, very close at hand, the experience of emigration and that sense of exile, of loss, but also of promise, of starting afresh, that comes with emigration. From his own circumstances, it was natural that two historical questions became central for him: what creates a nation and a national culture? And how do individuals and families situate themselves within that nation?

Early in his academic career, Bailyn identified three areas of interest which came to dominate his scholarly life. The first was that of the relationship between European and American life, and the linked question of the transmission of culture between closely related peoples but across space and in conditions of primitive technology. The technological continuity and constraint is exemplified by the fact that communication between the old and the new changed very little from the first voyages of discovery at the end of the fifteenth century through to the arrival of steamships around the 1820s and 1830s. The same is largely true of print technology before the invention of the steam press. Bailyn's whole period is in a particular technological band.

The second issue that interested Bailyn was the transition between pre-modern and modern worlds. He never had much use for the word "traditional", nor for the notion behind it. From the start Bailyn accepted that American society (the society of the Europeans in what was to them a New World) was pre-modern, but also that it was never traditional in the sense that, for example, some peasant societies in Eastern and Central Europe might have been considered traditional. And Bailyn has not been interested – and defiantly so – in the supposed condition of post-modernity. So what he has done essentially is to explore the multifarious ways in which what he terms a pre-modern world is changing fast, in the seventeenth, eighteenth and early nineteenth centuries, into a modern world. Bailyn has spoken of

> the fascination . . . of early modern history: the long era of transition to modernity – far enough away to provide a deep perspective on the present and to isolate critical turning points, yet close enough to modernity for one to recognize elements of a familiar world in their original form.

Thirdly, he has always attended to the interplay between social and cultural history and, within the latter, to the tension between cultural and intellectual history. He embodied a cultural turn long before it became fashionable to proclaim its arrival. But then he has always practised craft and applied common sense, not theory, and has abhorred "self-conscious intellectual posturing": there are glimpses of an Elton within Bailyn.

In each of these areas of investigation Bailyn was guided by two beliefs which he took from the historian Sir Lewis Namier, another emigré, living and working in England. First, he realized the centrality for the historian of uncovering "the informal structure by which social groups [compete] for state power". Secondly, he came to appreciate that reality outruns not only ideas but also commonplaces, and that the maladjustment between reality and assumption, prejudice, principle and idea sometimes becomes too great – and that, when that happens, customs and practices which have been taken for granted are suddenly questioned. Bailyn argued that some people (but not, note, a particular social class) accept the implications of such new social reality, while others cannot face up to its challenge. It was ultimately in this way that he came to think about the origins of the American Revolution, and to lay bare that revolution's implications. The circumstances of life in eighteenth-century America had become divorced from the principles by which people believed that they were living, and, indeed, by which they were formally living – and constrained (i.e. within a monarchical empire). At a certain moment the maladjustment between the lived reality and the (constraining) inherited principles was so great that some people tipped the balance and, accepting the implications of the new reality, embraced that "contagion of liberty" which was to produce the United States. Others could not face up to that challenge and they became the loyalists of the Revolution. I will say more about that, about the tragedy of men of good intentions, who choose what is apparently the wrong side, later.

Most of Bailyn's work has been on what a great historian, Charles M. Andrews, in the 1920s called *The colonial period of American history*. Now whether that title is apt, I am not sure. But that expression – the colonial period – tends, if the historian is not especially careful and especially imaginative, to narrow the focus of study down to the relationship of white settler and white governor. It becomes all too easy for such an approach to omit not only the central fact of slavery and the burden of race, but also to neglect the whole question of the interaction between those already occupying what we came to know as the New World and the European invaders of the fifteenth to the seventeenth century. Much teaching of "American history" in American universities in the last ten years has shifted dramatically away from concentrating on the role of Europeans in America to becoming a study, almost a meditation, on the impact of the existing inhabitants, native "Americans", on those purported discoverers. The whole word "discovery" has been analyzed, called into question, consigned in some cases to the scrap heap: it was merely that the Europeans discovered a continent which had been very well known for very many generations beforehand.

It is worth setting out the questions with which Bailyn has been concerned in the Anglo-American relationship of the pre-Revolutionary period. It is easy to say Anglo-American, but that needs qualifying at both ends: because he has really been concerned with Britain rather than merely England (that tension, of course, is always with us, not least in the European Cup, the World Cup and the Olympic Games!) and because he is not concerned just with that part of North America that became the United States, but with British North America, an even vaster expanse which stretched right through the West Indies and up to Hudson's Bay. Bailyn has concentrated on five aspects of that relationship: first, the integration of the North American provinces into British political and cultural life, or the reintegration by people who had emigrated; secondly, their subsequent separation from that political and cultural life and the implications of that separation for the nature of the subsequent American polity; thirdly, the dissolution of that cultural and political life; fourthly, the repudiation by those on the verge of becoming Americans of that life and its values; and fifthly, the replacement of those values by what might be understood as authentic American values, with all the richness and poverty of approach that that implies.

Bailyn shows that the political and cultural life inherited from the Old World could not (however hard settlers and promoters of settlement tried, right through to the 1770s) be sustained in the New. In the conditions of the New World the authority of property could not hold because, providing the individual had the confidence to confront the wilderness (what contemporaries intriguingly called "the skirts of civilisation"), they could always step westwards and avoid that authority. In these circumstances, the perpetuation of respect for, for example, age becomes the more remarkable. Generally, the blunt physical facts of the New World necessarily changed the culture of the people who arrived there.

So, from the very start America was a country, a nation, a place, in which authority was hard to sustain and independence was relatively easy to acquire. Historians differ in the way in which they balance the continuing purchase of English values on the New World settlers and the chilling and liberating impact of that physical (and, by European standards, empty) New World. And, for Bailyn, a double challenge is presented. First, that balance must be weighed. This is always an important task for Bailyn: hence his comment on abolitionism: "what strikes one [i.e. Bailyn] forcibly is not that Jefferson's generation did not get rid of slavery, but that so much was done at the time to eliminate it, even if it wasn't completely outlawed". But secondly, beyond that, the past, whether the English or the American past, is "a different world. The basic experiences are different from ours, yet they seemed to the people who experienced them then to be so normal that they did not record things that we would consider to be strange and particularly interesting". The exploration of the mundane presents a tough challenge: Bailyn cited in 1991, as I remember he had to me in 1967, the difficulty of our coming to terms with the smell of early modern life: the lack of smell, for example, renders unreal the experience of colonial Williamsburg.

Now Bailyn's British/American scene was wide-ranging and it is important to give some examples of the ways in which he approached and tackled it. It was maritime and mercantilist, it was joined by trade and, of course, it was an empire in which maritime and riverine connection always came naturally. The links largely went across the Atlantic and it was very difficult to develop links up, down and through what would become the United

States. Wind and tide essentially controlled communications around the Atlantic.

So Bailyn's is a maritime and mercantilist empire and a cultural world. His first exploration of the cultural shapes revealed by the pressures of quotodian economic life was his edition of an extraordinary text, *The Apologia of Robert Keayne*. Keayne, a seventeenth-century Boston merchant, a would-be strict Calvinist and a sometimes successful merchant, found it necessary when he came to sit down and write his will, to run on to 50,000 words, including an extensive explanation and justification for his past commercial practice: "Was the selling of 6d. nails for 8d. per lb. and 8d nails for 10d. per lb. such a crying and oppressing sin?" As an example of the compulsion of Calvinists to explain their activity, it is an extraordinary document.

Now the compulsion in many of these people is to explain everything. This becomes a very characteristic American phenomenon, which finds one outlet in a written constitution: there is a compulsion to write everything down and try and get everything clear and explained, and all eventualities covered. Of course it is a delusion: language and implication cannot be fixed. Does this mind-set betray a lack of confidence, the uncertainties masquerading as conviction, that might be characterized as provincial, as marginal?

Bailyn has always been attracted by the margin, the march. The frontier for many historians has to be written looking west: for Bailyn, the lived experience of the seventeenth- and eighteenth-century settlers largely hinged on facing east. These, he insists, were provinces. And in "England's cultural provinces: Scotland and America" an article of 1954 co-authored with John Clive, Bailyn made an attempt to define provincialism, to point out that the experience of the American Provinces was not unique and that in the seventeenth and eighteenth centuries Scotland and indeed, by extension, Ireland, felt alternately and simultaneously the attraction and the repulsion of the metropolis, London. London's attraction lay in its wealth, its civility. The repulsion was spurred by its corruption. The sense of shock felt by Americans, by provincials, when they visited London is quite palpable. The anti-metropolitan theme, exemplified by Jefferson, has remained central in American culture. With the exception of Philadelphia, itself perhaps only a twentieth the size of London, American towns were small, even tiny, places. If one were to attend the Pennsylvania legislature of the eighteenth century, one would knock on the door and enter almost directly. When, by way of contrast, Pennsylvanians went over to London seeking a favour, a decision, from the Board of Trade, they found the kernel of decision-makers surrounded by coarse layers of protecting fibre: doormen, porters, secretaries and the like. Gratuities oiled the complex path to power. England was easily stereotyped as a corrupt place. But it appeared a corrupt place because it was, by American provincial standards, such a vast place: it required guides and guidance: immediate access was not only culturally inappropriate but

167

also physically impossible. Whether it would be culturally appropriate in the United States was highly disputed: Andrew Jackson's high-minded, and snobbish, opponents deplored his throwing open the White House on Inauguration Day in 1829. And the apparent sale of access to the White House in return for donations, etc., remains an issue in the campaign against President Clinton.

A concern with the perception of corruption has been central to Bailyn's work on political culture. Bailyn is not and has never been a strictly polit-ical, or an institutional historian. His concern has been for the informal structures by which social groups competed for state power. He has writ-ten about the creation and ordering of an American political system, both on a colonial level (in an article on politics and social structure in colonial Virginia) and on a proto-national level in *The origins of American politics*. Here Bailyn is concerned not least to investigate the evolution of party and faction, and the debate over their legitimacy in America. This is a very important topic because the acceptance of party is tantamount to an acceptance of pluralism. Yet there is always within American history a tension between the belief that America is a plural society, in which one necessarily as well as willingly has to be tolerant of other creeds, views, and so on, and the belief that that all reasonable people should think alike. Bailyn's work should be read alongside another classic evaluation of the implications of New World settlement for the personalities of the settlers: Hector St. J. de Crèvecoeur, *Letters from an American farmer* (recently published in New York: Penguin, 1981).

And, finally, Bailyn has written about the ideological blanket that was cast over Anglo-America and then was sneaked, as it were away, from England and wrapped around America by Americans. He wrote about this in an essay called "Political experience and enlightenment ideas of 18th century America" and then, decisively, in *The ideological origins of the American revolution* which won the Pulitzer and Bancroft Prizes. This is not an ideal-istic interpretation, even though it is about ideology. Bailyn is not himself an ideologue. One blanket – "Americanism" – could not really cover the whole people. Many remain chilled while others were stifled by it. The point was the use that Americans made of the ideology available to them, how that intersected with lived experience and how people, as I said, were suddenly brought up short by what they had, often naturally and unthink-ingly, done. Indeed there is a sense in which Bailyn can be read as anti-intellectual, as emphasizing the ultimate spur to action of what he calls mundane exigencies and simple matters of social and political fact.

Bailyn is also interested – and this links in a sense with the anti-intellectual thread – in America as an opportunity for individual fulfilment. It is appro-priate that he turned from his *Ideological origins . . .* , with its conviction of the impact of the "contagion of liberty" on the whole people, to study the impact of the New World on individuals, and on a group. This project has not been completed, but its first stage has been marked by his extraordinary studies of what he termed *The Peopling of America*, *The Voyagers to the West* and *The Peopling of British North America*.

Intriguingly, while Bailyn's differing concentration on each of these topics over time has tended to mirror and reflect temporary occurrences in American society, at one level his has been a consensual view of the American past. He has not sought to make America the site of class struggle (though he has focused much of his enquiry on the devices which "social groups" use in their competition for "state power"), and as Gordon Wood rather ruefully acknowledged, Bailyn "seems to have developed a particular antipathy to social interpretations of the Revolution . . . The explanation of this aversion is not easy". Whether America is the site of class struggle; if not, why not; and whether the answer, no, implies a commitment to and a celebration of American exceptionalism, is a classic discussion, debate and argument within the American historical profession and indeed within the American people generally. Is America different? Why is there no socialism in America? Has there ever been a proletariat in America? Bailyn has endured to paint a picture of an America deeply indebted to the old world, but, under the pressures of distance and space, distance from the metropolis and space within the provinces, first unable, and then unwilling, to maintain the ties. Given the pressures of distance and space (and the consequential twists in the saga of the creation of a labour force, often of slaves), America necessarily became exceptional.

But, as well as being consensual from that point of view, Bailyn's has been a remarkably capacious view of the past (he himself has acknowledged the debt owed in this respect to the Jewish exiles from the Europe of the 1930s, "the least parochial people") and a remarkably humane vision and version of the multi-faceted creation of the American past. Throughout his career Bailyn has been keen to use agglomerations of material, and to deploy statistical analyses: but not as a goal in themselves, but rather as a way of revealing "categories" and "patterns", which can then be exemplified by an examination of "individual lives". For "in the end, one must talk about people, their activities and concerns". Bailyn has dealt both with what I am going to have to call the ordinary people, the common people, and also with the master theorists of the State. For Bailyn an important point is that all contribute to the definition and the experience of America and that includes the losers in the revolutionary – and the constitutional – struggle as well as the winners.

In this way Bailyn sets his face against what I think is the most awful passage I have read in 26 years of university teaching. The passage is in E. H. Carr's book "What is History?" (p. 126). Carr writes:

> History is, by and large, a record of what people did, not of what they failed to do: to this extent it is inevitably a success story . . . By and

169

large, the historian is concerned with those who, whether victorious or defeated, achieved something. I am not a specialist in the history of cricket. But its pages are presumably studded with the names of those who made centuries rather than of those who made ducks and were left out of the side.

Now I find that an extraordinarily patronizing and èlitist view of history. Historians, note, are terribly bad at writing about failure. They are, for example, much happier writing about MPs who get re-elected than MPs who don't. It is a bizarre compulsion that we have: I suspect that there is probably some kind of wish-fulfilment on our own part. Bailyn dealt with this issue about the "losers" in the Revolution struggle in his *The Ordeal of Thomas Hutchinson*, a biography of the Royal Governor of Massachusetts at the start of the Revolution. He depicts the fortunes of a conservative in a time of radical upheaval and deals with problems of public disorder and ideological commitment. Although Bailyn was actually writing in the late 1960s when Harvard students were doing terrible (and iconoclastic) things to authority outside his very window, it was not written as a tract for the times.

> It is part of the general effort I have been making over the past few years to develop a fuller picture of the origins of the American Revolution than we have had before and to exemplify an approach to history that emphasises balance over argument, context over consequences and the meaning of the past over the uses of the present.

This involves the elaboration of a tragic view of history. And this is important to Bailyn for, "if one can, up to a certain point, work sympathetically with the losers, one can – in some small part at least – overcome the knowledge of the outcome", that besetting sin, snare and delusion – anachronism. Thus one can speculate that it is not that he wrote his biography of Hutchinson because he objected to the activities of the student radicals of the late 1960s (although, of course, he might have done), but because he regarded as specious and anachronistic the often expressed claim to kinship with previous generations. Diana Trilling echoed this concern in 1971 lamenting the "marked shift . . . from an historical to a nonhistorical emphasis in instruction" since the 1930s. Quizzed as to her knowledge of the Spanish Civil War, one student told Trilling, "I don't know much [about it], but I do know enough to know it was our fault."

On the other hand, Bailyn is aware that "to explain – in depth and with sympathy – is, implicitly at least, to excuse". And it is for the historian to cut himself off, to sever the personal, if not the national, link between present and past:

> the historian, in his analysis and description, is no longer a partisan. He has no stake in the outcome. He can now embrace the whole of the

event, see it from all sides. What impresses him most are the latent
limitations within which everyone involved was obliged to act; the
inescapable boundaries of action; the blindness of the actors – in a
word, the tragedy of the event.

So Bailyn came to study what it is tempting to call the losers as well as
the winners in the revolutionary struggle and, as I say, this terribly difficult
and patronizing term, the ordinary people of America: to study what other
historians might call their "world view", or their "mental map". For example,
he exhumed the written remains of a Bostonian shopkeeper who rejoiced
in the name of Harbottle Dorr. Dorr did something that I think all of us
do at some stage in our lives, though he did it obsessively. He kept newspapers. Harbottle Dorr kept newspapers in Boston in the 1760s and 1770s
and put little messages at the top of them to remind him of the meanings
the news items had for him: Lord Bute is corrupt, the British Government
is tyrannical, standing armies are prohibited, etc, etc.

Bailyn's mercantile empire was made up not of principles, ideologies
or policies but of people, of individuals, of kin, of friends, enemies and
acquaintances struggling to keep in touch across the ocean, to make the
sum of Atlantic trade greater than its individual parts, and to come to terms
(as Harbottle Dorr tried) with the customs, values and prejudices of their
neighbours and their would-be masters. He was interested in the way in
which individuals interacted and tried to build and tried to perpetuate. But,
even though he was interested in the tension between, on the one hand,
building and perpetuation and, on the other, expansion and movement, his
was never just a Whig nor, despite claims to the contrary, a celebratory,
view of the past. Bailyn never held the view that the past was an improving
but inferior version of the present. He urges an analysis

> without any sense of inevitability or necessary progress; [critical
> transitions] have to be seen in all their complexity and with all the acci-
> dental, contingent elements highlighted – and . . . with no assumption
> that change means progress or that purpose determines outcome.

In Bailyn's view we must not expect too much of our ancestors: he points
to a comment by Rev. Andrew Elliott, who, at the crisis of independence,
could write "it is possible we may be mistaken, things may be very different
to others as upright as ourselves". That kind of sentiment, that tolerance,
is very important to Bailyn and it is in associating himself with such a
perspective that Bailyn has separated himself most decisively from more
impatient historians and from the movement for political correctness. Although Bailyn has insisted that "understanding early modern history gives
one a purchase on understanding the modern world" and he believes that
studying history "thoroughly and systematically [is essential] if our society

is to keep its sanity, its sense of reality and self-awareness", he is yet able to maintain that the past is just that, it is past. True historians "have an intellectual – but not a political or ideological – stake in the outcome" of their work. And we cannot impose our categories on people who were so unfortunate or so fortunate as not to have them at their disposal. That people in the past were confused and often fearful, Bailyn was not afraid to acknowledge: a criticism of his book on *The Ideological Origins* is that he has portrayed Americans as paranoid. He insists that they saw through a glass darkly, only subsequently coming to appreciate the implications, structural and ethical, of what they were doing. The consequence of that realisation was *transformation*, a word which appears often in his work, and which provides a chapter heading in *The Ideological Origins of the American Revolution*. This emphasis upon transformation separates him from those true consensus historians who have attempted to deny that there was a Revolution in and after 1776, but it is also this particular view of the Revolution that separates Bailyn from the Marxist and Marxist-leaning historians. For Bailyn insists that the Revolution was not a social Revolution and he has actually become increasingly strident in his repudiation of the idea that the Revolution was born of social dislocation and brought about social change in its wake. Bailyn argues that "the mind-set of the people who led the Revolution – merchants, politicians, planters, asnd preachers . . . were very broadly shared". This is a widely contested view.

Nor has Bailyn any truck with those who argue "that there is something immemorial, intrinsic to American life – a deep strain – that has always led to these kind of problems ['public problems with moral dimensions – poverty, social (including gender) inequalities, racism'] or that there was once a better world from which at some point we departed". Some of Bailyn's work has been criticized by historians on the left for its apparent glorification of an America characterized as white, middle class, achieving. For Bailyn, however, there is no ground for decrying past ages for not thinking in terms familiar to Arts faculties in and after the 1960s. Nor is there any justification for a refusal to come to terms with the past on its own terms: the past is another country and we are not responsible for it (although we have to live with its consequences).

Bailyn has been interested in American exceptionalism. But exceptionalism, he insists, has to be established, New World characteristics compared and contrasted with what held before, in the Old. In *The Ideological Origins . . .* , he argued that the particular cast of American thought had to be understood as taking off from its British predecessor. In *The Peopling of British North America*, he puts forward the propositions that:

> The peopling of British North America was an extension outward and an expansion in scale of domestic mobility in the lands of the immigrants'

origins, and the transatlantic flow must be understood within the context of these *domestic* mobility patterns

and that

> American culture in this early period becomes most fully comprehens-
> ible when seen as the exotic far western periphery, a marchland, of the
> metropolitan European culture system.

We see here the extraordinary scope of Bailyn's study and concern. Concentrating on core materials (e.g. the lists of emigrants to America, 1773–6),
he does not forget the context: the swirl of population mobility, beginning
"sometime in the early Middle Ages", that came to centre on "the massive
transfer to the Western Hemisphere of people from Africa, from the European
mainland, and above all from the Anglo-Celtic offshore islands of Europe,
culminating in what Bismarck called 'the decisive fact in the modern world',
the peopling of the North American continent". This passage has alarmed
Bailyn's critics. "What is strikingly absent . . . is any awareness of the historic significance of the non-Western world", wrote Appleby. "Reading the
book, I realized how strongly I felt about our collective responsibility to
write our own history with the consciousness that it is but one of many
histories". Bailyn, she fears, has patently refused her challenge to "American
historians [to] join other late-twentieth century writers in the endeavor to
stop making ours the culture of reference for the rest of the world". But
Bailyn explicitly flags the matter of Africa (e.g. in the third Proposition set
out above). Appleby's question ("why importance is attached to this group
of immigrants and not to a subset of 10,000 Africans who arrived in South
Carolina in the 1720s or to a subset of Irish who left for Pennsylvania during the famine years of 1727–30?") rests on a false polarity ("and not to").
Another reviewer, Kulikoff, points out that the subset of immigrants whose
careers Bailyn follows are those who became "communal leaders and those
who left letters and diaries, hardly a representative sample". These "success
stories" could, and should, have been placed in a more meaningful context.
Bailyn, therefore, has failed to attain the high standards he set for himself
in *Hutchinson*. While he does direct attention to fiasco, chaos and disaster,
it remains extraordinarily difficult to tell the stories of those who toiled in
vain, who did not marry, who left no descendants, whose families were
separated by war and economic pressure. Not all who did not succeed can
be written out of history as failures: but, for lack of evidence, their stories
often cannot be retrieved. Social mobility is usually easier to conceive of in
terms of upward mobility: that, after all, has been the experience of the
majority of University teachers in the post-war world. Downward mobility is
harder to discuss, and evidence is harder to come by. Social immobility is
even more testing as a theme. Only Richard Cobb has been able to convey
the sense that endurance, sticking it out in the face of the intolerable and

intrusive demands of ambitious men and grasping government, is itself a triumph, worthy of historical discussion, and, indeed, celebration.

Transformation, a realization of implication, took people into unexpected places and caressed them into adopting unexpected values. Revolutionary Americans moved on from liberty and independence, to anti-slavery, to a hostility to established churches, to democratic political structures and to Republican manners. And all of this, calling authority into question, suggested that Americans would be ungovernable, that independence was all-embracing and that America would be the nation of the young. Bailyn ends *The Ideological Origins* with this passage:

> seeds of sedition would constantly be sowed, and harvests of licentiousness reaped.
>
> How else could it end, what reasonable social and political order could conceivably be built and maintained where authority was questioned before it was obeyed, where social differences were considered to be incidental rather than essential to community order, and where superiority, suspect in principle, was not allowed to concentrate in the hands of the few but was scattered broadly through the populace? No-one could clearly say. But some, caught up in a vision of the future in which the peculiarities of American life became the marks of a chosen people, found in the defiance of traditional order the firmest of all grounds for their hope for a freer life, The details of this new world were not as yet clearly depicted; but faith ran high that a better world that any that had ever been known could be built where authority was distrusted and held in constant scrutiny; where the status of men flowed from their achievements and from their personal qualities, not from distinctions ascribed to them at birth; and where the use of power over the lives of men was jealously guarded and severely restricted. It was only where there was this defiance, this refusal to truckle, this distrust of all authority, political or social, that institutions would express human aspirations and not crush them.

So that was Bailyn's vision of the future afforded to confident Americans around 1800, but there is a dark side to this, of course. Americans were at that time deprived of external and hierarchical authority; authority which still sustains and constrains us here in the United Kingdom. Of course Americans sought to create constraints within themselves: Hector St. J. de Crèvecoeur's *Letters from an American Farmer* (1981) offers an extraordinary critique of the American, "this new man", whom he both loved and loathed. The sense of the cultural deprivation entailed by independence has nowhere been better expressed than by Henry James in his biography of Nathaniel Hawthorne. Bailyn can see that the absence of order and authority provided scope, possibility, flexibility. James provides a nice counterpart to Bailyn, indicating what is absent from the New World of America.

> one might enumerate the items of high civilisation, as it exists in other countries, which are absent from the texture of American life, until it should become a wonder to know what was left. No State in the European sense of the word, and indeed barely a specific national name. No Sovereign, no court, no personal loyalty, no aristocracy, no Church, no clergy, no army, no diplomatic service, no country gentlemen, no palaces, no castles, nor manors, nor old country-houses nor parsonages, nor thatched cottages, nor ivied ruins; no cathedrals, nor abbeys, nor little Norman churches; no great Universities nor public schools – no Oxford, nor Eton, nor Harrow; no literature, no novels, no museums, no pictures, no political society, no sporting class – no Epsom, nor Ascot! Some such list as that might be drawn up of the absent things in American life – especially in the American life of forty years ago, the effect of which upon an English . . . imagination, would probably, as a general thing, be appalling. The natural remark, in the almost lurid light of such an indictment, would be that if these things are left out, everything is left out. The American knows that a good deal remains; what it is that remains – that is his secret.

Bailyn has done more than most to reveal to us, from his profound, broad, and sympathetic understanding of the experience of settlers in the New World, just what lies behind the "American secret".

Suggestions for further reading

There is a bibliography of the writings of Bernard Bailyn in J. A. Henretta, M. Kammen and S. N. Katz (eds), *The Transformation of Early American History* (New York: Knopf, 1991), pp. 263–8. The best way to judge the impact of Bailyn's work is to read the reviews, especially those in the *William and Mary Quarterly*, the *Journal of American History*, and the *American Historical Review*: in her review of *The Peopling of British North America* and *Voyagers To The West*, Joyce Appleby categorized the books as "a sophisticated contribution to Whig history and an exuberant celebration of American exceptionalism": *William and Mary Quarterly*, 3rd series, **xliv**, p. 791, 1987. Bailyn's views on the nature of the historical profession and the obligations of the historian are quoted from his *On the Teaching and Writing of History*, E. C. Lathem (ed.), (Hanover, N. H., Dartmouth College, 1994). Bailyn's essay on Harbottle Dorr is in his *Faces of Revolution* (New York: Knopf, 1990).

Works by Bailyn's peers, relevant to the questions addressed in this essay, include E. S. Morgan, *American Slavery, American Freedom* (New

York: Norton, 1975); G. S. Wood, *The Creation of the American Republic* (Chapel Hill: University of North Carolina Press, 1969), and his *The Radicalism of the American Revolution* (New York: Knopf, 1992); I. K. Steele, *The English Atlantic, 1675–1740* (Oxford: Oxford University Press, 1986).

Chapter Fourteen

Writing women in: the development of feminist approaches to women's history

Gerry Holloway

Introduction

History is important to all human beings. The past is never dead or irrelevant. It shapes the present through our social, political, economic and cultural institutions and constructs our identity. The relationship between the past and the present is symbiotic. Our understanding of the past is shaped by that past. For, as E. H. Carr has explained to us in *What is history?*, our knowledge of the past is always partial and has been formed by groups who had the power to hand down to posterity their version of history. Consequently, our knowledge of history is always political, as are our ways of interpreting it.

Since Herodotus first began writing history around 450 BC, the construct of history has been a male product and has remained so for nearly 2,500 years. It has been the history of man, by man and for man and has played its part in the maintenance of patriarchal power. However, at specific points in the flux of economic, social and political change, there have been opportunities for subordinate groups to challenge the social and political order and offer new ideas for the future and revised versions of the past. In this century, the women's movement has been one such group and alongside its political, social and cultural challenges for the present, it has attempted to construct new understandings of the past. In this chapter, I will be examining the ways that the writing of British women's history has developed over the last thirty years and some of the different approaches that have evolved. I will then focus on a debate that is ongoing in feminist history circles. I shall conclude with a survey of the position of women's history in academia today.

A brief history of women's history

There are, I would argue, two conditions necessary for alternative readings of the past: first, a consciousness of a lack of knowledge and, secondly, the ways and means to produce alternative readings. In this country, in this century, at various points, both these conditions have been present and have given oppressed groups, such as women, the opportunity to challenge dominant readings of the past. With regard to recovering women's history, there have been two clear opportunities for women to challenge traditional forms of history – during the mass political movement of women in the early years of this century and since the Women's Liberation Movement of the 1970s.

However, even this assertion has been challenged. For example, Dale Spender in *Women of ideas and what men have done to them* has argued that until the last twenty years or so history has been written by men, about men and usually for men and that, mostly, these men were white academics. Spender is right when she argues that the omission of women from most history is a structural problem which has been built into the production of knowledge. Women have largely been excluded both as subjects and producers of history, and this exclusion is of tremendous significance both for women's consciousness and the way women are regarded in society. As Carr has argued, it is dominant groups which decide what is history. From a feminist perspective this means that it is men who have determined the parameters of history, decided what is problematic, significant, logical and reasonable and decreed who gets the funding to do the research. Further, Spender argues that not only have women been excluded from history, but that the process itself can enforce the "authority" of men and the "deficiency" of women. I will return to this issue later when I discuss the ways that gender has been constructed in conventional narratives.

Spender's position is, however, depressingly deterministic and overlooks an earlier group of women historians who tried to redress the gender bias of traditional history. Despite the odds being stacked against them, from time to time female historians have appeared and some have written about women's experiences. For example, the suffragist, Alice Clark, wrote *The working lives of women in the seventeenth century* in 1919 and Ivy Pinchbeck wrote *Women workers and the Industrial Revolution* in 1930. Both books are excellent empirical studies of the period, but offer us no theoretical framework and tend to reflect dominant notions of femininity. Similarly, there was a cluster of women suffragists writing in the 1920s and 1930s about the suffrage struggle – for example, Sylvia Pankhurst *The suffragette movement* and Ray Strachey *The cause*, but, useful as these are, they are written by interested parties and consequently suffer from the biases in favour of their own organizations that one would expect.

One of the first books to deal with women's exclusion from the production of history was written by an American, Gerda Lerner, *The majority finds its past*. In this book, Lerner examines the ways in which women have been written about historically. Further, in her essay "Women Lost and Found: The Impact of Feminism on History" Jane Lewis has argued that the writing of women's history can be divided into several developmental stages. First, there is the category which Natalie Zemon Davis in her article "Women in transition: the European case" has called the study of "women worthies". This refers to the chronicling of the lives of exceptional women such as Elizabeth I or Florence Nightingale or groups of women participating in exceptional activity, such as the suffragettes. This type of study has gone some way towards redressing the negative image of women that has emanated from their almost total exclusion from mainstream histories and, not surprisingly, this form of women's history still continues to be written. However, although it is important in contextualizing women in mainstream history, it still reflects traditional male concepts of the nature of history, and therefore ignores most of womankind.

An example of what I mean by "traditional concepts of the nature of history" can be seen in the ways in which two historians have chosen to write about the suffrage movement. Andrew Rosen's *Rise up women! The militant campaign of the women's social and political union* is an important account of the Women's Social and Political Union (WSPU) which appears on many course reading lists. Although he attempts to identify suffragettes by focusing on membership of the WSPU, he also follows a traditional approach which concentrates on the leadership's interaction with politicians and seeks to redefine militancy as a political strategy. This approach tends to be descriptive rather than explanatory. On the other hand, Susan Kingsley Kent seeks to explain the interrelationship between sexual politics and the demand for the vote and offers a more coherent explanation of, for example, Christabel Pankhurst's demand for "Votes for Women and Chastity for Men". This analysis demonstrates that Pankhurst was only echoing popular sentiment in the women's movement rather than deserving of being dismissed as merely typical of the bizarre preoccupation of a few misfits, as David Mitchell argues in *Queen Christabel*. Kent does not perceive the suffrage movement as purely a political strategy to enfranchise women, but regards the movement as a protest against the whole social condition of women and considers the power relationship between the sexes as crucial to the whole debate. This approach stresses the importance of the suffrage historian looking beyond the immediate details of the struggle itself to attempt to understand that struggle. Further, these examples exemplify the difference between women's history and feminist history. Women's history (Rosen) takes women as the subject matter, but is not necessarily feminist in its approach. Feminist history (Kingsley Kent) is informed by feminist theories and does not always focus just on women.

Another developmental stage in the writing of women's history takes movements or events already established as important by men and examines the role contributed by women. Lerner has called this type of writing "women's contribution history". Texts that fall into this group include Pinchbeck's *Women workers and the Industrial Revolution,* Sarah Boston's *Women workers and the trade unions* or Lucy Middleton's *Women in the Labour movement.* Again, although this work is important to our understanding of women's role in society, Lerner argues that this type of history follows male paradigms and offers no new reconceptualization of history. Further, women are judged in male terms rather than their own. For example, in *Women in the Labour movement*, Labour women are portrayed as being supportive of male leaders, which ignores the controversy which took place during the 1920s over the birth control debate. Party policy was opposed to birth control, but the Labour women's section supported free access. As Jane Lewis has argued, the desire to chronicle the activities of united women in a united movement diminishes the importance of women's experience and overlooks the power dynamics amongst men and women in the Labour movement. Further, it fails to examine the power dynamics between the leadership and membership of the women's Labour movement. Another study of women in the Labour movement, Christine Collette's *For Labour and for women* which examines the Women's Labour League before 1918, explores these internal dynamics and helps us understand why women-only organizations diminished after the First World War and offers us a useful interpretation of the decline of overt feminism in the 1920s.

Lewis argues that, if we want to know more about the lives of the majority of women, we have to develop strategies that go beyond studying "women worthies" or women's contribution to male-dominated organizations and discover what was central to women's lives. "Woman-centred" or feminist history is the next stage in the development and demands a rethink of what is "important" in the past and how we analyze it.

Women's relationship to the family has always been central to women's lives whether they were mothers or not, and this relationship has been a key focus of much research over the past twenty years. For example historians, such as Carol Dyhouse in *Feminism and the family in England*, have focused on how feminists in the past tried to analyze their relationship with dominant definitions of the family and have sought to reinterpret the family in ways that would be less repressive for women.

Periodization has also been a focus of feminist historians. Are the traditional foci of historical research of equal importance to women? This debate has led to some historians arguing that a new periodization for women's history is necessary, while others call for a gendered approach to the traditional periodization. For example, Jane Rendall in *Women in an industrialising society* examines the ideological constructs of woman, alongside changing work patterns and social relationships both in the public and domestic workplace. This study offers an illuminating view of the impact of industrialization on the lives of both men and women. The radical feminist Shulamith Firestone in *The dialectics of sex* argues that the theoretical task of feminism is to understand gender difference as a system of male domination, and the political task of feminism is to end it. The work that feminist historians have been carrying out over the last twenty years has encouraged other historians to focus on gender as an important tool in historical analysis. Central to this approach is the assertion that gender is a culturally-shaped group of attributes and behaviours given to the female or to the male and therefore is a social construct. Gender construction is based on the notion of polarity, since each gender is perceived as the opposite of the other. The French philosopher, Simone de Beauvoir argues in *The second sex* that in western society woman is regarded as Other or "not man" and this concept of otherness underlies categories of contrasting characteristics labelled masculine or feminine – strong/weak; active/passive; independent/dependent; competitive/co-operative, rational/intuitive, etc., which are all opposites that have gender connotations.

In feminist history, the concept of gender difference has been used to discuss the different roles of men and women in society – for example, through an examination of the ideology of separate spheres which was prominent in the nineteenth century. The ideology of separate spheres laid down two areas of social life – the public world of politics and business, and the private world of the domestic and personal relationships. From this notion developed gendered attributes for each sphere. The public world of work and politics was competitive and harsh, based on rational thought and science and was therefore designated male. The private world of domesticity and personal relationships was one of harmony and love and based on emotion and nature and therefore female. The project of the ideology of separate spheres was to ensure that these ideals were pursued. One approach to studying the history of the women's movement in the nineteenth and twentieth centuries is to focus on women's struggle to redefine the boundaries of these two spheres. An example of this sort of approach is Leonore Davidoff and Catherine Hall's ground-breaking study *Family fortunes* which analyzes this ideology, questions its dominance in the lived world of men and women, and produces a new gendered analysis of class formation at the beginning of the nineteenth century.

However, gender is not the only lens that feminists have used in their reconceptualization of history. Class, race, ethnicity, sexuality and other labels of oppression have been brought into the rewriting of history. I shall focus on two of these differences here – class and race – and reflect on the implications that this multifaceted reconceptualization of history offers us. Just as the new social history of the 1960s sought to reclaim the history of working-class men, there is now a commitment in feminist history to study the lives of working-class women. The definition of class is always difficult

181

and doubly so when considering women. The usual determinants of class are not straightforward. For example, a nineteenth-century woman could be the daughter of a professional man but, although this would place her in the middle class, she might well be uneducated and poor, only clinging to her middle-class status by an appeal to respectability. The daughter of a working-class man might well be poorly educated in the conventional sense, but her streetwiseness and economic independence would put her in a favourable position compared to the hapless, impoverished middle-class lady. On the other hand , the cultural capital accrued by the middle-class status of her family could open doors for the middle-class woman which would always be firmly closed to an equally talented working-class woman.

Feminist historians have not always paid enough attention to the issue of class between women. They have described the class differences in the experience of women but have not paid sufficient attention to the dynamics of class between women. For example, Lewis argues that Patricia Branca's work on middle-class women, *Silent sisterhood*, has challenged the stereotype perpetuated by male historians like Harold Perkin in *The origins of modern English society*, that the middle class woman was ". . . the completely ornamental, completely helpless and dependent . . . wife or daughter with no function besides inspiring inspiration and bearing children". However, she has not explored the relationship between middle-class women and their servants or the working-class women that middle-class women sought to help by their social work and philanthropy.

Others have questioned the relationships between middle-class women and working-class men but not women of different classes. For example, Mary Drake McFeely in *Lady inspectors* explores the relationship between middle-class women and working-class men in the Factory Inspectorate but does not explore class relations between the middle-class woman factory inspector and the woman factory worker, beyond noting that there was some resistance on the part of the workers to reporting misdemeanours to the inspector. However, in recent years, some feminist historians, such as Christine Collette, mentioned earlier, and Jane Lewis, in her essay "The working-class wife and mother and state intervention" which explores the relationship between middle-class health visitors and their working-class clientele, have addressed the problem of class relationships between women.

A further issue that has developed alongside the dynamics of class in women's history is the development of an examination of the dynamics of race. The omission of race until quite recently in British feminist historiography is symptomatic of western feminist thought which has had a tendency to regard women's history as white women's history, very much in the way that men have regarded history as white men's history. Despite this tendency, western women's history has not completely ignored issues of race; for example, women's relationship to slavery has been examined in texts such as Claire Midgley's *Women against slavery: the British campaigns*.

Yet, often women historians have focused on patriarchy and capitalism as the oppressors and used gender as a unifying concept. Consequently, women's role in imperialism has been neglected. Again, this omission is being rectified by the work of women such as Antoinette Burton who focuses on white women's contribution to the construction and sustenance of imperial ideology.

Women's history and poststructuralism: a current debate

So what is the current position in women's history today? When Jane Lewis wrote her article on the development of women's history in 1981, women's history was on the margins of academia. The profusion of studies and courses which have developed over the past fifteen years or so speaks of the success of writing women into history. However, there is no complacency or consensus amongst feminist historians. Recently, there has been a debate in the journal *Women's History Review* concerning the relationship between postmodernism/poststructuralism and women's history. This is a debate that has been continuing for some time in America and two of the protagonists in the *Review* were American scholars.

There are differences between postmodernism and poststructuralism, but, for the purpose of exploring this debate, they have been conflated in the articles, because they both question and deconstruct grand narratives such as feminism, or Marxism and this is the issue upon which I want to focus. As June Purvis has argued, the impact of these analyses has been to shift the traditional emphasis of most history writing from what is "true" to how we produce "truth". This shift has caused concern amongst some feminist historians who have focused on the recovery of women's past. Poststructuralist analyses have pointed out the fact that "woman" is not a unifying category and that questions of difference, class, race, etc. are important. This analysis has been useful in showing up differences between women, but, some poststructuralists have taken this further and argued that the concept "woman" is meaningless because of the differences between women, and this has caused controversy. The opponents to this argument have replied by arguing that, just because there are differences between the way women experience oppression, this does not negate the fact that all women share an experience of oppression. The task of feminists is, they argue, to analyze different forms of oppression and the power dynamics between women as well as between men and women. The tension between historians wanting to focus on the material lives of women and those interested in the way that we produce "truth" is ongoing. In *Women's History Review*, the debate opens with Joan Hoff's article "Gender as a postmodern category of paralysis". Hoff argues that history writing in the States is becoming paralyzed by an overemphasis by feminist scholars on poststructuralist theory. This, she argues, isolates scholarship from the political women's movement with history teachers in schools trying to integrate women's history into the curriculum, and counterparts working on women's history in Eastern Europe and what she calls "Third World" countries.

Her argument began an intense debate and June Purvis, the editor of the journal, wrote in her editorial that she had received letters and phone calls in response to the piece, many supportive, some with mixed feelings and some outrightly hostile to it. In reply, Susan Kingsley Kent fiercely defends poststructuralism arguing that Hoff's article is anti-intellectual and incorrect. She takes issue with Hoff's assertions that: 1) postmodernists dispute the existence of a real material world and that their analysis renders historical agency impossible and irrelevant; 2) that postmodernist theory is misogynist; 3) that postmodernist theorists are politically paralyzed. Caroline Ramazanoglu writes a more measured response. She argues that while Hoff "usefully shows that questions of *how* we know gender are displacing questions about *what* needs to be known about women's lives and *why* relations between men and women are as they are", it is still important to acknowledge that, although history is disintegrating into a multiplicity of voices, not all narratives are equal.

This debate is crucial and has implications for other histories too. Joan Sangster, an oral historian, also shares the concerns of Hoff and Purvis, amongst others, about the consequences of emphasizing form over content. In her essay on using oral history to reconstruct women's lives, she argues for situating poststructuralist insights in a feminist materialist context. She writes ". . . we do not want to return to a history which either obscures power relationships or marginalises women's voices".

The debate around poststructuralist approaches to the past is set to run for some time yet and we shall have to wait to see whether it will mean the demise of women's history writing. I am optimistic and do not think it will. Theory can not be totally divorced from experience, and empirical enquiry will continue to form the basis of theoretical work. Recognition of difference as an important concept has enabled us to focus on oppressed groups such as women. It has also helped us to understand that there are differences within oppressed sections of society as well as difference between groups. However, it is important that theory is grounded in material experience – what women say and do will continue to form an important part of feminist historical analysis.

Conclusion

The project to write women into British history is now well under way. Women's history as a taught subject began its life in the 1970s in independent women's studies groups and adult education classes, such as those run by the Workers Education Association. Since then, the field has grown and now many universities either have courses focused on aspects of women's history or include women in more general history courses. However, this inclusion is not automatic and is often the result of the numbers of academics writing about and wanting to teach women's history and the numbers of students wanting to study it. This demand has greatly increased and continues to challenge institutional resistance. Women's history is still often regarded as a specialism which it is not necessary to offer at undergraduate level. In addition, although women may be included in conventional history courses, this often means that the type of history taught falls into the category of "women worthies" or "contributory history" and there is no attempt to reconceptualize history in the ways that I have been suggesting. Schools are also attempting to include women's history in the National Curriculum, although this involves a willingness on behalf of teachers to read curriculum guidelines in a gendered way, and make the effort to search out appropriate texts and methodologies.

Furthermore, when I began studying history in the early 1980s it was still possible to keep up with the number of women's history books being produced. This is no longer the case, even if one is restricting one's focus to British women's history. Some journals have focused either in part or wholly on women's history. In 1982, *History Workshop Journal* became a journal of socialist and feminist historians, although it has since dropped both appellations and has been followed by further journals, *Gender and history* (1989) and the even more specifically focused, *Women's History Review* (1992).

Another challenge to institutional resistance has been the formation of the Women's History Network on a regional, national and international basis. This is a network of academics, students, archivists, schoolteachers and others interested in women's history. The network produces its own newsletter and publications, runs conferences and promotes the study of women's history at all levels and both inside and outside educational institutions. Nevertheless, the challenge to ensure that women are written into history still continues. When Lewis wrote her article in 1981 she was cautious about whether we were about to see the incorporation of women's history as a serious subject for academic research and teaching or whether it would be marginalized as a passing fad. There has been an increase in the numbers of women academics researching women's history being promoted to professorial status. However, there is still a feeling that women's history is only on the syllabus because it is popular and not because it is necessarily thought of as being of equal value to, say, political or economic history, even though women's history informs these fields. Publishers, ever sensitive to market demands, are nervous about publishing anything too innovative, and some feminist historians have trouble finding publishers for their more radical work. Further, institutions often find women's history courses

185

threatening and even a few can be too many. A colleague told me recently that her institution feels that the two women's history courses currently running are more than sufficient and that, although it concedes that there is a high student take-up on the existing courses, she is not allowed to develop any further courses. There is still a structural problem in academia which is based on a power hierarchy where traditional male ideas, structures and ways of seeing the world prevail, although they do not go unchallenged. I expect she will keep me posted on this ongoing battle.

Women's history is now firmly on the agenda and is a vibrant and controversial area of research. It is still marginalized to some extent, but its vibrancy offers a constant challenge to the "dry as dust" moribund history writing that Carr criticized over 35 years ago. Indeed, it has challenged Carr himself, for it would be impossible for him to write *What is History?* today omitting practically all mention of women either as subjects or writers of history as he did in 1960. This challenge is of vital importance. During her research in the development of feminist consciousness, Gerda Lerner discovered that over the last two thousand years, women have constantly reinvented the wheel with respect to female scholarship. Women, who were excluded from formal educational institutions, were ignorant of the work of women of the past, even their very recent past. For the first time in history, women's experience, agency and knowledge are being systematically collected and theorized by women scholars. However, the study of women's history has taught us that there are times when women's lives are on the agenda and other times when they are not. While academic institutions continue to be embedded in an ideology of inequalities of power in which male concerns have hegemonic dominance, we have to guard against complacency; otherwise, feminist scholars will constantly find themselves reinventing that wheel.

Suggestions for further reading

There are many useful books and articles on the development of women's history. In this essay I have referred to Gerda Lerner *The Majority Finds Its Past* (Oxford: Oxford University Press, 1979) and Jane Lewis "Women Lost and Found: The Impact of Feminism on History" in Dale Spender (ed.) *Men's Studies Modified: The Impact of Feminism on Academia* (Oxford: Pergamon Press, 1981) whose Introduction I have also referred to. For the discussion on "women worthies" I have used Natalie Zemon Davis "Women's History in Transition: The European Case" *Feminist Studies* (1976). For international perspectives on writing women's history, see Karen Offen, Ruth Roach Pierson and Jane Rendall (eds) *Writing Women's History: International Perspectives* (London: Macmillan, 1991). For histories of the development of feminist thought, I have referred to Dale Spender, *Women of Ideas and What Women Have Done to Them* (London: Routledge, 1982) for a radical critique and Gerda Lerner, *The Creation of Feminist Consciousness: From the Middle Ages to Eighteen Seventy* (Oxford: Oxford University Press, 1993). For methodological approaches to women's history see Joan Kelly-Gadol "The Social Relations of the Sexes: Methodological Implications of Women's History" in E. Abel & E. K. Abel (eds) *The Signs Reader: Women, Gender and Scholarship* (Chicago: University of Chicago Press, 1983), and June Purvis "Doing Feminist Women's History: Researching Lives of Women in the Suffragette Movement in Edwardian England" in Mary Maynard & June Purvis (eds) *Researching Women's Lives from a Feminist Perspective* (London: Taylor & Francis, 1994) and June Purvis "Using Primary Sources When Researching Women's History from a Feminist Perspective" *Women's History Review* 1(2) 1992. For a discussion of race see the special issue of *Women's History Review* "Feminism, Imperialism and 'Race'", Barbara N. Ramusack and Antoinette Burton (eds), 1994, 3(4). A useful text on definitions used in feminist theory is Maggie Humm (ed.) *The Dictionary of Feminist Theory* (London: Harvester, 1989). The debate on women's history and post-structuralism appeared in *Women's History Review*. The Hoff article appeared in 1994, 3(2) and the editorial by Purvis and responses by Kingsley Kent and Ramazanoglu appeared in 5(1) together with a reply by Hoff. Joan Sangster's article "Telling our Stories: feminist debates and the use of oral history" is in 1994, 3(1). Another relevant article in *Women's History Review* is Mary Maynard "Beyond the "Big Three": the development of feminist theory in the 1990s in 1995, 4(3). Membership details for the Women's History Network can be obtained from myself, the Membership Secretary, at the University of Sussex.

Chapter Fifteen

⁂

The new history:
the *Annales* school of history
and modern historiography

Peter R. Campbell

Throughout the nineteenth century the great majority of historians spent their time writing books on the history of governments, wars, treaties, the rise of nation states, the development of political institutions and the history of law. There were, for example, few historical studies of the peasants, and almost no serious analyses of the economy. History was about narrative; it told a story, based on documents. It was about "facts", and the German historian, Ranke, was the model. Many documents were published by learned societies, but they were all chosen for publication by men with largely the same preoccupations, the same idea of history.

In this situation two entirely new historical approaches began to make their presence felt – Marxism, and sociology. Marxist historical theory was, of course, something quite new, because the aim of Marx was to show how the economy was, in the final analysis, the most important factor. Within the economic structures, class struggle was generated. In the long run this emphasis on the role of economic factors was to have a very stimulating effect on historians. Nowadays all historians in the West, whether or not they agree with the other aims of Marx, recognize the importance of economic factors which condition and limit men in their individual actions. At the beginning of the twentieth century sociology was the other major influence. Durkheim and Max Weber developed theories about the study of contemporary society which put the emphasis on a new range of factors in human development. They pointed to the importance of social structures, of the family, of hierarchical or patrimonial conceptions, on the actions of men and women. They felt that they had discovered a science of society, and they thought that theirs was a better sort of analysis than Marxism.

All this had a profound influence on many intellectuals at the beginning of this century, although not all. Most continued to accept the traditional forms of nineteenth-century historical enquiry. Of the several who chose to be influenced by the new thinking, three Frenchmen in particular concern us. Like missionaries all three were inspired to change the definition of "history". The implication of both Marxism and sociology was that analysis was as important as narrative. Therefore, a political narrative had to be set in the context of the economy and of the structures of society. This was a move away from history-as-narrative towards history-as-problem-solving. It became complex on a different level. It set in train the development of a school of historians whose work has profoundly altered the way historical studies are approached all over the world. They have contributed to a new framework of explanation, a different sense of historical time, the investigation of new subject matter studied with new methods – popular mentalities, festivity, attitudes towards death, the family, childhood, magic and superstition. From these beginnings new approaches have become standard, such as the quantitative analysis of data, the history of mentalities, the idea of "total history", and from the 1980s a new kind of "cultural history", still in the process of finding its definition. Throughout, the key word of this diverse school has been interdisciplinarity, a concept particularly dear to Sussex University.

The forerunner was Henri Berr (1863-1954) who founded a periodical in 1900 to bring together all branches of knowledge in a synthesis. He had a plan to commission 100 volumes in a collection called "The evolution of humanity", which would use all the methods and subject matter of all the social sciences such as geography, economics, sociology and history, to explain human society. He greatly influenced two younger men, Lucien Febvre (1878-1956) and Marc Bloch (1886-1944), both professors at the University of Strasbourg.

Both of these men were against "history" as it was then practised in most universities. Controversy was a characteristic, a hallmark of their work. In 1929 they founded a learned historical periodical called *Annales d'histoire économique et sociale* (Annals of economic and social history). This journal was, especially from the 1950s, to become the the the largest and the most influential historical journal in the world. This is an extraordinary achievement. Why did it happen at all, and why in France? In fact, the rethinking of history was also beginning in America, but perhaps French culture was more suitable for the development of ideas than American or British. The latter are cultures that value pragmatism more than theories. Part of its extraordinary success in France is to be explained by the fact that by the 1950s the new historians had captured elite places in the centralized education system and were able to train students to continue their ideas and campaign for their historical beliefs from positions of power. Added to their missionary zeal and their conviction that theirs was the most stimulating analytical approach to the past, they were very adept at writing about and publicizing their cause. But these are inadequate explanations. The most important reason for their success lies in their doctrine, in what they were saying, doing and advocating. They have written some of the finest, most subtle, most stimulating history books in the twentieth century. This was recognized not just in retrospect but at the time of publication, in some cases in the 1930s, and the spirit of innovation still continues to the present day. Every historian today (and a much wider public) is familiar with the names and works of Bloch, Febvre, Fernand Braudel, Emanuel Le Roy Ladurie, Georges Duby, Jacques Le Goff, Roger Chartier, amongst the French, and Natalie Zemon Davis and Robert Darnton from America. For historians reading the articles in the *Annales* in the 1930s there was an excitement in them, a sense of discovery and intellectual adventure so often lacking in the drier studies of the history of the "old school". It was as if whole new perspectives were suddenly opening up before the scholar. And this approach was to bring about, in the long run, a most profound and permanent effect on Western historical studies. First, in studies of the medieval period; and soon after in the early modern period. It is to be regretted that historians studying the twentieth century have generally been much slower to take up these ideas.

What then do *Annales* historians think history as a discipline should be? Of course, their answer would be very different from the one given and practised by the nineteenth-century historians, including at that stage the Marxists. For Marc Bloch, history is the study of man, although it should not be defined too precisely because definitions can be very limiting. Bloch wrote one of the best books on history, entitled *The historian's craft*. It was published after he had been shot by the Germans for resistance activities during the Second World War. Allow me to quote to you from Lucien Febvre's review of this book. We should note in passing that it was written in 1949 when memories of the Second World War were still very strong, and France had recently been occupied.

> Is Marc Bloch going to make a lengthy, rigid definition of history at the start of his book? There are indeed plenty of precedents for that. What historian is there who has not at least once in his life fallen a prey to the disease? Marc Bloch resists. He does not define history. Because any definition is a prison. And because the human sciences, like men themselves, need freedom above all else. A definition of history? Which history? I mean at what date and in what framework of civilisation? Does history not vary, all the time, in its restless search for new techniques, new points of view, problems needing to be put more aptly? Definitions – do not the most precise definitions, the most carefully thought out and most meticulously phrased definitions run the risk of constantly leaving aside the best part of history ... Definitions – are they not a kind of bullying? "Careful, old chap, you are stepping outside of history. Re-read my definition, it is very clear! If you are a historian, don't set foot in here, this is the field of the sociologist. Or there – that is the

psychologist's business. To the right? Don't dare go there, that is the geographer's area . . . and to the left. the ethnologist's domain." It is a nightmare, madness, wilful mutilation! Down with all barriers and labels. To the frontiers, astride the frontiers, with one foot on each side, that is where the historian has to work.

Three methods are important: first, the comparative method, of which Marc Bloch was a great advocate. By comparative history he means choosing the same issue or problem in two or more different areas, and studying it. When you have come to conclusions about the same phenomenon in different areas, different cultures or different periods, you will be in a position to see what is general about the phenomenon and what is particular. For example, look at motives for popular rebellion by peasants in the seventeenth century in France, Russia and China, as Roland Mousnier has done.

Again Bloch was passionately interested in studying the peasantry in the past and especially their culture and mentality. In the early twentieth century, when France still had a majority of its population living in rural society, children were often brought up by their grandparents, because the parents would be working. If, therefore, you want to study the structures and operation of peasant culture in the more distant past, it is a good idea first of all to look at that slow-moving culture today. This will give you ideas about the right questions to ask about, say, sixteenth-century peasant culture. This sort of comparative approach is the second method, and is called the "regressive method".

Thirdly, there is the frequent use of models in history. By model we mean an artificial idea of what is normal. For instance, there is a Marxist model of revolution, which sees revolution as the product of certain historical forces: class struggle, economic crisis, political crisis and the rise of a new class to power. A Western sociologist might of course have a different model of revolution, although it might still be influenced by Marxism. The purpose of a model is to provide a framework to help you to know what to look for and what to try to explain. Models can be helpful and in a way we all use them unthinkingly, because a simple word can itself be a sort of model. "Modernization" is a word-model, as indeed is "child", as Philippe Aries has shown with his history of childhood through the ages, revealing that childhood as a specific stage of develoment was not recognized in earlier periods. In order to explain the direction these thoughts were leading, we must turn to one book in particular. It is *The Mediterranean and the Mediterranean world in the age of Philip II*, (1949) by Fernand Braudel. It is no ordinary history book. This large, very large, book in two volumes began as a history of the foreign policy of sixteenth-century Spain and Philip II towards the Mediterranean world. However, Braudel was influenced by Lucien Febvre who said to him: "Philip II and the Mediterranean is a good idea, but the Mediterranean world and Philip II is a better one". The book is divided into three parts, each corresponding to a certain type of historical time. The parts are called structures, conjunctures, and events. What he actually wrote was a book whose first part described the geography of the lands around the Mediterranean Sea, looking at the possibilities for human settlement and trade and communications. Next, he examined the economies of the Mediterranean basin in the sixteenth century and the influences on them, for example, the size of the population and the amount of precious metal for exchanges. Finally, he turned to the politics of the period and showed that it was constructed within a set of assumptions and aims that had been conditioned, unbeknown to the men of that time, by trends far beyond their control.

This "dialectic of space and time", as Braudel calls it, had a profound impact on the structure of explanation in history books and researches. Most general history books in France and the majority in other countries are now written with Braudel's structure in mind. They begin with economy and society, move on to cultures or "mentalities" and then turn at last to politics. There are some helpful criticisms to make of the structure of explanation so much praised in Braudel's work. Braudel, in writing about events in the context of structures, put the emphasis on the "long-term". A phrase he often used. It has led to a virtual abandonment of political history by *Annales* historians, as they concentrate on social phenomena over a long period. This has been useful and beneficial, but now, perhaps, is the time for historians to come back to political history with all the new understanding provided by the exciting developments in historical studies. There are problems in the uncritical acceptance of the idea of the long-term and the influence of structures.

First, people at the time could not see them, and were, at least consciously, unaware of them. Secondly, to describe the long-term structures and the century-long conjunctures is not the same as to explain them. The problem of the relation between causes remains unsolved. Thirdly, is it really possible to observe a neat division between types of time? As Hexter has argued, the eruption of a volcano like Vesuvius on 24 August AD 79 was a geological event of short-term significance – but long-term to people living on the edge of the volcano. And is not the Catholic Monarchy that lasted in Europe for six or seven centuries a phenomenon of the long term? In the final assessment we may prefer to keep the inspiration of Braudel, and not adhere too strictly to the specific relationship between the structures he emphasized. But let us not be discouraged by these problems. The criticisms themselves come from within the *Annales* school. They testify to the vigour of the new history and the flexibility of its philosophy. Let us not forget that these ideas have permitted whole new areas of history to be developed, and that these areas are a major and permanent contribution to knowledge. In my opinion the truest inheritor of the mantle of Marc Bloch and Fernand Braudel is Georges Duby, the medievalist. His works have all the brilliant originality in finding answers to questions in unexpected places that was the special quality of Marc Bloch. He himself has made illuminating comments on the history of mental structures over the long term. He believed that the study of particular crises can also give us a privileged access to an understanding of the way people thought. I quote:

> It is possible, by analysing certain explosive events, which reveal or bring to the surface a large number of latent factors, and which will generate a large amount of evidence, to make important advances in the history of structures, and to find out more precisely what makes it significant.

Indeed, he himself has used the event to illuminate the structures and has done as much as anyone to develop the new history of popular mentalities.

"We must count" is a characteristic saying of the *Annales* school. Since the early 1930s the economic historians had been writing a statistical history of prices and wages in France. Newer economic theories about the development of economies and the notion of "take off" put the history of prices and its value in a different context. However, it is not just in economic history that the need was felt to produce data in a systematic form. If history was to become a valid human science, as the pioneers of the New History hoped, it had to prove that it had methods comparable to real sciences. It had to prove that the writing of history was not just a matter of insight and imprecise flashes of understanding about a past in which each case was unique and unrepeatable. It had to show that, even if we cannot use experimental method on the past, we can use systematic collections of information in the form of figures and statistics. This would defend history from the imperialism of the other social sciences, and show that it was not mere guesswork.

It therefore became important for historians to know how to count. You say the bourgeoisie is rising in the seventeenth century? Prove it to be with statistics of social mobility of the purchase of manors by the middle classes! You say the Spanish empire is in decline in the seventeenth century? Measure the amount of gold and silver imported into Spain from the New World, and measure the amount of trade that Seville, the major port, has with colonies on the other side of the Atlantic! Measure! Quantify! Count!

Without doubt the most fascinating new type of study is the history of mentalities and ideologies. Neither of these words has the narrow political meaning usually attached to it. Instead, the meanings have been enlarged to suggest the ways in which cultures in a given period see and interpret their world. The history of mentalities is the study of the beliefs and the ways of seeing in a given culture. Ideology means something much broader than a political creed; it means the attitudes and values people hold. The classic text on the history of mentalities is by Lucien Febvre, and is called

The problem of unbelief in the sixteenth century: the religion of Rabelais. Febvre was angered by a scholar who claimed that the great sixteenth-century writer Rabelais was an atheist rather than a Christian. He felt that the accusation was unhistorical and he set out to show why. It was true, he admitted, that Rabelais had been called an atheist, but this was just a common term of abuse in that period which meant little in practice. He wrote a study in three parts of the perception by men in the sixteenth century of the world and God. The first part is about Rabelais himself as seen through his writings; the second is about his friends and his intellectual circle; and the third is a very brilliant and bold explanation of the general thinking in sixteenth-century France. Febvre thus gave us a history of the mental universe of men in a certain period in the past. The conclusion of the book was that all thought had the concept of the existence of God as an unchallengeable assumption, and so Rabelais could not have been an atheist!

We needed the *Annales* school's redefinition of History for the history of mentalities to be possible, and we needed their redefinition of historical time as well. This is because we are not dealing with events, but with attitudes. Therefore, we need first to make use of the new sense of historical time that has been developed. An attitude must be studied over a longer period, perhaps over a century, and a change of attitude will not take place suddenly, although sometimes it may seem to do so. It will have been prepared over many years, but may suddenly become visible at the time of a great event. In general, then, mentalities and ideologies deal with ways of thinking over the "long term".

The second important point to realize is that the history of the mentality of an era will need to include the history or description of many attitudes. A noble in the sixteenth century could believe both in honour and in witchcraft, but a peasant may have believed in magic but not the noble idea of honour (he knows it exists but his idea of it is different; he may prefer to stay with his family than to go on campaigns, but would take another peasant to court for impugning his wife's "honour"), and so mentalities may change according to social groups.

A third point to note is that each social group will have a slightly different mentality. This mentality, or vision of the world, may include ideas and attitudes shared by everyone at that time, and it may also contain some ideas confined to a particular group. The study of mentalities is therefore very closely connected to the study of groups. Mentality is one of the things that makes groups different. Journeymen artisans have a different mentality in some respects (probably those most noticeable to other people in society) from their masters, and the master artisans see the world differently from the nobles or the rich bourgeois. Yet, they all share some attitudes and ways of reacting and behaving, because they are all members of the same society.

An interesting conclusion follows from this. It is not just the economic role that determines social structures in society; the mentality and the shared set of values and attitudes also create the differences between groups. Allow me to make this clearer by two contrasting quotations:

> Men, developing their material production and their material intercourse, alter, along with their real existence, their thinking and the products of their thinking. Life is not determined by consciousness but consciousness by life. (Karl Marx)

> Social realities are a whole. One could not pretend to explain an institution if one did not link it to the great intellectual, emotional, mystical, currents of the contemporary mentality. (Marc Bloch)

While Marx is suggesting that ideology is the consequence of material conditions of life and production, Bloch is suggesting that the apparently material institutions in life are to be understood in the light of mentalities. I think that it is true to say that Marx did not adhere consistently to his view, as is revealed by the idea that the Protestant religion and capitalism were linked. They may well have been connected, but did the religious belief make better capitalists, or did frustrated potential capitalists choose the Protestant religion? This relationship between ideology and infrastructure is perhaps one of the least clear. On the other hand, Bloch would certainly agree that the material conditions of life also structure the mentalities. Take the example of peasants and their volatile emotional state: is this not a consequence of a life led on the edge of the precipice of poverty? Is not the peasant sense of time less precise than that of an urban dweller? It is precisely because there is a large and legitimate area of overlap that both Marxists and liberals have been able to work so well together in the same field of history. And, of course, the *Annales* school itself was influenced from the beginning by Marxism and sociology. Leading and influential Marxist historians of mentalities are, in England, E. P. Thompson, and, in France, M. Vovelle, former professor of the French Revolution at the Sorbonne in Paris.

In more recent years we have come through study to realize that, even though a period of history and a culture that has certain characteristic mental structures, there is a lot of variation between different subcultures in that society. Thus sailors and shoemakers share general assumptions about the world, but have very different cultural practices and some specifically different beliefs. One might compare and contrast two famous studies of the history of mentalities: first, Natalie Zemon Davis's study of marriage and family life in a village in the 1550s. The disappearance of Martin Guerre and his apparent return (he was in fact an impostor), and the court case provide the basis of a wide exploration of attitudes and personal strategies in a village. Secondly, Robert Darnton's much debated discussion of the "great cat massacre" in eighteenth-century Paris uses this little-known episode in cultural history to shed light on the mentality of artisan print workers and their relations with their employer, as expressed in symbolic form through their villainous prank.

The history of witchcraft and folklore is truly fascinating. The discipline historians have borrowed from it in order to study its cultural anthropology. But instead of using certain theories and techniques to ask questions about modern non-European societies, we historians prefer to use the same methods to study cultures of the past. "The past is another country", as Fanon said, so why not study and discuss the society in which our own ancestors lived in the same way as you would study a foreign culture? After all, is it not misleading to think that we British or Americans have clung to the same sorts of attitude over the centuries? In some ways we have, but the differences may be as important as the similarities, and the similarities may be more apparent than real. Thus, we can study the types of festival in a society, and try to understand the role and function of festivity in the past. Why is it that the world is so often turned upside down in rituals? For example, why is carnival characterized by plenty and waste, when there was so little food in society? Why is authority allowed to be mocked by the inversion of its symbols, and why do groups of young men at carnival time behave as if everything is permitted and pretend to be kings or bishops? It is not enough just to say this is the spirit of carnival – what else is going on? There are historical questions to be asked, and answered. What is the role of magic in the village community and why did witches suddenly become the objects of persecution? It is not enough to say that they were persecuted because they were women; why were they not persecuted as witches before the sixteenth century? The answer must lie partly in the attitudes of men towards women, and these attitudes must have changed in some way, or have been given different expression. So it is that new and important questions come to our attention just as we are trying to understand a society at the point at which it is most obscure and incomprehensible. To do so we need to use the tools provided by other disciplines, but we must still ask well-formulated historical questions. In the last decade the history of mentalities has fed into an emerging discipline of cultural history. Exploiting developments in literary theory and cultural anthropology, and responding to criticisms of the history of mentalities, historians like Roger Chartier have studied the culture of printed books, their readership and reception, notions like private and public spheres of life, or concepts like civility and religious piety. This kind of history is more theoretically driven, it emphasizes culture as appropriation at a given time, rather than unchanging attitudes. Its questions are important, and they are transforming our understanding of the past and how we got here. But a fuller exploration must await its own chapter in a second edition!

History will never be truly scientific. It can use all the methods of the other social sciences; it can use hypotheses and theories and models, just like them; but it should retain a literary quality that makes it of interest to everyone. History is not an empire, it is the past of Everyman. History is everything that happened in the past. It is the great achievement of the *Annales* school to have taught us to accept this statement, and to have given us the methods to attempt the study of the history of everything.

Is history the most important science among the humanities? *Annales* historians believe it is. It is the most complex, precisely because it has to deal with the specific relations between models, structures and events that are unique. It is the most important because it can make use of the techniques of all the other social sciences, even the most modern, in order to study the totality of the past. There is no doubt that the work and the ideas of the historians of the *Annales* school has been, and continues to be, an inspiration to us all. Moreover, it is in the great humanist tradition.

Suggestions for further reading

It is better to read the historians themselves than introductions to their approach, but J. Le Goff and P. Nora (eds), *Constructing the past* (Cambridge: Cambridge University Press, 1985) is almost a manifesto. Marc Bloch's *The Historian's craft* (Manchester: Manchester University Press, 1954) is an inspiration, as are his longer works mentioned in the text. Lucien Febvre's essays collected in *A New Kind of History*, P. Burke (ed.) (London: Routledge & Kegan Paul, 1973), open many windows on to the past, as does his *Life in renaissance France* (Cambridge, Mass.: Harvard University Press, 1977). Febvre's *The problem of unbelief in the sixteenth century* makes an excellent read (Cambridge, Mass.: Harvard University Press, 1983). Braudel's works remain widely available, and his essay on "Structures and the long term" is reprinted in English in *On history* (Chicago: University of Chicago Press, 1980) while a special edition of the *Journal of Modern History* in 1972 was dedicated to "Braudelian History". Philippe Aries opened new vistas with his *Centuries of childhood* (New York: Vintage, 1975) and *The hour of our death* (London and New York: Knopf, 1981). Many have written exemplary works in the footsteps of these masters: Le Roy Ladurie's *Peasants of Languedoc* (Urbana: University of Illinois Press, 1974), *Carnival in Romans* (Harmondsworth: Penguin, 1981) and his best seller *Montaillou* (Harmondsworth: Penguin: 1978) are representative of the *Annales* approach, as is Pierre Goubert's *The ancien régime* (London: Weidenfeld & Nicholson, 1973 and 1996); Michel Vovelle's *Mentalities and ideologies* (Cambridge: Polity, 1990) contains stimulating essays on popular culture and religion, as does Natalie Zemon Davis's collection of essays *Society and culture in early modern France* (Cambridge: Polity, 1987), which she followed up by *The return of Martin Guerre* (Cambridge, Mass.: Harvard University Press, 1983). Robert Darnton's *The great cat massacre* takes a jolly and varied step towards cultural history, debated in the *Journal of Modern History* in 1985 and 1988, while his *The kiss of Lamourette* (London: Faber, 1990) is more reflective, and Roger Chartier's *Cultural History* (Cambridge: Polity, 1988) helps to define a new sub-discipline. Carlo Ginzburg is the leading Italian exponent of the history of mentalities, and his *The cheese and the worms, the cosmos of a sixteenth-century miller* (London: Routledge & Kegan Paul, 1981) is a fascinating glimpse into someone's mind. The multi-volume series edited by Georges Duby and collaborators on *A history of Private life* (5 vols, Cambridge, Mass.: Harvard University Press, 1987–91), and *A history of women in the West* (4 vols, Cambridge, Mass.: The Belknap Press of Harvard University Press, 1992–4) show just how great the achievement of the *Annales* school has been, in a very accessible form. Peter Burke has written a brief history of the *Annales* school, *The French historical revolution* (Cambridge: Polity, 1990), and a special issue of *Review*, 1978 was dedicated to the *Annales* achievement. Most of these are in paperback.

Chapter Sixteen

Opiate of the people and stimulant for the historian? – some issues in sports history

John Lowerson

A notable, if not widely noticed, encounter between historians and sport took place when the editor of this book, William Lamont, attended the 1980 Wembley Association Football Cup Final with one of the greatest Tudor historians of this century, the late S. T. Bindoff. West Ham beat Arsenal (the editor's favourite) 1:0. Bindoff had last attended a Cup Final in 1923 when West Ham was also playing, but against Bolton that time – they lost 2:0. That match has passed into footballing legend because of the one policeman on a white horse who controlled the large crowds coming to what was Wembley's first Cup Final. Neither of these two historians exercized his clinical judgement on anything but the quality of play; they were there for recreation, spectators rather than observers. Few of Bindoff's generation of historians would have regarded football as worth a scholarly thought – it was a game, a pastime, an escape from the archives and the footnotes which were the sign of the true academic. Sport might appear in the sort of books designed for popular consumption, pastimes of the people and so on, but it was history without seriousness; even G. M. Trevelyan's deliberately popular *Social history of England* (supposedly "history with the politics left out") made little reference to it. Such treatment might now seem surprising in view of the development of sports history as part of the secondary or tertiary spin-off from historiography since the 1960s, yet it still lurks in the suspicions of those who drift slowly along what is left of the old historical mainstream, while many of the rest of us dance about the more fascinating eddies. The nature of historians' engagement in the study of sport has its own narrative history, but it also mirrors many tensions within the scholarly profession and wider controversies about the uses to which history is put, as well as over interpretations of general trends and particular events. In this brief discussion I can only outline some of the main issues – roots, political usage and divergence.

British sports history emerged as a consciously defensible sub-skill of the historian's craft in the early 1980s, the time it had taken for the key strands of initial research to be worked through in the wake of the turmoil the 1960s produced by shifting the focus and loosening the boundaries of many intellectual disciplines. It would be reasonable to argue that almost all major British work in the field since then counts as an offspring of one key text, E. P. Thompson's *The Making of the English working class* (1963). A substantial number of scholars have now locked themselves into working through the ramifications of both his uneasy populism and his commitment to modernism, either placing cricketers, footballers and even lawn tennis players or golfers alongside Thompson's stockingers and impoverished handloom weavers as deserving rescue from the "enormous condescension of posterity", or questioning the whole assumption that "popular culture" is the preserve of the working classes in sporting terms. The two milestone texts in this process were Tony Mason's *Association football* (1980) and Tony Mangan's *Athleticism in the Victorian and Edwardian public school* (1981), apparently concerned with opposite ends of a social spectrum. The division was never quite so sharp as that suggests, but they did focus on the tensions produced before 1914 by the emergence of the professional player as against the manly amateur. Since then we have seen a number of papers with the loose generic title of "The state of sports history", usually offering a descriptive review of the literature together with a suggested agenda for further research designed to clarify the author's hegemony in the field. That is something which I am trying to avoid here, since there are wider questions to be asked about the cultural milieu of sports history which make it a lively and occasionally perilous arena into which to venture. Any professional activity which defines itself as only existing within the confines of its recent outpourings runs into serious difficulties by concealing some key agendas which go beyond the convenient modernist/postmodernist dichotomies which offer an easy route into late twentieth-century controversies.

Sports history owes a great deal to antiquarian beginnings which most current practitioners fail to recognize, let alone celebrate, so obsessed have they become with academic respectability. The professionalization and near-abstraction of much modern writing divorces it quite frequently from the concerns of its subjects, avoids a popular audience and also conceals the uses to which the history of sport was put in the past. Not least of these applications was the assertion of national identities. The first significant attempt to write any sports history in England came in 1801 when the engraver Joseph Strutt produced *Glig-Gamena Angel-Deod; or the sports and pastimes of the people of England . . . from the earliest period to the present time*. Shorn of the fantastic first part of its title it went through another seven editions over the next century, feeding an increasing concern to find the "real roots" of so many English games, as the recreations of an old country seemed to be threatened both by urban industrialism and by the bureaucratization and economic opportunities which the late Victorian sports boom produced. It spawned many minor successors, books devoted to particular sports such as stoolball in Sussex or cricket anywhere, and articles in a string of turn-of-the-century encyclopaedias, of which those in the 1911 *Britannica* are probably the best representatives. Such works have continued to appear and can still produce a remarkable degree of disagreement, particularly among amateur historians who delight in angry letters of rebuttal to newspapers, publishers and even individual authors when an apparently sacred text is misquoted or even interpreted differently from the customary explanations – the history of cricket seems particularly prone to this. These writings may lack the apparatus of modern scholarship, but they have long fed into a popular sense of the sporting past in which a fabricated tradition is often more important than rigorous thematic interpretation.

The discovery of sporting tradition is not, however, just the harmless antiquarian pursuit that I have just suggested, particularly where the survival of traditional games is concerned. The loosely constructed history of these activities played a not inconsiderable role in fostering nationalist identities in late nineteenth-century Europe and in some of the odder sideshows of Hitler's Germany, propping up racial fanaticism with an apparently dotty romanticism. It has since found other international settings, of which two examples must suffice. One major imperative in spreading late nineteenth-century reorganised sports lay in their being assumed to be "improving" by their very nature, the models for peaceful competition and co-operation that the French baron Pierre de Coubertin hoped for when he reinvented the Olympic Games in the 1890s. But by 1912 there were national teams and nationalist supporters; Hitler's Berlin Games of 1936, so remarkably filmed by Leni Riefenstahl and the international newsagencies, demonstrated just how far the ideal had deteriorated. After the Second World War the Olympics became an extension of the Cold War, the eastern bloc's successes prompting several studies in which histories of state intervention in places like East Germany were compared with the British laissez-faire experience. But it went even further than this. By the 1980s these international sporting circuses, each accompanied by a Scientific Congress which included a growing number of historians offering what appeared to be competitive papers, were seen as essential to the symbolic modernization of the Third World, and it was the modern games which were adopted, almost as a new cultural colonialism. So we were presented with televized images of emergent nations' fielding small groups of athletes, who marched proudly behind their new flags, matched by their countries' teams turning out in football internationals, all at a financial cost which represented a huge element in each country's GNP.

In reaction against that, there emerged significant nationalist movements in which historians have played no small part. Many smaller states, particularly

in Africa and the Pacific Rim, turned individually or collectively to redis-
covering their traditional games, with the usual corollaries about inventing
them where their roots were inconveniently vague. In many senses this process had its own history, particularly where competing groups in a sometimes artificially drawn "nation" sought to establish cultural as well as political
hegemony. Their new dominant "tradition" was that of a different ruling
group from the previous colonial or semi-colonial occupiers. Throughout
much of the world there emerged a minor industry of sports history writing
tailored to those demands, propping up the legislation of oil-rich Gulf states
or meeting the needs of African or Chinese political masters. At international
conferences controversy emerged in ways which were much more direct
than the published proceedings of conferences sometimes suggest. When
the International Economic History Congress met in the still-Communist
Budapest in 1982, including a leisure and sports group in its offerings, many
participants were aware just how much the representatives from Eastern
Europe seemed to be looking over their shoulders towards the "correct"
interpretations offered by Russian scholars. Subsequent conferences on sports
history have revealed similar tensions but a more open sense of grievance.
Such issues surfaced at a major conference on the role of traditional games
in modern society, held in Berlin in 1993. The distinguished American
scholar Allen Guttmann, in a keynote paper, suggested that the United States'
exporting of their sports as an element of economic liberalism represented
an unmitigated good by replacing the near-barbaric primitivism of many
local games. The anger of many in his audience was almost palpable, reacting against both the claims and the neo-imperialism which supposedly dispassionate western scholarship offered to them as a model for interpretation.

Against such an international setting and the agendas of self-determination,
the concerns of much modern British sports history writing often seem
culturally parochial, representing the inbreeding of academia rather than
the poetic anger with social injustice which drove Thompson to write as
he did. Some would argue that, as with so much other social history, there
was a shift into a minor key, festooned with semantic and semiotic coun-
terpoints. But that is unfair, since there were other roots and routes from
which it also emerged, including the politics of national antiquarianism
already discussed. One of these roots was functional, another lay within
the varieties of scholarship to be found in modern liberal democracies and
broad groupings of scholarly styles.

The functional was simply that: born in a series of attempts to widen the
understanding of sports practitioners themselves. This was not, however,
popular history for the weekend footballer – we are talking here about the
training of sports professionals and their ancillaries. In Britain the old physical education colleges, designed to produce generations of sports teachers
who might also offer an "academic" subject to the lower forms of their

schools, were steadily absorbed into the old polytechnics and then trans-mogrified into coverall departments of the "new universities" which followed the 1988 Education Reform Act. Abroad, there are similar departments in the higher education institutions of North America and Australasia and some German universities; in Cologne, for instance, there is a long established Sports Hochschule with an Olympic Studies branch in Athens. The trend towards the widening of their students' horizons and the growing demands for academic "respectability" in both their courses and their products generated an almost inevitable bolting on ("integration" is not always the best word) of other disciplines, particularly sports physiology, philosophy, and sociology alongside history. Pressure towards research and promotion meant that many key sports historians appeared in departments of kinesiology and their ilk rather than in mainstream history teaching. Undoubtedly an older generation of these tended towards a rather mechanistic approach to the use of history, as a framework for more compelling activities, but the diaspora of capable doctoral graduates from the more usual breeding grounds of modern historians led to a sharp increase in interest and intellectual demands. It will undoubtedly be some time, particularly in Britain, before inherent intellectual snobberies are overcome and the quality of the work recognized for what it is, rather than being judged by its authors' source of employment.

The boost in the British approach owed much to the major shifts in historical thinking of the 1960s, although any self-respecting historian would argue that its roots went deeper than that. Indeed, the nature of the British experience of industrialization and urbanism led many scholars from else-where to concentrate their early works at least on features of the British stereotype as an operating model for work in their own countries. Many British scholars, however, do not operate easily in a comparative frame-work, the exception being studies in the spread of sport throughout the old Empire, useful in terms of the sources being largely in English and also for the continued scholarly expiation of post-colonial guilt. Many American writers, most noticeably Allen Guttmann, have gone both for a much wider syncretistic approach and for a longer chronology. The "it is not my period" syndrome which still besets many, if not most, British historians, despite the fact that many of them were taught on university courses which assumed a basic knowledge of over a thousand years of national and European change, has tended to produce an obsessive concentration on the modern, both in terms of the last two centuries and of the process of "modernization" to which the major sports have been so noticeably subjected. I shall return to those below, but there have been few British attempts to explain sports his-tory in a span which often begins with the ancient Egyptians, or in a choice of philosophical or aesthetic themes. For studies of eroticism in sport one turns largely to the United States, although there has been a British concern with games as a vehicle for manliness which shows a nodding acquaintance with Graeco-Roman culture, but largely as moderated by Victorian dons and public school masters. Often foreign scholars have seemed ready to build large theoretical explanations on thin documentary evidence, never a happy situation for the empirically-minded British, even when they were at their most Marxistly modern, let alone with the fragmentation of context and issues which emerged to haunt them in postmodernist writing. Foucault's works have occasionally been nodded at, but rarely absorbed.

American work has been received most happily in Britain when its attention is limited spatially – sport in Boston, New Orleans or wherever, or to individual games which are seen to represent acceptable national peculiarities – baseball and American football spring most readily to mind. The subjects may be unfamiliar but the methodology is reassuring. Nor has the other major alternative tradition has much influence on the British approach – that of "scientific" German historiography. That approach may now lack the assumptions of totality that von Ranke sought to achieve when he invented "scientific history", but it still combines a very heavy factual/narrative approach with a claim that all the work is underpinned by a firm hypothesis. The growing British concern with fluidity, paradox and the complex intertwining of historical strands has owed little to German writing, although contact between individual scholars has flourished in sports history. Even where German historians have written on such issues as sport and *burgertum*, and the role of nationalist sporting associations in bolstering the Second and Third Reichs, another expiation for past wrongs, the approach has been very different from that employed in Britain. Respect, rather than intellectual cross-fertilization, has remained the norm.

Within British practice, a great deal of writing focuses on sport as phenomenon, "because it is there" to borrow the words of a famous mountaineer about the Everest which killed him. There are, perhaps, fewer dangers in preparing, say, a narrative history of cricket and such works have laid a solid foundation on which more adventurous thinkers have built. Some of these books – Raymond Carr's on foxhunting coming most readily to mind – were substantial pieces written by academics about sports in which they participated enthusiastically, and the tradition continues even amongst the wielders of the latest critical apparatus – I admit happily to writing about fishing and bowls, for instance. But the impacts of sociology and the various "new" social historical approaches of the later twentieth century have opened new sight lines. Social class, gender, language, region, urban space, the exercise of power and so on have all become major targets for interpretation in approaches where the history of modern sport is treated as a useful seismograph for detecting shifts and changes in wider society. It was that usage which attracted scholars from the more traditional routes of historical apprenticeship and which has led to continued tensions with the users and practitioners from the more instrumental tradition of training I described above. Occasional signs of convergence have flickered, but the culture of the professional historian predominated and the internal politics of a number of associations devoted to the history of sport here and abroad demonstrated a continued unease and a resistance to takeover by the "professional" historians. There are times when the tribal alignments and cultures of academic groups can count for as much as the supposed pursuit of objectivity.

Such observations are not quite the digression they might at first appear. The influx of the new historians with all their analytical baggage shifted the nature of British sports history considerably, particularly when the employment of cultural stereotypes is considered. Perhaps the greatest attention has been paid to the various branches of football, but with most going to soccer as typifying the commodification of spectator sport for the working classes. It occupies in sports history the place the the music hall came to enjoy in the parallel burgeoning of the history of popular culture, and with all the drawbacks of that emphasis. It was perhaps its visibility, its role as a "mass" activity and its professionalization which prompted such favour, and it depended on a group of writers who were not content solely to watch from the terraces. But it also slotted into a wider debate, that of the role of crowd violence in modern society, with groups of writers who have found the fans more interesting than the game and its structures.

The key text, already noted, for the new approaches was Tony Mason's *Association football and English society, 1863–1915*, published in 1980. It went far beyond narrating the emergence of a working-class game from regional roots into professional organization and it became a model for a more holistic approach to sports history. Its strength remains its closeness to its documentary sources, interpreted with the mild Marxism that E. P. Thompson had left as his legacy to social history at the University of Warwick. Mason's subsequent work has included both a more popular interpretation of the role of sport generally in British society and a general analysis of South American football, but has continued to avoid the simplistic assumptions of capitalist "social control" which were first used to explain mass recreations. His *Association Football* provided an historical base for what was becoming a major issue in British society in general as economic crisis coincided with the first years of Margaret Thatcher's new radical Conservative government. The growing concern with the behaviour of fans both at home and in Europe and the assumptions about a new subculture of youth violence pushed football into being an index of British (in this case, largely English) decline in general. A short-lived joint venture between the Sports Council and the then Social Science Research Council in the early 1980s led to a number of case studies, and then more detailed enquiries, on the social role of modern leisure patterns, supposedly as working papers for influencing government policy. There is little sign that they achieved that aim.

Worries about possible social disintegration went hand in hand with arguments about the relative roles of state and private enterprise in providing for what was widely assumed to be the "leisure society" of the future, offering "meaningful" activities in almost Victorian terms, a purposeful containment of potentially dangerous energies away from the disciplines of work. In this process sociologists, planners and geographers had a head start in collaborative "leisure studies" which were often curiously ahistorical. It has to be said that the growth of sports history has done little to alter this, although there is considerable dialogue on the fringes. Attention to the phenomenology of football in terms of social policy has remained very largely firmly in the hands of the "Leicester school" of sociologists, the paradox being that one its key members, Eric Dunning, had collaborated in producing an imaginative sociological history of Rugby Union, *Barbarians, gentlemen and players*, in 1979. The divergence has continued, although scholars who might regard themselves primarily as sociologists, such as Grant Jarvie and both John and Jennifer Hargreaves, have continued to make inroads into sports history on other topics. At its simplest, the division over interpretations of crowd violence as an index of wider social disintegration has remained unresolved, with historians calling repeatedly for a wider understanding of past contexts against claims that football violence is of relatively recent origin. Meanwhile crowd control at Wembley continues to demand more than one mounted policeman.

If anything, historians have turned back to some safer grazing: few work on the post-1945 period and many prefer the First World War as their cut-off date. There is a working-over of much ground that has already been heavily ploughed in other branches of history. The exception has been Richard Holt, whose first work, *Sport in Modern France*, was a prime example of the new *British* historical approach to sport, one not on the whole matched by French scholars. Holt has offered a number of lively, but essentially synthesizing, books on sport in twentieth-century Britain whose broad, general assertions remain to be tested by more sharply focused studies. Football, meanwhile, has attracted other scholars, still held by its supposedly overarching symbolic role. One question Mason could not really answer was the role of local businessmen in club formation – there was an almost total block in refusing access to club archives. He has not been alone in this experience; when I was writing on golf I found a similar resistance. The public stereotype of the academic anarchist poking his nose into other people's business dies hard. Inevitably, one's deepest suspicions of sleaze, fixing and so on are reinforced – it is not only governments that hide their archives. The notable exception to this pattern was a study of West Ham Football Club by the American Charles Korr, whose book remains a model in explaining how considerations other than hopes of direct profitability may influence investment in sport; the idea of local networks and influence patterns offering a postmodernist interpretation without the jargon.

With the broad delineation of its history accomplished, football has now joined other sports in being more closely dissected. There have been studies of its role in reinforcing subordinate national identities within the United Kingdom, Smith and Williams on Welsh Rugby, Murray and Jarvie on Scotland, and so on. Similarly, questions have begun to emerge about regional loyalties, attachments to particular teams and the creation of sporting heroes in terms somewhat different from Thomas Carlyle's approach to the idea of the charismatic. One major input has come from discussions of the role of professionalism in which Wray Vamplew demonstrated that expenditure on players does not always guarantee results – what the sceptical reader of weekly scores in the press might have imagined was now reinforced by the apparatus of econometrics. Because of the broad similarity of individual historians' approaches, no great field of controversy has opened up yet, however, beyond the ever-present issue of crowd behaviour. Differences are best found in minor footnoting quibbles or in pernickety reviews, so closely now does sports history match its academic foster parents. It is in breakaways from this intensive focus on one game that creative disagreement has surfaced more readily.

Perhaps the major unresolved issue remains that of the role of social class, and here football has become part of a wider concern, one with which British scholars are frequently accused of being obsessed. What is often clear is that there has been a greater embarrassment in approaching the topic in, for instance, both the United States and Canada.With rare exceptions the major British attention has remained glued to working-class experiences. There was some outstanding and contentious work done in the early 1980s by Stephen Jones, whose tragic early death robbed sports history of one of its best practitioners. His Marxism was modifying slowly when faced with empirical evidence which did not fit, but it is still difficult to find studies of working-class sport which cope with the essentially apolitical nature of many local sporting associations in such industrial cities as Sheffield. The relatively small Labour-organised Clarion Cycling Clubs and the British Workers' Sports Federation have proved far more attractive to younger students than angling, whose participants are numbered in millions. Similarly, the middle classes have only entered many studies either as villains, with snobbish ethical codes, or as convenient investors in mass sports for profit. Mangan's key work on the development of a manly ethic and my own more comprehensive work, including studies of golf, went some way to redress this imbalance. This was part of a general process of opening up the middle classes to historical investigation. The revulsion against the heroic portrayals of entrepreneurs who were lauded in such optimistic works as T. S. Ashton's *Industrial revolution* (1948) has taken an unconscionably long time to die away. But, even as the necessary corrections were being made, sport history was touched by other intellectual enthusiasms questioning the suitability of past approaches and arguing that class as a topic, for instance, has been as limited as reliance on narrative. Gestures in the direction of regional or local sporting variations and loyalties, studies of Northumberland miners or Bolton football, have trickled through, but by far the most significant impact has been in gender studies. Actual publication numbers remain small, reflecting the imbalance within the academic establishment of women as well as the dominance of male games in the overall picture. But the new gender approaches, growing away from the more simplistic feminism of the early 1970s, came to question male sexuality as well as women's self-identity. Although the ubiquitous American, Allen Guttmann, produced a loosely structured history of women's games and looked for the erotic elsewhere in sport, it has been women scholars on both sides of the Atlantic who have made the most decisive contributions – Park, McCrone, Vertinsky and Hargreaves leading the field. Scholarly attention moved slowly away from such topics as the early women's hockey movement towards constructions of the feminine, both in terms of demands for self-realization and of the boundaries imposed by male attempts to prevent the erosion of a never-too-closely-defined hegemonic masculinity. Such studies have so far been bounded by the overall concern with western ideas and the experience of economically developed capitalisms, with side nods to the old Soviet experience. New work on images of the body was released from over-concentration on its sporting expressions into wider questions of models and interpretations of the physical in historical cultures examined both anthropologically and aesthetically.

British historians have had one focus which is not enjoyed by most of their foreign counterparts, but which has tied sports studies in with wider current questions; that of the British Empire and the colonial legacies. Not least of these was the stimulus given to them by work done in Canada and Australasia, where the dominant white ethic has proved easier to handle than in either India or Africa, let alone the Caribbean. In all those areas, however, there has been considerable attention paid to what is often seen as *the* British (read "English" as in so many other cases) export – cricket, the major remnant of the white diaspora. Its attraction for research lies not in the centralizing image of an imperial octopus, but as a factor in fostering separatist national identities, mostly in the white Pacific Rim. The Australians will probably rerun cricket's Bodyline Controversy of the 1930s as a model for Pom arrogance *ad nauseam* but, in Don Bradman and others, they also have their own Carlylean heroes. More difficult to examine in those terms has been the understanding of the British exploitation of the Empire as an extended public school playing field or slightly more ragged version of the hunting Shires of the English midlands. Gradually, the racism of the managers of Africa and India has been explored *in situ*, as well as in its survival in the sporting attitudes of a multi-racial Britain, where West Ham and Leeds supporters sharpen up their inherited xenophobia on ethnic minorities before their trips to the European mainland.

At the beginning of the twentieth century many British social commentators identified an obsession with sport as a major symbol, but also a cause of a supposed Darwinian decline in national strength. Fond of classical analogies, they compared the passion for "bread and circuses" at the end of Imperial Rome's magnificence with the spread of football, golf and lawn tennis amongst late Victorian Englishmen. The former game was held to reduce them to unhealthy spectators, the latter to rob them of the virility implicit in manly sports. There may well be some academics who view the development of sports history as affecting their own discipline similarly – where is the rigour of the close analysis of constitutional or foreign policy documents? They may well have a case – there are times when the writing of some scholars who are heavily dependent on analyzing newspaper reports takes on the gushing frenzy of their sources. But I have suggested otherwise in this chapter.

Sports history is an almost inevitable outcome of the "knowledge revolution" of the last thirty years of the twentieth century and of the increasing spread of scholarly tentacles. One might ask, however, whether the octopus is as useful a model as the amoeba in examining that process. Many academic disciplines and their subdivisions might be best understood by reference to their own tribalism as well as to their claims of the intrinsic value of their chosen territories. Scholarly networks have become increasingly international, as have the markets for publishers, particularly in the English-speaking world. The web of conferences has matched, if not exceeded, that of other historical subdisciplines, symbiotic as they are with major sporting foci such as the Commonwealth Games. And national groupings, such as the British Society for Sports History, proliferate, each with their own journals, brought together internationally under the broad umbrella of ISHPES (International Society for the History of Physical Education and Sport).

Because of this growth, sports history has shared some of the difficulties of the older History Workshop Movement. What began often as a loosely defined series of overlapping activities shared by academics and amateur enthusiasts became increasingly professionalized and removed from both popular and antiquarian interests in sport. Sports history, however, is still one area where the scholarly "amateur" (best defined as someone not paid to practise the historian's craft) can make valuable contributions, despite its domination by research students and established academics whose early work was probably done in other branches of history. Sometimes this has been resented and there are instances of parallel "learned" societies being established to escape from university domination.

Whilst all this has happened, sports history in general terms continues to reach huge numbers of readers who would not touch one of the scholarly texts or journals targeted by the new practitioners. As the twentieth century ends, for instance, there has been a spate of centenary histories of golf clubs. These sell to their members as part of the process by which traditions

211

are established, along with the general histories of football clubs, the Grand National and sporting records of all sorts. In the weeks following its production, each year *Wisden's Cricketer's Almanack* sells more copies than many popular novels and many thousands more than even the most successful book by a professional sports historian. Together with the apparently ceaseless popularity of biographies of heroes, ranging from Babe Ruth to Stanley Matthews, these works feed a hunger for sports history to which academic exercises often resemble the expensive offerings of a delicatessen. Many of these popular works exploit local memorabilia and oral history as their sources, materials around which the professionals still hover uncertainly, although the growth of sports-specific museums and new approaches to cultural history is pointing in a direction some are reluctant to explore. As with so many other aspects of the nostalgia and heritage industries, professional historians have remained largely aloof.

We finish by returning to that with which we began, with our two early modern historians at Wembley. In subsequent years they might have found many more of their colleagues on the terraces but would they be treating it as relaxation, or had it become another necessary visit to a slightly different sort of archive, with a rather different result hoped for? Given what they are now expected to produce, would they dare to enjoy themselves as much as Bindoff and Lamont did?

Suggestions for further reading

The largest and most convenient critical listing of sports history works, including many foreign language books and journals, is to be found in the footnotes of Richard Holt, "Sport and History: the state of the subject in Britain", *Twentieth century British history*, 7(2) pp. 231-52, 1996. The less ambitious or more hesitant might find a number of general works as a sound starting point. Tony Mason has provided two of these, with broadly similar titles. His *Sport in Britain* (London: Faber & Faber, 1988) is a useful general survey, not afraid of theory, whilst his *Sport in Britain, a social history* (Cambridge: Cambridge University Press, 1989) is a collection of papers on individual sports by a number of historians. Richard Holt, *Sport and the British: a modern history* (Oxford: Oxford University Press, 1989), offers a useful synthesis of work available at the time but is less strong on the later part of the twentieth century. A different, more thematic approach is offered by the sociologist John Hargreaves, *Sport, power and culture; a social and historical analysis of popular sports in Britain* (Cambridge: Polity, 1986). It is worth comparing these approaches with that of leading American scholars, with their longer timespans, international comparisons and stress on cultural themes. R. D. Mandell offers *Sport, a cultural history* (New York: Columbia University Press, 1984) whilst the doyen of the United

States writers, Allen Guttmann's prolific output is best represented by two books; *From Ritual to record* (New York: Columbia University Press, 1978) and *Games and empires* (New York: Columbia University Press, 1994).

The British emphasis on individual sports and social history themes saw its first major outing in Tony Mason, *Association Football and English society, 1863-1915* (Brighton: Harvester, 1980); his strong empiricism should be compared with E. Dunning, P. Murphy and J. Williams, *The roots of football hooliganism* (London: Routledge and Kegan Paul, 1988). A rather breathless input to this debate was made in James Walvin, *Football and the decline of Britain* (London: Macmillan, 1986). Another perspective, on the players themselves, is offered by W. Vamplew, *Pay Up, Pay Up and Play the Game: professional sport in Britain 1875-1914* (Cambridge: Cambridge University Press, 1989). Charles Korr, *West Ham United; the making of a football club* (London: Duckworth, 1986) remains a unique insight into the directors' box. Keith A. P. Sandiford, *Cricket and the Victorians* (Aldershot: Scolar, 1994) is very good on the exploited professionals. In general working-class terms, the best work is still to be found in two books by Stephen Jones; *Workers at play* (London: Routledge and Kegan Paul, 1986) and *Sport, Politics and the Working Class* (Manchester: Manchester University Press, 1988). Correctives to this focus can be found in J. A. Mangan, *Athleticism in the Victorian and Edwardian public school* (Cambridge: Cambridge University Press, 1981) and John Lowerson, *Sport and the English middle classes, 1870-1914* (Manchester: Manchester University Press, 1993). An interesting comparison further up the social ladder may be found between Raymond Carr, *English foxhunting; a history* (London: Weidenfeld & Nicholson, 1976) and D. C. Itzkowitz, *Peculiar privilege, a social history of English foxhunting, 1753-1885* (Hassocks: Harvester, 1977). An English regional approach began to emerge with J. Hill and J. Williams, *Sport and identity in the North of England* (Keele: Keele University Press, 1996) and D. Russell, "Sport and Identity: the case of Yorkshire County Cricket Club, 1880-1939", *Twentieth century British history*, 7(2) pp. 206-30, 1996.

Non-English coverage within the United Kingdom may be found in Bill Murray, *The old firm; sectarianism, sport and society in Scotland* (Edinburgh: John Donald, 1984), G. Jarvie and G. Walker (eds), *Scottish sport and the making of the nation* (Leicester: Leicester University Press, 1994), D. Smith and G. Williams, *Fields of praise; the official history of the Welsh Rugby Union* (Cardiff: University of Wales Press, 1980) and A. Bairner and J. Sugden, *Sport, sectarianism and society in a divided Ireland* (Leicester: Leicester University Press, 1993). For another spatial approach, that of the historical geographer, turn to the various books of John Bale, notably *Sport and place* (London: Hurst, 1982). The Physical Education roots can be found in P. C. Macintosh (ed.), *Physical education in England since 1800* (London: Bell, 1968), the sub-Carlylean hero in R. Holt, J. A. Mangan and

P. Lanfranchi (eds), *European heroes: sport, myth and identity* (London: Cass, 1996).

Much of the exciting work on sport and gender can be found in the very contrasting approaches of Allen Guttmann, *Women's Sports* (New York: Columbia University Press, 1991), Jennifer Hargreaves, *Sporting females* (London: Routledge, 1994), K. E. McCrone, *Sport and the physical emancipation of English women* (London: Routledge, 1988), P. Vertinsky, *The eternally wounded woman* (Manchester: Manchester University Press, 1990), J. A. Mangan and R. J. Park (eds), *From fair sex to feminism* (London: Cass, 1987) and J. A. Mangan and J. Walvin, *Manliness and morality* (Manchester: Manchester University Press, 1989). A rather smaller study of gender confusion may be found in John Lowerson, "Stoolball; conflicting values in the revival of a traditional Sussex game", *Sussex Archaeological Collections*, **133**, pp. 263–74, 1995. Imperialism can be seen through J. A. Mangan, *The games ethic and imperialism* (London: Viking, 1986) and J. M. Mackenzie, *Imperialism and the natural world* (Manchester: Manchester University Press, 1990). J. A. Mangan, *Pleasure, profit, proselytism; British culture and sport at home and abroad, 1700–1914* (London: Cass, 1988) covers individual sports and themes of racism and hegemony. Those wanting other sources than the printed should try *Oral History*, Spring 1997, with its series of articles on sport based on interviews.

The bibliographies of all these will provide some years of follow-up. Huge detail may be found in Richard William Cox, *Sport in Britain: a bibliography of historical publications, 1800–1988* (Manchester: Manchester University Press, 1991). To locate this and other approaches to history within academic tribalism, try T. Becher, *Academic Tribes and Territories* (Milton Keynes: Open University Press, 1989).

E. P. Thompson: witness against the beast

Eileen Janes Yeo

Edward Palmer Thompson (1924–93) left giant footprints across the historiography of eighteenth- and nineteenth-century England. His work was spectacularly controversial and, wherever he moved, he was followed by adoring acolytes and splenetic critics (sometimes resembling careerist terriers snapping at his heels). One of the few historians of modern (and postmodern) times to attract verdicts like "one of those extraordinary people who inspired whole generations" and "one of a select band of historians who have fundamentally changed the ways we can look at the past", Thompson's reasons for studying history and his major contributions to historical (and political) analysis deserve close attention. This essay will give a short account of his life and political commitment, before addressing his developing concerns with class and culture in England in works which have shaped research all over the world concerned, as they are, with widely-differing societies and historical times.

Class and culture

E. P. Thompson was the son of Methodist missionaries with, perhaps, surprising interests. His American mother, Theodosia Jessop, had worked first in the Lebanon, while his father, E. J. Thompson, became a scholar-poet of India, a friend of the Nehrus and of Rabindranath Tagore, whose work he translated. E. P. Thompson attended the Methodist Kingswood School before going up to Cambridge, but he broke off his university studies to serve in a tank regiment in Italy during the Second World War, in the course of which his brother Frank was executed in Bulgaria as a partisan and has since become a national hero. After finishing at university, E. P. Thompson became an extra-mural tutor at Leeds University in 1946, the same year that he married fellow-historian Dorothy Towers. Having joined the Communist Party as a student, he was active in the Communist Historians Group (1946–50) which also boasted such luminaries as Christopher Hill, who called it the "most stimulating intellectual experience I ever had" and underlined how "totally undogmatic" and "agreeably fierce" discussions were. In 1955, Thompson published a biography, *William Morris: romantic to revolutionary* which reinstated Morris as an important socialist thinker whose politics and art were intertwined and whose vision of work-pleasure and way of communicating it were capable of engaging desire, an issue of continuing interest to Thompson. Thompson left the Communist Party in 1956 over the savage Soviet suppression of the Hungarian uprising and, from then on, as a founder of the *New Reasoner* and then the *New Left Review*, became one of the most eloquent proponents of socialist humanism in the English-speaking world.

His principled defection from the Communist Party and his search for a new political landscape outside the conventional labour movement (articulated in *Out of apathy*, 1960 and in the *May Day manifesto*, 1968) helped him also to chart a new terrain for historical studies. Up to that time, two main sets of assumptions had prevailed in labour history. The first was a crude version of the Marxist model of base and superstructure which gave determining power to an economic base of productive relations and activity which produced a class structure. Culture (as way of life), consciousness, ideas and political and legal forms was seen as part of a superstructure which was considered to be reflective of the more basic level of reality. The second assumption was that once the working class became conscious of its economic exploitation and potential, it would organize into the kinds of institutions, like trade unions, co-operatives and political parties, which were usually seen as the sections of the labour movement and provided the conventional subjects of study for historians wishing to dignify the working class and help accelerate its forward march.

Thompson's *The making of the English working class*, published in 1963, broke both of these older assumptions. He insisted on class as a relationship between groups which develops over time and is lived out in cultural forms. In a now classic definition he wrote,

> the notion of class entails the notion of historical relationship. Like any other relationship, it is a fluency which evades analysis if we attempt to stop it dead at any given moment and anatomise its structure. The finest-meshed sociological net cannot give us a pure specimen of class, any more than it can give us one of deference or of love. The relationship must always be embodied in real people and in a real context. Moreover, we cannot have two distinct classes, each with an independent being, and then bring them *into* relationship with each other. We cannot have love without lovers, nor deference without squires and

216

labourers. And class happens when some men as a result of common experiences (inherited or shared), feel and articulate the identity of their interests as between themselves, and as against other men whose interests are different from (and usually opposed to) theirs. The class experience is largely determined by the productive relations into which men are born - or enter involuntarily. Class-consciousness is the way in which these experiences are handled in cultural terms: embodied in traditions, value systems, ideas and institutional forms. If the experience appears as determined, class-consciousness does not.

The lived experiences of men and women, which used to be relegated to the superstructure, Thompson argued, were important in forming classes and their consciousness of social identity. This way of looking at class created a new agenda for research within labour history. The lives and struggles of groups of working people, regardless of whether or not they resulted in institutions of the labour movement, now became legitimate areas to study. *The making of the English working class* put this approach to work and evoked working-class experience in a particularly vivid way, not least because Thompson's polemical, sarcastic and passionate style was always engaging regardless of whether it made the reader sympathize or splutter. As he wrote in a famous manifesto passage, "I am seeking to rescue the poor stockinger, the Luddite cropper, the obsolete hand-loom weaver, the utopian artist, and even the deluded follower of Joanna Southcott, from the enormous condescension of posterity". The political battles in which working people were embroiled received careful attention from the period of the French Revolution, when organizations like the Corresponding Societies all over the country, for the first time in history, tried to attract unlimited numbers into the political process, right through to the postwar radical revival and its culmination in the tragic events of Peterloo in August 1819. Thompson also explored the experiences of work in the section appropriately called "The Curse of Adam". He showed how new capitalist priorities and work disciplines affected field labourers, artisans and weavers who interpreted their experience with value systems which judged the changes to be not progressive but oppressive - for example, to be in violation of the constitutional rights of the freeborn Englishman to a fair day's wage for a fair day's work and to shatter people's pride in their craftsmanship.

In a famous section on the Luddite protests, Thompson argued that the artisans involved were not just mindless dinosaurs obstructing modern paths of development, but highly conscious craftspeople with clear ideas of the correct way to make their product, and of the fair way to treat working people, and who used constitutional modes of appeal to protective legislation through their trade societies (both important in armoury of the defences of the poor) and only turned to direct action when these interventions were dismissed as perpetrated by Jacobins. In his analysis, Thompson gave a model demonstration of how any historian studying a dissident group or a group without easy access to the public record has to reconstruct the sensibility and culture of that group from hostile evidence. By reading the actions as well as the words of the Luddites, Thompson produced a completely different idea of their motivation and their thinking within a mental framework of a moral economy which prioritized customary justice as against deregulated markets.

The making of the English working class was an immediate sensation and attracted not only applause but also attacks, from the left as well as from the right of the political spectrum. His historian critics levelled their assaults mainly at his claim that an underground tradition linked the Jacobins of the 1790s with the post-Napoleonic War reform movements, his interpretation of the Luddites, his arguments about the psychological function of Methodism at moments of political defeat (the "chiliasm of despair") and at his conclusions about the clear development of class relations and class consciousness by 1832. He replied to these criticisms in the "Postscript" to the second edition of his book in 1968. Feminists were also worried about the relative absence of working women compared with working men from the analysis, and several have produced substantive research to redress the balance (Anna Clark's, *The struggle for the breeches: gender and the making of the British working class*, 1995, is an example) which indicates, as Leonore Davidoff and Catherine Hall put it when speaking particularly of the middle class, that "class consciousness always takes a gendered form". More recently, historians influenced by postmodernism, like Patrick Joyce, have challenged the "master narrative" of class development and increasing class consciousness by arguing that the terminology of class was not the favoured language of radicals in Thompson's period and after; rather, the construct "the people" predominated and tended towards inclusiveness and harmony between classes. This view has been contested by other historians, including myself, who have argued that resonant rhetoric and symbols are contestable and capable of carrying contradictory meanings.

To his Marxist critics, Thompson responded with an article on "The peculiarities of the English" in 1965 which clarified his analysis of class and which set out the agenda for his subsequent historical work. He presented a set of proposals about the development of social relations in eighteenth-century England, not only arguing for the existence of what he paradoxically called an agrarian bourgeoisie, agricultural capitalists equally at home on their country estates and in the sophisticated London season, but also for the nature of the State as a parasitic structure not clearly allied to the emerging capitalist classes but controlled by banditti Whig Lords who made their fortunes largely out of the public purse. He was sensitized to this kind of formation by his understanding of state elites in the communist countries of Eastern Europe, an understanding which, in turn, was nourished by his continuing study of the eighteenth century. In "An Open Letter to [the

Polish dissident] Leszek Kolakowski" in 1973, Thompson elaborated the analogy between the two kinds of society and entertained a cautious optimism that the parasitic structures of Communist governments could be toppled from below, although he hoped that the popular uprising would be committed to more genuine socialist democracy than to the dash for capitalist market society that actually ensued.

Having moved to the University of Warwick in 1965, Thompson was already deeply involved, along with his postgraduate seminar, in studying social relations in eighteenth-century England. Their research resulted in a collective volume, *Albion's fatal tree: crime and society in eighteenth-century England* (1975) and in Thompson's own study of *Whigs and hunters: the origins of the Black Act* (1977). (I too was able to experience E. P. Thompson's generosity to young scholars when our mutual admiration for Henry Mayhew's ability to let working people speak for themselves and his analysis of the London trades resulted in a jointly edited volume on *The unknown Mayhew: selections from the Morning Chronicle 1849-1850* in 1971.) *Whigs and hunters* was, in some ways, the obverse of *The making of the English working class*, an elegantly crafted small gem compared to the earlier sprawling *tour de force*, but able, as Blake insisted, to make the universe visible in a grain of sand as well as in the vast panoramic view. By carefully tracking an episode of contention about the Royal forest of Windsor, which led to the passing of the Black Act in 1723, and created an enormous new inventory of capital crimes, Thompson showed how one mental universe was being defeated by another. A view of property involving customary but differential access and use rights was giving way to the idea of absolute private ownership which was the central feature of capitalism as a social formation; the Whig elite made fortunes out of both types of customary or contractual property.

In the same period, Thompson was also taking the view from below in a series of famous articles on popular culture which finally reached book form in *Customs in common* in 1991. Of these the most seminal and controversial was that on "The moral economy of the English crowd in the eighteenth century" (1971). Again, as in his study of the Luddites, Thompson explored episodes like food riots which had largely been seen before as spontaneous and violent eruptions of a mindless and hungry mob. Once more using hostile sources, like letters to the *Gentleman's Magazine* and to the Home Office as well as the proceedings of trials, Thompson paid careful attention to the timing of the outbreaks, to their ritual form as well as to the words that the rioters can be overheard speaking. He argued that these outbursts were strikingly restrained in their violence, which was targeted at symbolically loaded property not at persons, and which often involved the crowd commandeering grain or bread and selling these at what it considered to be a just price. He concluded that the crowd was acting in terms of a sensibility which he called a "moral economy" view,

219

which saw the market as a locus of customary rights and not of unrestrained economic behaviour, a place where the consumer, especially the poor consumer, ought to be protected in times of dearth, and the profiteer treated as an outlaw.

Putting together the view from above and from below, Thompson challenged the prevailing historiographical commonsense about eighteenth-century English society being paternalistic or being characterized by gentry paternalism on the one side and, on the other, deference from the labouring poor. Such a bland conception, he felt, concealed the amount of active reciprocity and conflict between the groups which his close studies had disclosed. As a concept, paternalism "tends to offer a model of the social order as it is seen from above; it has implications of warmth and of face-to-face relations which imply notions of value; it confuses the actual and the ideal". Instead, in his 1974 article on "Patrician society, plebeian culture" and again in his article on "Eighteenth-century English society: class struggle without class?", (1978), Thompson developed his view of the basic shape of eighteenth-century English social relations by drawing upon the metaphor of the field of force familiar to physics students from the school experiment with magnetic poles and iron filings which cluster towards the stronger force, but nonetheless are held in a dynamic equilibrium. He constructed a model of social relations which involved a power equilibrium between the gentry, whom he sometimes called the patricians (their own self-characterization), and the common people in the crowd, whom he called the plebeians or plebs.

These two basic groupings exerted their distinctly unequal power in highly theatrical ways to call each other to order within the bounds of a commonly understood set of duties and obligations, what Thompson called "the moral economy of the poor". The crowd who tipped their caps by day also posted anonymous threatening letters by night, reminding the gentry that freeborn Englishmen had customary rights: to food in the land where they laboured, to a fair day's wage for a fair day's work, and to freedom from arbitrary incursions by the armed force of the state. If not appeased, for example by market regulation or philanthropic gestures, the crowd might stage a riot by day, particularly in times of bad harvest and high food prices. The ruling classes had their own theatrical ways of displaying their authority. By and large the actual landowners only met the plebs face-to-face when regaled in the majesty of the law, or prepared to shower mercy and charity to cool plebeian discontent. Otherwise they operated as employers and landlords through a range of less benevolent middlemen, who then became the convenient focus for popular rage during riots.

In the eighteenth-century field of force, the gentry established their rule less by coercion and armed force and more by a theatrical style of rule. This was necessary and possible for two important reasons. First, until the period of the Napoleonic Wars and the raising of a force of armed volunteers, there was no standing army powerful enough to provide a police presence except at really critical junctures. Secondly, the labouring poor (another gentry term) could cohabit within this framework because, although they depended on the gentry and the industrial employers for their livelihood, their popular culture was given a wide berth and their times of enjoyment could be anticipated and remembered without fear of disruption by the powerful classes whether from the church or state. Thompson spoke of the church having detached itself from the emotional calendar of the poor at the same time as the gentry could position themselves as distant patrons of popular recreation.

This delicate balance of social forces exploded in the period of the French Revolution, after having been undermined in the preceding decades. Agrarian capitalists had already been organizing the production of crops for free movement and profitable sale in far-flung markets, statute law was enshrining absolute powers of ownership rather than use rights to property, employers were imposing new labour disciplines and redefining as theft what artisans regarded as customary prerequisites of their trade, and a new science of political economy was theorizing all this behaviour as compliance with the natural laissez-faire laws of economic life. But it was only with the French Revolution and the fear of an English replay that "the rulers of England conceived that their whole social order might be endangered". Before "the insubordination of the poor was an inconvenience; it was not a menace". From now on all collective actions of the crowd or their activities in political associations, trade unions or friendly societies were painted or smeared with lurid Jacobin colours. At this point "we move out of the eighteenth-century field-of-force and enter a period in which there is a structural re-ordering of class relations and of ideology. It is possible, for the first time, to analyse the historical process in terms of nineteenth-century notations of class". And this is where *The making of the English working class* enters once again to take up the story.

This iconoclastic view of the eighteenth century, which disrupted the patrician self-image of a polite, ordered, elegant and benevolent society, needless to say, disturbed the composure of many historians as well. A large number of critics lined up to fire shots at the article on "the moral economy of the crowd" and Thompson made spirited riposte to them in a chapter on "The moral economy reviewed", in his *Customs in common*, 1991. He largely targeted them as people who misunderstood, or refused to allow the legitimacy of, his questions and concerns, largely because they insisted on the monopoly of their own disciplines over the relevant issues: "intellectual history, like economic history before it, becomes imperialist and seeks to overrun all social life". Intellectual historians, he grumbled, "are rebuking me for writing an essay in social history and in popular culture instead of in approved Cambridge themes. I ought to have grabbed a bell-rope and pealed out Quesnay along with Pufendorf, Pocock, Grotius, Hume and the rest". But he expressed sympathetic interest in the way that the concept "moral economy", which he had fathered on the academic community, was being reshaped elsewhere, particularly in peasant studies to denote the "equilibrium of bargaining between unequal social forces in which the weaker still has acknowledged claims upon the greater" or "the social dialectic of unequal mutuality (need and obligation) which lies at the centre of most societies", whether in lower Burma and Vietnam, or among the Hausa in northern Nigeria, or in Bengali famine situations, or in class relations in eighteenth-century Ireland.

Ostensibly retiring to his house in the country to write *Customs in common* and also a long-projected book on William Blake, he came thundering on to the public scene once again in the late 1970s with apocalyptic attacks on the authoritarianism of the British secret state, on the one hand, and the French socialist theoreticism on the other. Confronting the work of structural Marxist Louis Althusser in "The poverty of theory", Thompson produced his most sustained and brilliant defence of the craft of the historian and of historical categories as explanatory concepts continually honed in an ongoing conversation between models and empirical materials. Here too he returned to the theme of identifying and challenging forms of elitism which he felt the obsession with theory was reproducing. He reminded his readers that "experience arises spontaneously within social being, but it does not arise without thought; it arises because men and women (and not only philosophers) are rational, and they think about what is happening to themselves and their world" and further insisted upon reminding the Marxist philosopher:

> that knowledges have been and still are formed outside the academic procedures. Nor have these been, in the test of practice, negligible. They have assisted men and women to till the fields, to construct houses, to support elaborate social organisations, and even, on occasion, to challenge effectively the conclusions of academic thought.

His deep concern about the terminal scenario that the authoritarian Thatcher government was happily embracing, partly as a result of its romance with the nuclear "deterrent", led him to produce some of his most stunningly satirical pieces, collected together in *Writing by candlelight* and in the influential pamphlet *Protest and survive*, ridiculing a government pamphlet, *Protect and survive*, which actually gave instructions on how to build a do-it-yourself understairs bomb shelter in order to survive nuclear attack! Active in the 1980s revival of disarmament activity, he helped launch the European Nuclear Disarmament group which appealed to the people of Eastern and Western Europe over the heads of their rulers to create a buffer zone of non-aligned powers who "unequivocally" rejected the ideology of both blocs. Not surprisingly he was accused of being a member of the KGB by the British right and a CIA agent by the Chair of the Soviet Peace Committee!

His last work, which appeared posthumously, was on William Blake. So many of the concerns of a lifetime clustered together here. With great scholarly pains, Thompson tracked surviving antinomian traditions from seventeenth-century radical dissent into the eighteenth-century London artisan world. Here was a tradition of knowledge, separate from and sometimes antagonistic to the "polite knowledge" of the Enlightenment which intellectual historians often study, but nonetheless vigorous and capable of offering robust alternatives to the materialism of capitalist market relations and to the powerful culture-makers who produced its paramount values. Thus Blake could lambast the moral or Mosaic law, guarded by institutions like the Anglican Church, while, at the same time, embracing Christ's Everlasting Gospel of forgiveness and love. In a song like *London*, Blake could encapsulate the blighted lived experience of a market society where all human relations become a matter of buying and selling, a tragedy made even more explicit in a deleted fragment from the *Human Abstract*:

> There souls of men are bought & sold
> And milk fed infancy for gold
> And youth to slaughter houses led
> And beauty for a bit of bread

To counter such a socially and psychically powerful formation as market society required a leap of imagination, intellect and will. Thompson found William Blake and William Morris particularly attractive because both tried to prise people loose from existing notions of common sense and ideas about the supposedly natural order of things. And both paid attention to the education of desire. Blake drew upon a religious tradition which eschewed oppressive purveyors of knowledge (like Enlightenment materialists "and priests in black gowns . . . walking their rounds/and binding with briars my joys & desires") and urged people to have confidence in a higher authority: be "haughty to man" and "humble to god". Morris tried to create a politics which would make people long for a better society "with the unreasonable passion of a lover". Like Morris and Blake, Thompson yearned for a more human world and like them, throughout his life, he stood firm and railed loud as a "Witness against the beast".

Suggestions for further reading

An extensive bibliography of E. P. Thompson's published writings, historical and political, is to be found in: J. Rule and R. Malcolmson (eds), *Protest and survival. The historical experience* (London: Merlin, 1993). The works by E. P. Thompson cited in this chapter, in roughly chronological order, are: *William Morris: romantic to revolutionary* (London: Lawrence & Wishart, 1955; Merlin, 1977); *Out of apathy* (London: New Left Books,

1960); *The making of the English working class* (London: Gollancz, 1963), (2nd edn, Harmondsworth, 1968 with postscript, 1980 with new preface); *The May Day manifesto*, rev. edn, R. Williams (ed.) (Harmondsworth: Penguin, 1968); *The unknown Mayhew: selections from the Morning Chronicle, 1849–50*, (ed. with E. Yeo) (London: Merlin, 1971); *Albion's fatal tree: crime and society in eighteenth-century England*, (ed. with D. Hay et al.) (London: 1975); *Whigs and hunters: The origins of the Black Act* (London: Allen Lane, 1977); *The Poverty of theory and other essays* (which includes "The Peculiarity of the English", 1965, and "An Open Letter to Leszek Kolakowski", 1973) (London: Merlin Press, 1978); "Patrician society, plebeian culture", *Journal of Social History* 7, 1974; "Eighteenth-century English society: class struggle without class?", *Social History* 3(2); *Writing by Candlelight* (London: Merlin, 1980); *Protest and Survive*, with D. Smith (Harmondsworth: Penguin, 1981); *Customs in Common* (Harmondsworth: Penguin, 1991) which includes the original "The Moral Economy of the English Crowd in the Eighteenth Century", 1971, and also "The Moral Economy Reviewed" discussing criticisms and developments; *Witness Against the Beast: William Blake and the Moral Law* (Cambridge: Cambridge University Press, 1993). Work about Thompson includes B. Palmer, *E. P. Thompson: objections and oppositions* (London: Verso, 1994); H. Kaye, *The British Marxist historians: an introductory analysis* (Cambridge: Polity, 1984) and *The education of desire: Marxists and the writing of history* (New York and London: Routledge, 1992).

Thompson lists his main critics and replies to them in the "Postscript" to the 1968 edn of *The making of the English working class* and also in "The Moral Economy Reviewed" in *Customs in common*. The most sustained critique from a Marxist viewpoint is to be found in P. Anderson, *Arguments within English Marxism* (London: New Left Books, 1980); for feminist revision, see Joan Scott, *Gender and the politics of history* (New York: Columbia University Press, 1989) and Anna Clark, *The struggle for the breeches: gender and the making of the British working class* (London: Rivers Oram, 1995); for post-modern critique, see Patrick Joyce, *Visions of the people. Industrial England and the question of class, 1848–1914* (Cambridge: Cambridge University Press, 1991) and for rejoinders, J. Epstein, *Radical expression: political language, ritual and symbol in England, 1790–1850* (New York: Oxford University Press, 1994) and Eileen Janes Yeo, "Language and Contestation: the Case of 'the People', 1832 to the Present" in *Languages of Labour*, J. Belchem and N. Kirk (eds) (Aldershot: Scolar, 1997).

Chapter Eighteen

Soviet historians and the rediscovery of the Soviet past

B. Williams

Changes in the present result in changes in the way we look at the past. For the historian one of the most exciting parts of the Gorbachev era between 1985 and 1991 was the rediscovery of the Soviet past, a process which, it can be argued, played a surprisingly large role in the collapse of Communism and the end of the Soviet Union. It is not possible here to consider all the reasons for that collapse, which would cover economic and ecological problems, nationality issues and the effects of the democratization of the political system. Of Gorbachev's three slogans, *perestroika, glasnost* and democratization, I want to focus on one area of *glasnost;* the rediscovery of the past. *Glasnost*, or openness, was introduced to get popular support for *perestroika*, or economic restructuring, and involved a virtually free press, and the discovery of a western-type, investigative journalism. Gorbachev miscalculated, however. Instead of encouraging support for the new policies, *glasnost* proved to be a licence to grumble, and fatally undermined support for the Communist Party. As was the case with Alexander II in the 1860s, by allowing greater freedom of ideas, Gorbachev was to create his own opposition. The Congress of People's Deputies in the summer of 1989 – the first partially freely elected assembly since the Constituent Assembly was dissolved in January 1918 – was a turning-point. As debates were broadcast live on television, the nation watched spellbound as deputies talked frankly about the problems facing Soviet society, such as pollution, the drying up of the Aral sea, and crime, and openly mentioned previously forbidden facts about the past – the impact of collectivization on their villages or their experiences of the purges. The myth of party infallibility was publicly and rudely broken.

The process of rediscovery of the past was not part of Gorbachev's original policy. In early 1986 he stated that "Stalinism" was an invention of the West, but in February 1987 he gave a speech to representatives of the media and said that "there should not be any blank pages in either our history or our literature. History has to be seen as it is." In fact the re-evaluation of the Stalin years had already started. Novels, such as Rybakov's *Children of the Arbat*, which had been written under Khrushchev in the 1960s but never published, began to appear. The Georgian film *Repentance*, an allegorical account of the Stalin years, had been shown before Gorbachev's speech. Nevertheless, after it, the flood gates opened as the media took up the challenge. Films and novels published abroad, such as *Dr Zhivago*, Grossman's *Life and fate*, set at the time of the battle for Stalingrad, and finally even the works of Solzhenitsyn appeared in Russia for the first time. Newspapers like *Moscow News*, *Ogonyok*, and *Argumenty i Fakty* attracted large readerships with their re-evaluations of the Stalin years. The last named had a circulation of 31.5 million by 1990.

Gorbachev made it clear in later speeches, in November 1987 and again in February 1988, that he intended the criticism to be restricted to the Stalin and Brezhnev years, and that he was not attacking socialism. "We are not retreating a step from socialism and Marxist-Leninism", he declared. Nevertheless he repeated that "we decisively renounce the dogmatic, bureaucratic and voluntarist legacy . . . Critical analysis, not avoiding anything, not fearing the truth, only such an analysis can work for socialism". Writers, journalists and filmmakers were in the forefront of this reconsideration of the past. Professional historians were, with few exceptions, much more reluctant to get involved, and to understand why we need to examine the history profession under Soviet rule. History had long been a dangerous pastime in the Soviet Union, and twentieth-century and party history was the most controlled and the most politically sensitive area. Trained separately through the Institute of Marxism–Leninism, party historians had more prestige but less freedom than their colleagues. Moreover they were an ageing profession with reputations to worry about, apart from the constant threat that party policies might change. Soviet history was a very different discipline from its Western counterpart. The early Bolshevik historian, M. N. Pokrovsky, once defined history as "politics fitted to the past".

History was a vital part in the creation of a new society for the Bolsheviks after 1917. Education and propaganda played an important role in building socialism. During the early years of the Russian Revolution mass theatre, cinema, posters, literature and art were all harnessed to the task of changing society and history was no exception. The battle on the historical front, like the battle on the military one, was fought out over the civil war years. Early texts like Trotsky's *History of the Russian revolution to Brest Litovsk* and John Reed's *Ten days that shook the world*, stressed the mass nature of the uprising as an encouragement to the European proletariat to copy the Russian example. By the early 1920s Lenin was insisting on the essential leadership role of the party, both in explaining the success of the Bolsheviks in Russia and in setting up foreign Communist Parties through the Comintern.

In 1924 *IstPart* was set up to study the party's role. Some left-wing Bolsheviks wanted to abolish history altogether as bourgeois and unnecessary, but Lenin emphasized the need to learn from history. "The Communist", he wrote, "must first be able to take from the old school what is absolutely necessary for him. It would be a great mistake to believe that you can be a communist without assimilating all human knowledge of which communism itself is the result". This did not alter the fact that all existing history books were bourgeois and had to be rewritten. There was need to legitimize the Bolshevik takeover and provide the proletariat with its own account of the past. Pokrovsky set himself the task of presenting the Bolshevik regime as the inevitable culmination of a millennium of history of worker and peasant struggle against exploitation. History was to explain the future as well as the past by presenting it in terms of Marxist stages and class struggle. This remained true of historical writing throughout the Soviet period.

In 1960 *Voprosy Istorii*, one of the main Soviet historical journals, wrote, "the study of history has never been a mere curiosity, a withdrawal into the past for the sake of the past . . . Historical science has been and remains an arena of sharp ideological struggle and remains a class, party history". And again in 1962, "an historian is not a dispassionate reporter who identifies facts or even places them in a scientifically valid pattern . . . He is a fighter who sees his goal in placing the history of the past in the service of the struggle for communism". Pokrovsky would have agreed with such statements. He called history "the concrete investigation of concrete social questions, study of which will reveal general laws governing social change and which may then be utilised in shaping the future course of society". An old Bolshevik who had been a member of the party since 1905, he became the commander of the new army of Red historians after the revolution and trained the next generation of students. His *Brief history of Russia*, written in 1920, became the textbook for the new regime, a strictly Marxist account based on economic determinism, where all changes in society were related to changes in the methods of production and exchange, and the individual was eliminated from the process of causation. Russian history from the ninth century was placed within the various Marxist stages of development, although Pokrovsky added his own stage of merchant capitalism in order to be able to argue that Russia had had a form of capitalism from the seventeenth century and was, therefore, now ready for socialism. As deputy commissar for education, the head of the Institute of Red Professors, founder of the Society of Marxist Historians and chair of the Central Archive Administration, Pokrovsky was indeed the history man of early Soviet Russia.

Nevertheless, non-Marxist historians were allowed to survive the 1920s, in line with Lenin's policy of using bourgeois experts, as long as they did not oppose the regime, until new Soviet ones could be trained. Pokrovsky himself seems to have seen such people as useful targets on which his new students could sharpen their skills. Such tolerance stopped, however, with the First Five Year Plan of 1928. Non-Marxist historians were arrested as part of a campaign to proletarianize society, and the radicals were allowed to take over in history as in other professions. Pokrovsky benefited from this, but was also criticized as a vulgar Marxist, as Stalin's new policies emphasized the willpower of the proletariat over economic determinism, party leadership and the cult of Stalin himself, and even a growing nationalism with the policy of socialism in one country. Torn between his acceptance of the party's right to dictate and his disagreement with the new line, and criticized as reactionary by his more radical students, Pokrovsky admitted his errors and died, loaded with honours in 1932. By then, however, Stalin had firmly taken over control of the history profession. Many of Pokrovsky's students were in their turn purged and the *Brief history* was replaced by Stalin's own *Short course* by the end of the 1930s. Between 1931 and 1934 only three universities, all in the provinces, taught history at all.

Under Khrushchev the historians were given greater freedom, as Stalin and the cult of personality were repudiated in 1956, but again the party line was firmly maintained if historians attempted to go too far. The entire editorial board of *Voprosy Istorii* was dismissed in 1962 and historians like Roy Medvedev, who had written a critique of Stalin with *Let history judge*, or A. M. Nekrich, who had produced an account of the early days of the war which went further than the official line would allow, were silenced or forced into exile. Given such a background, it is hardly surprising that historians were slow to respond to Gorbachev. The camps or exile could await those who guessed the political situation wrongly. Nevertheless a few historians were prominent in *glasnost.* Yurii Afanasiev was made director of the State Archive Institute and Professor V. P. Danilov's work on collectivization of agriculture was published. Young researchers began to delve into the archives. But the main work of history in these years was by a maverick. General Dmitri Volkogonov was an army general who became head of the Military Historical Institute and published the first Russian biography of Stalin since his death in 1988, a typically *glasnost* work called *Stalin, Triumph and tragedy.*

Soviet commentators started to attack the policies of the Stalin years and not, as had happened in 1956, just the cult of personality. Collectivization of agriculture, the famine (for the first time openly admitted in the Soviet Union), the terror and nationality policies were the main fields on which the attack was to focus. The Stalin years were firmly blamed for the problems facing Gorbachev as he struggled to reform. The command administrative economy, the over-centralization and the quota system which emphasized quantity not quality, pollution, apathy and the inability of the population to adapt to new technology, were all blamed on Stalinism. For the first time it was argued that there had been a direct break in 1928 from the true Leninist route to socialism as laid down in the 1920s, thus repeating in the Soviet Union an argument which had raged in the West for many decades.

Critical Western writing on the collectivization of agriculture in 1930 and the resultant famine of 1932–3 was now borne out by Soviet research. The drive to complete the First Five Year Plan in four years, and the widespread use of terror and excessive speed which accompanied it, devastated the countryside. Collective farms were ordered to be set up in one to three years according to area. Agricultural experts were sacked as "bourgeois specialists" and local cadres, who often opposed the policy, were not used. There was little planning and few instructions, even as to the exact nature of the collective farm envisaged. 25,000 proletarian volunteers and youth movement enthusiasts were sent into the villages, and the setting-up of collective farms was spearheaded by the local police. Party officials, faced with quotas and desperate to avoid criticism, raced to collectivize before their neighbours. Opposition was blamed on the *kulaks* or rich peasants as class enemies who were to be eliminated as a class, that is, shot or deported to Siberia. The peasants slaughtered their livestock to avoid handing them over to the new farms. Half of Russia's horses, 45% of cattle and two-thirds of sheep and goats were lost. Original utopian ideas of agro-industrial complexes with peasants living in towns and being bused out to work on a farm as to a factory, and enjoying collective lifestyles with sauna and solariums and modern technology, soon evaporated. As quotas of grain owed to the state were raised year by year, the seed grain was taken, leading to one of the most catastrophic, and unacknowledged, famines in Russian history.

Sholokhov's novel, *Virgin soil upturned*, written at the time, had given a realistic account of the suffering and chaos involved, including the wholesale slaughter of animals, but had attempted to justify the policies followed. By the late 1980s no such inhibitions existed. New articles showed young party activists from the towns, frantic to obey orders, looting and stealing property, inventing *kulaks* to fulfil quotas set from above. New figures of 150,000 households sent to Siberia in 1929, rising to 285,000 by 1931, were issued. The editor of *Novyi Mir*, Tvardovsky, in an influential poem, described his shame at having participated as a young enthusiast and his refusal to help his father and his starving family, who had been labelled as *kulaks*. It became clear that the term "*kulak*" in the early 1930s produced much the same reaction among convinced communists as "jew" did in Nazi Germany; as vermin, sub-human enemies of the state to be shown no mercy. Stalin himself referred to them as "bloodsuckers, spiders and vampires". Again the lesson was drawn that such policies left a broken and alienated peasantry responsible for the failings of Soviet agriculture. As no less a person than an academician of the Agricultural Academy put it, "What and who did the peasants become after such a bloody lesson? Alienated from his land and from the distribution of what he produced he turned from a master into an executor of jobs and orders".

Revelations of the extent and severity of the famine, new to the Soviet public, were deeply shocking. One author described his home village on the Volga where only 150 of 600 households survived. Stories of cannibalism were common. Posters were put up in the Ukraine saying that it was wrong to eat dead children. The internal passport was reintroduced to stop the peasants fleeing the areas affected. No aid was forthcoming and grain was in fact exported to the West to aid the drive for industrialization. The Soviet regime was amazingly successful at keeping details of the tragedy from the outside world. It was revealed under Gorbachev that the extent of the famine was greater than realized. Robert Conquest's *Harvest of sorrow*, now translated into Russian, concentrated on the Ukraine, but it is now known that the famine stretched across Southern Russia into Kazakhstan. Up to seven million people died. The famine was an area where historians did contribute. Danilov called it "Stalin's most terrible crime, a catastrophe of which the consequences were felt in the whole subsequent history of the Soviet countryside". Volkogonov referred to it as "a holocaust".

With regard to the purges of the 1930s similar revelations, often in the form of television documentaries or in popular magazines, gave rise to what one commentator described as a collective trauma. *Memorial*, the organization set up to commemorate Stalin's victims, turned to oral history and set up data banks. Stalin's personal responsibility and detailed involvement in arrests, trials and executions was documented. We now know that he did attend trials in secret and personally signed death warrants. Mass graves of victims were discovered; 150,000 bodies at Kuropaty near Minsk, 50,000 near Kiev, two graves near Leningrad. What remained of labour camps were turned into museums. Television programmes on individual camps interviewed survivors and guards. The KGB archives started to release details of the deaths of intellectuals and lost poems and other literary works were released from police archives. The debate, long raged in the West, as to the numbers of Stalin's victims, took on new impetus as more details emerged. The latest figures are 10–11 million "unnatural" deaths by 1939 alone, most connected with collectivization and the famine. The excess death rate of the Stalin years as a whole would be much higher, perhaps of the order of 20 million. According to recent testimony, as many as 18 million people were "repressed" in labour camps or colonies between 1934 and 1952. Reports have also claimed that seven million of these were shot, but such figures cannot be confirmed by evidence now emerging from the archives. What is clear is that the death rates in the camps rose considerably during the war, up to 25% a year in the middle years of the war. The overall losses in the years of the Second World War are now put at 26 million; some certainly accounted for by deaths in the camps, the deportation of whole nations accused of collaboration with the Germans, and repression against the populations of newly annexed territories in the West and of returning Russian prisoners of war. While the arguments as to death figures continue, there is little doubt that these run into many millions, far higher than Western "revisionist" historians estimated in the early 1980s. Comparisons with the Nazi's camp system began to be made. More revelations were issued as to the army purge, that it had been prepared by 1936 and that, as well as the killing of top army generals, some 400,000 party cadres in the army were shot.

More details emerged as to Stalin's own character; his vindictiveness and cruelty to those around him in the government, his dread of assassination and his fear of flying. We know that by the 1930s he shut himself into the Kremlin and spent much of his time watching films, which idealized Soviet life. We now have details from participants in the Seventeenth Party Congress in 1934 that Stalin was defeated in the vote for members of the Central Committee by Kirov and that the vote was changed, although direct evidence of his involvement in Kirov's murder remains elusive. Gorbachev initiated judicial rehabilitations of some of Stalin's victims, foremost among them Bukharin, but also over a million ordinary citizens. The Soviet Union accepted responsibility for the murder of Polish army officers at Katyn in the Second World War and admitted for the first time the details of the Nazi–Soviet pact of 1939, which handed the Baltic States and East Poland to Stalin. Apart from the Baltic States, these revelations had considerable impact on other national minority areas of the Soviet Union. Collectivization and the famine affected the Ukraine and Kazakhstan in particular. The 1930s saw attempts at centralization which led to purges of many of the leaders and intellectuals of the republics and an end to the relative autonomy given these areas in the 1920s. At the end of the war whole nations, including the Volga Germans, the Crimean Tatars, the Chechen–Ingush and others, were deported to Siberia or Central Asia, accused of collaboration with the Germans. As the Gorbachev era opened the Crimean Tatars were still campaigning to be allowed to return. In the new atmosphere of *glasnost* the national minorities rediscovered their own histories and their own national heroes, many of whom had fought against Russian dominance in the past. The response was demands for increased autonomy, the rise of anti-Soviet and anti-Russian feeling and, increasingly, demands for outright independence.

Gorbachev's aim had been to criticize Stalin but not Lenin. Lenin was to be used to legitimize changing policies, as both Stalin and Khrushchev had done before him. *Glasnost* was to be sanctioned by an appeal to the Lenin of 1917 and "all power to the soviets". A book called *Lenin on Glasnost* was issued and in January 1990 a round table discussion of the ideological committee of the Central Committee met to discuss the relevance of Leninism to *perestroika*. The policies of *perestroika* itself were to be sanctioned by the New Economic Policy, and much was made of the 1920s as a model in both economic and cultural affairs. Gorbachev was in effect saying that the whole of Soviet history after 1928 had been a mistake, and that a suitably modernized, late Leninism could take Russia forward into the twenty-first century. However, the attempt to use Lenin to underpin the third plank in the policy, that of democratization, and the introduction of

231

some degree of political pluralism, was to prove more difficult. The calling of the Congress of People's Deputies, the sanctioning of unofficial organizations and of popular fronts for the support of *perestroika*, and finally alternative parties, led to the abolition of Article six of the Soviet constitution by February 1990 which guaranteed the monopoly of power in the hands of the Communist Party. Like Dubcek in Czechoslavakia in 1968, Gorbachev was relying on popular support for a reformed socialism. If that had existed the revelations of the Stalin years had fatally undermined it.

Moreover, such a policy involved a radical reinterpretation of Lenin. Gorbachev and his advisors were influenced by Medvedev's ideas of an alternative, "democratic" Leninism. As Gorbachev allowed first a choice of candidates within the Communist Party at elections and then alternative parties and interest groups to be represented at the Congress of People's Deputies, so his supporters began to argue that, if Lenin had lived, the New Economic Policy would have been transferred into a New Political Policy, the Mensheviks would have been legalized and a degree of social democracy introduced. "Lenin prepared us for that" wrote one commentator in *Literaturnaya Gazeta* in 1988, "but he didn't manage it, he didn't live long enough". Plimak published a work on Lenin's testament which encouraged the view of a liberal Lenin, a sort of closet democrat, as did Volkogonov's view of Lenin in his Stalin biography. It was stressed that Lenin changed his mind with the introduction of NEP and brought in a semi-market economy. He was presented as human and humane, willing to admit his mistakes. By July 1990 Gorbachev was arguing that it was necessary to return to the Leninist version of the party, as an educative vanguard to influence society in a moral direction, and that this did not imply a monopoly of power.

By 1989, however, it was clear that the effects of *glasnost* meant that, unlike his predecessors, Gorbachev was unable to control the process he had started. The use of the past, the Soviet leader was beginning to learn, could be a double – edged weapon and could be used against him. The idea of a "democratic" Lenin, so crucial to Gorbachev's strategy of legitimizing his new policies, was by no means universally accepted. As one critic put it, "in my opinion Lenin's viewpoint is blatantly liberalised nowadays. The person bearing Lenin's name is a kind of Chekhovian intellectual". As the government stressed the promises of "all power to the soviets" and Lenin's encouragement of the creative power of mass action in 1917, on the one hand, and the late Lenin of the New Economic Policy, on the other, so the democrats focused on War Communism and Lenin's use of terror and dictatorship during the Civil War. These policies were, moreover, directly linked to Stalin and the policies of the First Five Year Plan and the purges, as the democrats rejected the recent attempts to separate Lenin from Stalin. The Civil War was portrayed by Gorbachev's opposition, not as the heroic years of the revolution, but as an unnecessary disaster, blamed on Lenin's refusal of a socialist coalition government in 1917 and his utopian and draconian policies after 1918. Books and articles were published, fiercely critical of Lenin's repression of the Cossack rebellion during the Civil War, and of the Bolshevik policy of forcible requisition of grain from the peasants, now seen as responsible for the famine of 1922–3, as Stalin's policies were for the famine ten years later. Above all Gorbachev's critics focused on Lenin's use of, and justification for the terror, and his creation of the *Cheka*, the forerunner of Stalin's NKVD and the later KGB.

As early as May 1988 the economist Selyunin compared Lenin with Stalin in this respect, and blamed both the Russian tradition, going back to Peter the Great and Ivan the Terrible, of modernization by force from above, and what he saw as the utopian strand in Marxism, involving the sacrifice of the individual for the good of the cause. Arguing that during the Civil War the use of terror spread without boundaries, affected whole sections of the population and involved the taking and shooting of hostages, Selyunin claimed there was no real distinction between Lenin's terror and that of his successor. In a very influential series of articles six months later on the origins of Stalinism, the philosopher, Tsipko, took a similar line, tracing the problems with the Soviet system not just to Stalin, but to Lenin, Marx and Engels. The fault, he said, "lay not with the mustaches but with the beards". As it became clear that a lot of Lenin's writings remained unpublished and that the Soviet public, accustomed to the cult of Lenin, had a somewhat sanitized view of their founding father, incriminating documents began to appear. One notorious example was the publication of a letter from Lenin in March 1922 using the need to raise money for famine relief as an excuse to launch an attack on the orthodox church. In language typical of him, but not what his readers were used to, he wrote:

> famine is the only time when we can beat the enemy (i.e. the church) over the head. Right now when people are being eaten in famine stricken areas we can carry out expropriations of church valuables with the most furious and ruthless energy. We must crush their resistance with such cruelty that they will not forget it for decades.

Such writings undermined the legitimacy of the Communist Party and Gorbachev's attempts to salvage an earlier, reformable, epoch of democratic socialism.

With Gorbachev's political turn to more conservative and hard-line policies during the autumn and winter of 1990, attempts were made to reverse the process of reconsideration of the past. In January 1991, on the anniversary of Lenin's death, an attempt was made to reconsecrate the traditional image of Lenin. *Pravda* published an article on its front page entitled "Forgive us, Vladimir Ilyich!", but it was too late. By then democrats, including Yeltsin and the mayors of Moscow and Leningrad, soon to be renamed St. Petersburg, had resigned from the party and were standing for free elections on non-party tickets. Democratization had made the Communist Party increasingly irrelevant. Not only were national minority areas beginning to demand independence or greater autonomy but in Russia itself a rising nationalism was undermining Gorbachev's position as president of the the Soviet Union. By the early summer of 1991 Yeltsin was to be overwhelmingly elected as president of Russia and the failed coup in August was to herald the end of the Soviet Union, the power of the Communist Party and Gorbachev himself. Statues to Bolshevik heroes, and in the republics even to Lenin himself, were pulled down. As one disillusioned communist supporter wrote "a country lives not only on its economy and institutions but also on its mythology and founding fathers . . . It is a devastating thing for a society to discover that their greatest myths are based not on truth but on propaganda and fantasy".

This extraordinary period obviously had great impact on how history was actually taught and learnt in schools and colleges across the Soviet Union. In 1988 Gorbachev ordered that all exams in history were to be cancelled at secondary school level and above and history text books were withdrawn for rewriting. As we have seen, this had happened before in Soviet history and the initial assumption was that a new approved text, incorporating the *glasnost* line, would be issued. However this time there was pressure for not one but several different versions to be allowed. After a heated debate as to whether or not there could be more than one correct Marxist line, Gorbachev sanctioned a number of alternatives. The teams of scholars set about their work, to find that when they had completed it that it was already out of date, and in some cases the country they were writing about no longer existed. Meanwhile teachers had to use their own initiatives and whatever resources were available. Some embraced the opportunity with enthusiasm, using newspaper revelations, oral accounts, and newly rehabilitated dissident writings. Others turned back to pre-revolutionary historical writing and the bourgeois historians, regarded as useless by Pokrovsky, were reprinted. Western accounts of Russian and Soviet history, for so long castigated as hostile capitalist falsifications, were now translated into Russian. A series of round table discussions took place between Soviet and Western historians and the proceedings were published in Soviet historical journals.

As was proved in 1990–1, what had been learned could not be unlearned. Pandora's box could not be closed again. As had happened in Poland under Solidarity in the 1980s, when dissident historians had lectured to factory audiences on the Nazi–Soviet pact, Katyn, Jewish Poland and other topics of Polish history which did not appear in the official textbooks, so now in the Soviet Union itself history became a popular preoccupation and a great influence on the political scene. In 1988 a cartoon appeared in *Moscow News*, reprinted on the cover of R. W. Davies's invaluable book. It showed a spotty youth answering a question from his history teacher with the words "Shall I give you the text book answer or the real one?". Once that could be said, the Soviet Union in its old form was doomed. As Khrushchev had said in the 1960s "historians are dangerous, they need to be controlled".

Suggestions for further reading

The bulk of this essay has been taken from the Soviet press and periodicals during the Gorbachev years. For English language accounts of the *glasnost* revelations R. W. Davies offers the best introduction in *Soviet History in the Gorbachev revolution* (London: Macmillan, 1989) and his follow-up to the book, "History and *Perestroika*" in E. A. Rees (ed.), *The Soviet Communist party in disarray* (London: Macmillan, 1992), pp. 119–47. See also A. Nove, *Glasnost in action* (Boston: Unwin Hyman, 1989), T. Ito (ed.), *Facing up to the past. The Soviet historiography under Perestroika* (Sapporo, Japan: 1989), and W. Laqueur, *Stalin. The Glasnost revelations* (London: Unwin Hyman, 1990). The Radio Liberty publication, *Report on the USSR* is also invaluable. D. Volkogonov's biography of Stalin has been published in English as *Stalin: triumph and tragedy* (London: Weidenfeld & Nicholson, 1991). His newer *Lenin, life and legacy* (London: Harper Collins, 1994) is, in contrast to the earlier work, very critical of Lenin. Roy Medvedev's *Let history judge*, first published in the West in 1971 has been reissued in a revised edition (New York: Oxford University Press, 1989). For a short, up-to-date and analytical account of the Stalin period see C. Ward, *Stalin's Russia* (London: Edward Arnold, 1993). For Soviet historiography generally there are two books by A. G. Mazour, *Modern Russian historiography* (Princeton: van Nostrand, 1958) and *The Writing of history in the Soviet Union* (Stanford: Hoover Inst. Press, 1971). See also K. F. Shteppa, *Russian historians and the Soviet state* (New Jersey: Rutgers University Press, 1968), C. Black, *Rewriting Russian history* (London: Atlantic Press, 1957), N. W. Heer, *Politics and history in the Soviet Union* (London: MIT Press, 1971) and S. H. Baron and N. W. Heer (eds), *Windows on the Russian past. Essays on Soviet historiography since Stalin* (Ohio: AAASS, 1977). There is a good biography of Pokrovsky by G. M. Enteen, *The Soviet scholar bureaucrat. M. N. Pokrovsky and the Society of Marxist Historians* (London: Pennsylvania State University Press, 1978) and an account of historians in the Five Year Plan years in J. Barber, *Soviet Historians in Crisis. 1928–1931* (London: Macmillan, 1981). Pokrovsky's *Brief History of Russia* has been translated into English (London: Martin Lawrence, 1968) and other works by him are also available.

For the classic Western account of the purges see R. Conquest, *The great terror: A reassessment* (London: Hutchinson, 1990), first published 1968, and for a detailed examination of the current available evidence and controversies see E. Bacon, *The Gulag at war* (London: Macmillan, 1994). The best known "revisionist" account is J. A. Getty, *The origins of the great purges* (Cambridge: Cambridge University Press, 1985). Richard Pipes's two volume history of the revolution, *The Russian Revolution 1899-1919* (London: Collins Harvill, 1990) and *Russia Under the Bolshevik Regime* (London: Collins Harvill, 1994) was the first Western account of the revolutionary period to appear after *glasnost* and was fiercely critical, not only of the Bolshevik regime and of Lenin, but also of the revisionists. For Western approaches to the Russian Revolution, including revisionism, see E. Acton, *Rethinking the Russian Revolution* (New York: Edward Arnold, 1990), and R. Suny, "Revisionism and Retreat in the Historiography of 1917; Social History and its Critics" in *The Russian Review*, **53**, 1994. For a Western Revisionist response to the fall of Communism see S. Smith, "Writing the history of the Russian Revolution after the fall of communism", in *Europe - Asia Studies*, **46**(4) 1994. O. Figes, *A people's tragedy. The Russian Revolution 1891-1924* (London: Jonathan Cape, 1996) is an excellent and very readable example of a new approach to the subject. The best general history of the Soviet period remains G. Hosking, *A history of the Soviet Union*, final edition (London: Fontana, 1992).

Index